Marginalia
A Cultural Reader

Mark Kingwell

Penguin Books

PUBLISHED BY PENGUIN

Penguin Books Canada Ltd, 10 Alcorn Avenue, Toronto, Ontario, Canada M4V 3B2
Penguin Books Ltd, 27 Wrights Lane, London W8 5TZ, England
Penguin Putnam Inc., 375 Hudson Street, New York, New York 10014, U.S.A.
Penguin Books Australia Ltd, Ringwood, Victoria, Australia
Penguin Books (NZ) Ltd, cnr Rosedale and Airborne Roads, Albany,
Auckland 1310, New Zealand

Penguin Books Ltd, Registered Offices: Harmondsworth, Middlesex, England

First published 1999

1 3 5 7 9 10 8 6 4 2

Author representation: Westwood Creative Artists
94 Harbord Street, Toronto, Ontario M5S 1G6

Printed and bound in Canada on acid-free paper ∞

CANADIAN CATALOGUING IN PUBLICATION DATA

Kingwell, Mark Gerald
Marginalia: a cultural reader

ISBN 0-14-028699-3
1. Popular culture.   2. Civilization, Modern, 1950– .   I. Title.

HM101.K56 1999   306'.09'049

C99-931272-3

Visit Penguin Canada's Website at **www.penguin.ca**

Contents

Marginalia

A Cultural Reader

My Marginal Attachments

The essays, columns, and articles in this book are, in a sense, the story of a decision, the only really difficult professional choice I have made. In 1987, in the face of a job offer from *The Globe and Mail*, where I had worked for two years as a summer intern, I decided to go to Yale and continue my graduate studies in philosophy. In doing so, I left behind the profession, but not the practice, of journalism. I continued to write for newspapers and magazines even as I made my way, slowly, into the academic world. I continue to do so to this day. Working this way, I probably get to do more of the kind of journalism I like than if I had opted for the other path. I certainly get to do more of the kind of thinking I like.

And so, in the way that a shape can be discerned by shading in what is at its edges, this material is about what my life is not. You will find here none of the academic writing I have done over the years. You will hear nothing of the lectures and seminars I give every week of term time. Harsh critics of academic life would say that the former are invisible anyway, except to a small coterie of dutiful academic librarians and dedicated fellow-travellers in political theory. Equally harsh commentators on contemporary youth culture might wager that, given the sound of ringing cellphones and portable CD players, the latter are likewise inaudible.

Be that as it may. The point is that these writings represent my marginal attachments and enthusiasms, the things that give me pleasure and fire my interest when I am not struggling with the details of the ideal speech situation, or trying to boil down Hume's argument on induction for the consumption of first-year students. They are marginalia not in the sense of being less important to me, only in being the journalistic sidebars of my academic work. Indeed, even to use the term might suggest a sharpness of distinction, and an order of priority, between the two forms of writing and thinking that I don't actually endorse. Writing at the margin is often more important, certainly more interesting, than the main body next to which it stands. Moreover, the mind does not split itself so cleanly into compartments—even if it is undoubtedly true that one of my academic articles, say that effort on metaphysics and the tropes of common sense from the *Journal of Speculative Philosophy*, might look like the work of a wholly different person from the one who briskly assessed "Monday Night Football" in *Saturday Night.*

Academic opinion remains divided on the precise worth of the latter kind of writing, of course, and ranges from one cherished colleague who gets quite angry when it is suggested that such work does not "count," to another who once advised me to "write a second book" if I wanted a promotion—despite the fact that I'd already written three. What gets called mere journalism or (still worse) popularizing remains in poor regard within the academic world, for reasons that continue to baffle me, especially when that disdain is paired with a sullen sense of grievance that the world does not pay more attention to scholarly work.

There is no way to settle this tiresome dispute here, maybe no way to settle it at all, given the nature of academic opinion. In any event, the fact of the dispute provided one reason for my decision to include some literal marginalia on the metaphorical marginalia in this volume. I wanted to play with the relationship of centre to side at one more level, to set up a dynamic of different voices and tones, and so to suggest some of the destabilizing effect of moving back and forth between moods and discourses. My non-academic writing has, I think, helped me to be a better professor of my subject, comfortable with the techniques, reference points, and flexibility that come with writing for mainstream publication. From the other direction, philosophy's insistence on precision has helped with the necessary discipline of making good arguments briefly, and with knowing (sometimes anyway) when less is more.

I don't suggest this path of mutual reinforcement is for everybody, or even hope that everybody will see it my way. I merely say that this is the marginal life I have chosen to pursue. It is, in a sense, the way I managed to avoid having to make that difficult career decision after all.

The articles included here might be considered marginal in another way, too. Most of them address topics that some people consider of only passing interest: sports, television, fashion, gardening, underwear, kissing, travel. In the main, and with some exceptions (such as a couple of longish articles about politics), they are examples of what is usually called "cultural criticism."

That may make them sound grander than they are, and I am certainly not about to suggest that, taken together, they add up to a treatise in cultural theory. Though my non-academic work is often about culture, and though (like anyone writing sensibly about movies, television, fashion, or popular music today) I am deeply indebted to the work of people like Roland Barthes, Theodor Adorno, Fredric Jameson, Dick Hebdige, Gilbert Adair, and Walter Benjamin, I make no claim to have entered the fold of academic cultural studies. I want these efforts to be taken for what they are: attempts to read aspects of experience—with some sense of direction and commitment, yes, but without diverting the discussion into a detailed theoretical effort. That effort belongs, if anywhere, in a different forum.

For the most part, I have tried to follow an approach that Marx, himself a journalist of no mean talent, identified as *Kulturkritik*: careful but lively attention to the texture of daily cultural affairs, in order to expose their hidden assumptions and ideological tendencies. That means in practice that I have turned my attention to a fairly wide variety of topics, the things that I find interesting or irritating or funny, and tried to say something non-obvious about them. That has meant, in turn, that I have become known as "a guy who writes about popular culture," and I have taken my lumps from crusty colleagues and self-hating media hacks alike for allegedly being interested in too many things. I confess I cannot make sense of that charge.

In Marx's hands, this sort of close attention to the flotsam of culture was in the service of a larger political project, a project to which one cannot any longer be unproblematically committed. It is even possible, as many people will argue today, that there is no connection to be made between the analysis of culture and politics. (This includes, prominently, people on the Left whom I mostly admire, like Todd Gitlin and Richard Rorty.) That leaves cultural criticism in a dreary position, as Adorno recognized quite early on. Without a program of social transformation to back it up and give it point, such criticism falls into modishness, mere hand-wringing or, worse, the sort of moralizing assessment that reinforces dominant ideas, as when people spasmodically complain about television violence or suggest that rising hemlines on "Ally McBeal" are evidence of a breakdown in family values.

On the other side, though, a too-successful theoretical structure can have unforeseen negative effects. Fredric Jameson, writing of Michel Foucault's theory of power, put the problem this way: "Insofar as the theorist wins, therefore, by constructing an increasingly closed and terrifying machine, to that very degree he loses, since the critical capacity of his work is thereby paralyzed, and the impulses of negation and revolt, not to speak of those of social transformation, are increasingly perceived as vain and trivial in the face of the model itself." A theorist of this capacity is in the dangerous position of suggesting, conservatively, that resistance is futile because resistance is always taken up, celebrated, and thereby neutralized by the overwhelming influence—the "hegemonic ideology," I should say—of the mainstream consumer culture. Within minutes, apparently, we are confronted by the clean, Gap-clad version of the grunge rocker or the cheerful, strangely compliant Microsoft model of the cyber-anarchist.

If, furthermore, everything is ideological, is it ever possible to say anything that is not itself ideological? Is the critic not forever implicated in the practices and assumptions—and, more practically, the capital transactions—of his cultural milieu? Could he ever criticize it effectively without stepping outside it? But then, even assuming that such stepping out were possible—I do not—wouldn't it simply put the critic in the position of the aggrieved and probably reactionary old fart? Marshall McLuhan once said that the fact he was writing about something was *prima facie* evidence that he disapproved of it—a rather precarious position for a good critic to take up.

There is middle ground to occupy here. Throughout my working life as a critic, I have assumed what I probably cannot demonstrate, namely, that the position of *participant-observer*, which cultural anthropologists use to describe their own necessarily implicated and disruptive presence in other forms of life, is likewise appropriate when it comes to describing one's own form of life.

That undertaking is a tightrope walk, and sometimes we may fall. Always we remain open to charges that we have not criticized the culture so much as celebrated it, have not penetrated the surface so much as polished it. We have to be aware of the seductions of cultural consumption, to which we are all prey. We have to be aware, further, of the seductions of thinking we understand consumption, for that very sophistication is something we also consume, often in ascending orders of reference and faux-acknowledgment of "what is really going on." (Think, for example, of the way television advertising has become progressively more nuanced and self-reflexive over the past decade in its efforts to please a more culturally savvy viewer.)

I try to acknowledge those risks, and to accept the culture's seductiveness as a crucial part in any writer's tactic of critical immersion. I have not always succeeded in this, but an approach that simply ignored these forms of appeal would risk a much deeper kind of self-deception. Besides, my approach is more fun! "This way of 'looking awry' at Lacan," the critic Slavoj Žižek has said of his own preoccupation with Hitchcock and Stephen King, "makes it possible to discern features that usually escape a 'straightforward' academic look. On the other hand, it is clear that Lacanian theory serves as an excuse for indulging in the idiotic enjoyment of popular culture."

In the end, only the reader can decide whether I have succeeded in making my interests interesting. For myself, I will continue to take my chances and try to practise what Albert Camus once called "the modest thoughtfulness which, without pretending to solve everything, will always be ready to give human meaning to everyday life."

These are essays, not closures—radical in orientation, but not utopian. They do not point towards a more ideal culture, merely seek to tease out some implications of this one. I hope they are conversational rather than declarative in tone.

Like any conversation, they embrace a number of different voices. Reading them again, I was struck by the variety of tones I have used in order to get something said: sometimes ironic or wry, sometimes expository or arrogant, sometimes wistful. The earliest included pieces, most of them written for *The Globe and Mail*, date from the four years I spent as a graduate student in New Haven during the 1980s. The latest is scheduled for publication sometime between the writing of this introduction and the appearance of the book. In between there are essays written for *Descant*, television columns written for *Saturday Night*, culture columns from *Adbusters*, and various commissioned reviews and articles from about a dozen other publications. Together they represent a decade of listening to, and playing with, the different voices of my mental party line.

The book includes thirty-seven articles both slight and substantial. There was no very systematic principle of selection at work here, more a simple effort at winnowing. When I gathered together all the occasional writing I had produced over the last ten years or so, I found it amounted to more than seven hundred typescript pages, much of it rubbish. (Scribble, scribble, scribble!) My first effort at cutting down this pile, easy enough, simply involved leaving out anything I judged too academic or odd or time-sensitive, or anything I simply no longer cared for. I was, of course, too easy on myself: that brought that number of relevant pages down to about four hundred.

I decided not to include anything that had made its way into one of my books, or that no longer struck me as even a little original. That created some borderline contenders. I kept all the things that I really liked, or that other people really liked, or that had appeared in rather unusual places. I even included a few pieces that other people really disliked, just for the hell of it, but I was not deliberately provocative. The article of mine that so far has produced the most hostile reactions—a *Saturday Night* TV column on the children's show "Sailor Moon," which prompted more than fifty angry letters, some of them from frustrated male collegians clearly in love with the show's animated schoolgirl characters—is not here. I was never that fond of it.

Anyway, these and other decisions brought the number of pages down to about 320, and from there I just had to grit my teeth and slash another fifty or so pages to make the book a manageable size. Any such selection is necessarily less than ideal, unavoidably personal, and incapable of pleasing everyone. There may be one or two articles here, like the essays on Pierre Trudeau and Stanley Cavell, that are of slightly specialized interest. My brother Steve will probably notice the absence of a certain article about the Toronto Blue Jays; a *Harper's* essay on memes appeared too late to be included. My main hope is that the final selection does not omit anything really worth revisiting, and adds up to something slightly greater than the sum of its parts.

Certain general themes do emerge, almost despite themselves. I notice (as you might) some favourite words and writerly tics spread over the years and pages. I also see several ongoing preoccupations, obsessions, and influences that have until now played below the surface of my full awareness. Things like irony and its limits; the need for transcendence; the importance of play and connection; the danger of false dichotomies; the complex relation of technology, speed, and boredom. These ideas (and a few others) are what might be called the furniture of a mind, discrete but related elements ever in the process of being rearranged, edging forward or back in response to different opportunities and impulses.

I like to think they make for a coherent world-view, but contradictions or gaps loom here and there, *aporiae* of greater or lesser import. This is probably the cost of working out one's thoughts in public. Maybe it's just the nature of the beast we call thinking. I have not tried to smooth out these bumps, but I have noted a few of them in the margins—that being, after all, one thing that marginal notes are good for. Others, as you will see, record changes of heart, acknowledge minor acts of literary theft, give references or bits of backstory, and generally do just about anything else that came to mind. Feel free, as always, to add your own.

Writing for publication is never easy. Writing for magazines and newspapers adds to the already tricky business of committing thought to page the stringent demands of deadlines, audience expectation, desired liveliness, and the limits of space. It is harder than most people—and especially most academics—think. It also cannot be done alone, safe in the cloistered study. It involves dealing with editors, proofreaders, designers, and fact-checkers, most of whom are paid to have ideas of their own. There is bargaining and feinting, offer and reply, compromise and disappointment. Every professional writer knows the sinking feeling that comes from seeing a piece improved by an edit, only to face late-night haggles over the fifty additional lines that must now be cut to fit the art director's page layout before the issue is closed.

I have great respect for all the editors I have worked with over the years. Some are brilliant; many saw a topic that suited me when I would not have seen it myself; each one paid me the high compliment of thinking my work worth printing. Still, complete agreement has not always been possible, and I have taken this opportunity to restore a few original formulations that, whether for the sake of plainness or a kind of prudery, were altered by well-meaning revisions. Thus what was, for example, rendered in *Saturday Night* as "a New York edge" is returned to the more straightforward "fuck-you edge" that I wanted; and instances of words like "post-modern," "chthonic," or "ineliminable" are left intact, together with passing allusions to Martin Heidegger, Curt Gowdy, and John Woo. It goes without saying that in all cases of factual corrections or improvements in sense, I have retained the benefit of sage editorial advice.

For in the end no writer can be good without good editors. I therefore gratefully dedicate this book to the following people, who made it possible: Ryan Bigge, Carolyn Gleeson, Hilary Keever, and Kalle Lasn of *Adbusters*; Julie Crysler and Nelda Rodger of *Azure*; Jennifer Ruark of *The Chronicle of Higher Education*; Allan Hepburn and Karen Mulhallen of *Descant*; Katherine Ashenburg, Warren Clements, Victor Dwyer, Philip Jackman, Jerry Johnson, Martin Levin, Sarah Murdoch, Elizabeth Renzetti, and Constance Schuler of *The Globe and Mail*; Ian Garrick Mason of *Gravitas*; Roger Hodge and Lewis Lapham of *Harper's*; David Warren of *The Idler*; Ann Dowsett Johnston of *Maclean's*; Catherine Cole of *Muse*; Aernoud Witteveen of *Nijenrode Management Review*; Boris Castel of *Queen's Quarterly*; Mark Stevenson, Dianna Symonds, and Kenneth Whyte of *Saturday Night*; Douglas Bell, Nadine Kriston Csathy, Joanna Pachner, and Evan Solomon of *Shift*; Andrew Cohen and J.L. Granatstein of *Trudeau's Shadow*; George Cook, Karina Dahlin, and Margaret Macauly of *University of Toronto Magazine*.

Full citations for all articles are included at the end of the book. Additional thanks, finally, to Gail Donaldson, Sara Borins, Naomi Klein, Ceri Marsh, Suzanne Stein, Jennifer Barclay, and Jackie Kaiser, for their help with this book. They are never marginal.

"The starting point of these reflections was usually a feeling of impatience at the sight of the 'naturalness' with which newspapers, art and common sense constantly dress up a reality which, even though it is the one we live in, is undoubtedly determined by history. . . . I wanted to track down, in the decorative display of *what-goes-without-saying*, the ideological abuse which, in my view, is hidden there."

–Roland Barthes, *Mythologies*

"I am not Roland Barthes (though I have diverted myself, here and there, by pastiching his style)."

–Gilbert Adair, *Myths and Memories*

Beginnings

Underwear, Kisses,

Transcendence

An alternative (and obviously less catchy) title for this section might be this: not-quite-random thoughts on manners, mores, and modes of both travel and rest. One of the great pleasures of occasional journalism is that almost anything can present itself as an occasion worthy of an article. You find that stray insights—from late-stage parties, re-reading a familiar book, or one of those long trundles down the jetway towards the open, flush-riveted door—sometimes mould themselves into a larger argument.

Well—insights, arguments. That may do them too much credit. Scattered thoughts; intellectual rambles. There are a few linkages here that I will leave to fend for themselves: airplanes, memory, beauty, limits, love, home. But these articles are responses to occasions. Each of them is, in its way, a stroll in the garden, where you never quite know what you might find. I hope more flowers than weeds, anyway.

Running Low on Posing Pouches?

Come to the Cabaret

I think it has been far too long since I last went shopping for underwear.

I came to this conclusion when, after several years of happily maintained underwear status quo, I recently decided to add a few new pairs of drawers to the drawers of my dresser. Now don't get me wrong. It's not that I've allowed my smalls wardrobe to get into tatters, or that I never go shopping. It's just that I tend to buy for quality rather than fashion. Also, as a matter of superstition, I buy underwear only in multiples of three. (Don't ask.) The result was that I hadn't been to the underwear department in a while—at least some time before they apparently decided to turn it into a cross between a rock-video set and the dancefloor of a "men's cabaret" I once visited in Amsterdam.

I believe it was called "The Manhole." And yet the American undergraduates I was with persisted in thinking it was some kind of Chippendales club.

I have to admit I was a little taken aback at the change. I remember the underwear departments of our staid old department stores as rather subdued places. They were populated by mothers who dragged mortified sons through the aisles, and serious-looking grown men who bought solid, conservative stock with an eye to the bottom line, not the bottom.

Not so any longer. Now, everywhere you look, abs are rippling, biceps are flexing, quads are popping, and, ahem, undershorts are being (as they say in certain novels I've never read) *amply filled.* In fact, by my non-professional estimation there's enough ampleness around to fill something like twice the number of Y-fronts on display.

But of course, they're not just plain old Y-fronts any more. No sir. You've got bicycle shorts, bikini shorts, high-cut bikini shorts, and full bodysuits. You've even got things that look suspiciously like "posing pouches"—those infinitesimal garments overmuscled body-builders

4

use to show off the hideous disproportion a human body is capable of assuming under severe duress.

The male analogue of the Lewinsky thong.

These variations on the male short are displayed in subtle black-and-white photos, all executed in the tasteful soft-porn "School of Herb Ritts" manner. And because the models displaying the wares are without exception such fine anatomical specimens, the underwear all looks somehow fabulous. The bodies, beautifully toned and proportioned, strike poses reminiscent of Greek statues, except they have a noticeable addition of unsubtle erotic charge: Achilles on the dancefloor, doing amyl nitrate.

I even find that underwear has become a subject of serious political and philosophical debate, especially in those journals devoted to the new but rapidly growing field of queer theory. I don't find this all that strange, because I can easily imagine how underwear, like any form of clothing, might signal important sexual and (maybe) political messages. For instance, I'm willing to believe it matters a lot under what circumstances you feel okay wearing your underwear as outerwear. But what I can't imagine is me, myself, actually wearing any of the stuff I see in the stores—under any circumstances at all.

The day this article was published, I walked into my Aristotle class to find the words "amyl nitrate?" written on the blackboard. Obviously I am cooler than my students.

Or under anything at all.

The reason is simple. If you focus on the shorts and not the body, you can't help realizing that knee-length Y-fronts are pretty goofy looking. What's more, I can't think of many people who, knowing that, would still want to wear them. Maybe that just demonstrates the limits of my imagination, because presumably *somebody* is buying all this steep under-apparel. Here it is for sale, after all, and not obviously putting anybody out of business.

Since not many of the buyers of this underwear can look as terrific as the sculpted models in the photos—who actually look like sculptures, when you think about it; most of them don't even have heads—it follows that *a lot of men look ghastly in the underwear they're wearing right now.* That's right. Look around carefully as you read this. See the banker across the aisle in the subway? See him reading his *Globe and Mail* with such dreary concentration? Now picture it. Beneath that grey Harry Rosen suit, that guy is wearing . . . a posing pouch!

Maybe it's too early in the morning to imagine anything like that.

If you're a man, please try to recall the unease you feel right now when you're next out shopping for underwear. It's hard to hear, I know, but the fact is you probably don't look like Jean-Claude Van Damme or Marky Mark. More disturbing still, only somebody who *does* look like them could look any good in knee-length jersey Y-fronts. Face it, my friend: Kate Moss will never lean her naked body against your rugged chest. Buying Calvin Kleins will not help you. Don't be fooled. Short of a magic wand, *nothing* will help you.

In fact, the next time you find yourself in the underwear department, you might as well be sensible. It's difficult, of course, surrounded by all this eye-popping male flesh trying to work its subtle envious magic on you. You will start to think, "Hell, I don't look so bad in my black Speedo bathing suit. I'm no Fabio, but I can still flex a muscle or two. Why not a pair of high-thigh bikini briefs? They look pretty hot on that model." But believe me: you do look bad in the Speedo. It's just that nobody has had the heart to tell you. Your wife has been hiding it at the back of your closet for three summers now, but you keep finding it.

Here's my advice. There's probably a Marks & Spencer nearby. They've been selling underwear since before you were born. What's more, the underwear they sell looks like it was designed that long ago. Go there right now and *buy some boxer shorts.* Be sensible and don't start getting any silly ideas. Don't fool with jersey material or high-leg tailoring. And I think I'm right in saying silk is not really a practical underwear material. Buy the plain cotton boxers. The ones that come in various tartan patterns. The ones that bag in the back.

While you're at it, buy nine or twelve pairs so you don't have to come back for a long time.

You'll thank me someday.

6

The Party That Ended Too Soon

The millenarian glee with which harbingers of "the new values" have been castigating the poor 1980s has reached such a pitch that the truly shocking thing now would be to learn that Michael Milken was really a philanthropist, the savings-and-loan scandal just a misunderstanding among gentlemen, and Ronald Reagan (what *he* clearly thinks is true) the greatest living American. True shocker: 1980s really a good decade!

This article marks, for better or worse, the beginning of my obsession with the idea of the millennium.

But instead this fever of self-laceration and new-found piety lives on. We know "the new values" are here to stay when they begin emerging from the mouths of television commercial actors, whose rumpled down-home appearance (blue chambray shirts, worn jeans for men; floral-print dresses, pastel cotton sweaters for women) is a semiotic clue to their sincerity. What are they actually selling? As usual, it hardly matters. Greed and flash and insane careerism are out, they tell us in earnest voices meant to exude mature good sense. Loyalty, family, commitment, conservation—all that stuff is in. *All that stuff?*

But these revisionist robots are only the latest, and friendliest, actors in the Evil Eighties morality play. We have seen the Yuppie burned in effigy. People have been sent to jail. Long shots of deserted Wall Street have filled our television screens. How many times have we been told, since rounding the corner on the Eighties and embarking on this ten-year pilgrimage towards the new millennium, that the Party Is Over? Has anyone missed it? The Party Is Over.

This was sheer cultural inoculation, deflecting attention from the smooth triumph of global capitalism.

And good riddance! We all hated (didn't we?) those 500K-a-year Wall Street traders, with their Ivy League diplomas and red suspenders. We all hated the wolfish Ivan Boesky and the wicked witch Leona Helmsley (are these fairy-tale images a fluke?). We all *really* hated the aggressively gelled character played by Michael Douglas in Oliver Stone's *Wall Street,*

Gordon Gecko: a man named, not coincidentally, for the little lizards New Yorkers keep in their apartments to eat cockroaches.

Sure, we hated them. But I hate these new touchy-feely moralists even more. For one thing, their regret and conversion to good sense smacks of the hangover. I have friends who force themselves to jog on bleak Sunday mornings when the consumption of liquor has left them in a dehydrated condition comparable to five non-stop air journeys around the world. They claim vicious exercise is the best cure for what ails them. It's not. They're just pointlessly punishing their *bodies* for a *spiritual* malaise called guilt. But hey, fitness is "in."

I should probably acknowledge that this is actually me. But I know I am not alone. Admit it.

Another thing that bothers me about notices that the Party Is Over is that I wasn't invited to the Party in the first place. Like most of us, I lived through the Evil Eighties. I even lived part of them within easy striking distance of Party City itself, New York. But did I get to the Party? Nope. I did go to one cocktail do in Manhattan during the 1980s, where I stood next to thuggish young men in dinner jackets who talked of reverse triangular mergers, giving points, making killings, and so on. It was pretty boring; but the food was good.

An accurate description of life in graduate school.

I feel a little bad about this now. I missed the Party! I imagine children coming up to me in ten years and asking, "Hey, mister, what was the Party really like? What did you do during the Evil Eighties?" "Well, kids, mostly I was hunkered down with some fat tomes by dead German guys. I wrote a couple of dissertations nobody has read. I ate a lot of breakfast cereal and tinned soup." I'll be the equivalent of somebody who spent the Gay Nineties in a dour funk, or weathered the Roaring Twenties being sensible and modest.

In 1998, Nike CEO Philip Knight took a forty percent pay cut, bringing his annual compensation to a slimline level of $1,680,000 (U.S.); Albert Belle, who once threw a baseball at a fan trying to take

I can live with that, I guess. What really bugs me is that I'm not really convinced the Party *is* over, and I suspect that all this new morality might be a diversion to draw our attention away from those people still at the Party. These include every politician currently in office, the many people still making hundreds of thousands on the Street (Wall or Bay, as you like), and all professional athletes, who show no signs of thinking greed is "out."

To the extent that they represent a false (that is, both insincere and inaccurate) conversion, "the new values" are just a late twist on an age-old theme. Responses to a new millennium, as to a lesser extent to a new century, are essentially two. One involves optimism, high spirits, loosened morality, and lots of first-class alcohol. The other involves dark prophecy, self-flagellation, the castigation of handy scapegoats, and the preaching of simplicity, plainness, and a puritanism that passes for good sense.

Make no mistake. Our response to the 1980s has nothing to do with a real sea-change in values, or even the downturn in the economy (though that's real enough). The fact that an entirely arbitrary event—the passage of 1989 to 1990—marked it is proof enough for that. No, we are merely doing what humans have always done: approaching a new era with deep misgivings and anxiety. Some try to lash themselves into shape; others seek oblivion in celebration. We *all* wonder desperately what the future will bring.

Our mistake, I think, was to have the Party peak too early. We are bad hosts, bad party-goers. (One minor effect of this: everybody read *Bonfire of the Vanities*; nobody will go see the movie.) Instead of ending it with a flourish of recriminations and angry preaching—Dad getting home too soon—we should have allowed the Party to spread, invited the neighbours, rolled out into the street in a superfluity of high spirits.

But no. We will enter the new century and millennium like guests who drank too much too soon, began to slump, and wept at the sound of midnight striking—already a little hungover, regretful, and punishing themselves for their excess. What a shame.

his picture, will make $11.9 million (U.S.) playing for the Baltimore Orioles in 1999.

By 1998, annual U.S. growth rates were once more booming at 3.9 percent, and unemployment was bottoming out at 4.3 percent; on the other hand, 70 percent of Indonesian businesses were in bankruptcy as of March 1999.

9

On Hitting the Chic

and Missing the Buss

There is a scene in Steve Martin's *L.A. Story* where his character, a gormless weatherman, says to his wife: "I'm not kissing anybody on the cheek anymore. I *hate* that." Yet later, bowing to social pressure at a horrible yuppie brunch, he leads the pack in exuberant cheek-bussing.

I hate cheek-kissing too. But like most people, I find myself submitting whenever I'm faced with a friend or acquaintance offering the small patch of facial flesh. Not that I do it gracefully. My intense dislike of cheek-kissing translates into gross physical awkwardness, with much bumping of chins and scraping of noses, many total misses of lip and cheek, and the occasional sound crack to the head.

I don't really. If you saw me at a party, bussing away like mad, you'd realize I am being a little disingenuous here.

Once, I missed the offered cheek by such a wide margin that I ended up giving one of my friends an unexpectedly intimate kiss to the ear. As I leaned back in alarm, she winked at me.

Her name was (and is) Marie Adams; she's the older sister of my high-school buddy David Adams, and this happened on a train platform at King's Cross in London.

You would think that my female friends, after some years of injuries both trivial and serious, would keep their cheeks to themselves. But no. At dinner parties, book launches, academic wine-and-cheese parties, even (yes) brunches, here they come. Our heads bob and weave like punch-drunk boxers. Her cheek swims into view and I dart my mouth at it like a fish in a feeding frenzy. I hear lips smacking under my right ear.

Meanwhile, my arms entangle gauchely with hers, or they wrap tentatively around her ribs. But where do I put my hands? High on her back? (Bra strap!) Down lower? (Love handles!) Must the cheek-kiss *always* be followed by the gingerly hug—the hug otherwise reserved for the patient with a contagious, life-threatening disease? Sometimes? Never?

Matters are complicated by the fact that some of my friends are European, and others, though Anglos, live in Montreal. These people favour kisses to both cheeks—but not consistently. They switch from one cheek to two apparently at whim. Sometimes they lead to my right, sometimes to my left. Are they trying to keep me on my toes? Do they think my life so humdrum it requires an enlivening uncertainty about the cheek-kiss?

There are even some people who throw caution to the wind and attempt to kiss me on the lips. This often happens even as I am still aiming for their cheeks. The result is a more than usually wicked nose-bump.

The cheek-kiss obviously began as a chaste, and therefore acceptable, displacement of the lip kiss. It is suitable for friends and ex-lovers (especially if your spouse is looking on as you greet them). It also fulfils a clear social need. I usually shake hands with my male friends, but shaking hands with women smacks of the corporate world, and I feel more affection for my female friends than I do for, say, my bank manager.

So the cheek-kiss must stay. Its problem is really that it's *not formal enough*. You just don't know what to expect.

Elsewhere, this is not an issue. I've seen teenagers in Paris getting through four ritual cheek-kisses without difficulty, partly because they always do it the same way. Grasp hands; first kiss to the left; bump cheeks and don't worry where your lips are. Repeat as necessary. Or consider European politicians: clad in their bulky overcoats, grasping each other's shoulders, bumping chests, they manfully slam their heads from side to side. No problem.

I don't think we can standardize the North American cheek-kiss, though. There are too many variations already. Besides, this is the New World; we don't hold with that degree of formality here. Kiss free or die!

What we can do is give people a split-second to prepare themselves for what's coming in the cheek-kiss. I have devised a simple system for making this warning known. You simply telegraph a set of coded intentions as you approach your friends. At your next party, say, walk towards people while shouting something like this: "One, no contact, go left, little hug!"

This code would do for, say, an acquaintance, short-term friend, or spouse of a colleague. One cheek-bump kiss (no lip on skin), followed by a brief hug. The beauty of "go left" is that each person will move their

This now includes one or two male friends, who still haven't overcome their hilarity concerning an article in a gossip magazine, which reported me kissing a boy in public.

I have often thought the four-kiss ritual would serve to slow the rate of people moving on to more powerful and/or attractive people; but no doubt true schmooze-artists would master the art of looking over your shoulder even while kissing you.

head to the correct side. For a good friend or ex-lover you might step up the warmth a bit and yell: "Two, contact, go left, big hug!" Or if your spouse is over at the drinks table: "One, contact, go straight, big hug!"

As the evening progresses, and *you* go over to the drinks table a few times, you might even want to move on to: "One, ear contact, go left, sly wink!" Just remember to specify your instructions loudly as you close with your prey.

There are dangers, of course. At loud or particularly bibulous gatherings, communication breakdowns are inevitable. If your voice is not robust, try a simple system of hand signals, like those used by NFL quarterbacks. If you've had a lot to drink, stand still and let yourself be handled. It's simpler.

It's also possible that the kissing parties, closing for contact, will be shouting quite different things. You, bolstered by three mimosa cocktails, are hollering about "wet contact" and "reverse hugs," while the fashion-model wife of your publisher is quietly suggesting: "One, no contact, thank you, go way left, hug in your dreams."

The rule here is: lowest common denominator. The two parties, assuming they can still hear and understand each other, perform whatever the least demonstrative person has called for. This rule will breed frustration, it is true, but it will cut down on fistfights. It should be observed without exception.

My system is a clear improvement over the chaos and uncertainty that now marks our social interaction. It will also limit social injury. It's not excessively formal—you still never know what's coming. And it leaves lots of room for social geniuses to devise clever variations without unsettling their acquaintances too much. Adopt it without delay.

I find this is good advice in general.

I'm sad to report that, as of this date, my system still lies unused, my etiquette acumen mostly unacknowledged.

Brideshead Revisited, Revisited

Ann Thwaite, introducing a volume of memoirs called *My Oxford*, noted how, in common with many other readers, she was surprised on re-reading it to find how little of *Brideshead Revisited* is about Oxford. The experience cannot be unusual: only Chapter Two and part of Chapter Five of Evelyn Waugh's most famous novel are actually set in Oxford, and the plover's egg luncheon that in memory seems to last forever occupies in truth only a few pages.

Why then is *Brideshead* considered by most people "an Oxford novel"? Or, better: why is it that the memories most people harbour of it feature those elegant, languorous young men, Charles Ryder and Sebastian Flyte, reclining (probably drunk or getting there) amid tinkling fountains and dreaming spires, briskly dismissive of scurrying dons and swots in black gowns?

It is surely partly because *Brideshead* is and remains a young man's book, a collegiate paean, an ode to youthful love. The dire consequences of Charles's infatuation with the charming young aristocrat, Sebastian, and his warped Anglo-Catholic family are left for later. Sebastian's horrible drinking bouts, the family's heavy-handed disapproval, his final degradation enacting the whims of a gruesome Foreign Legion deserter in Morocco, are not dwelt on by the glow of remembrance.

Still, to say these things is only to examine the popular dimensions of a literary, and cultural, myth. We think of *Brideshead*, and of what Humphrey Carpenter has called "the Brideshead generation," with our own university memories wrapped up in a Burberry overcoat of Anglophilic good taste and idealized, champagne-flavoured romance. But is that how we ought to think of it?

My own first reading of Waugh's book came in high school, not university, and it was already a guilty pleasure. My English teacher, a Jesuit priest, had first placed it on our curriculum and then removed it. (We read *The Pickwick Papers* instead, a substitution I came fully to appreciate only much later.) I have no way of knowing whether this piece of literary give-and-take was intentional, but it certainly piqued my curiosity and I devoured the book one weekend of the spring vacation.

It would be cliché to say it changed my life, but it literally did. I had applied to study geophysics at university, because I thought that was the sort of thing one did with higher education. I saw myself, somewhat implausibly, drilling for oil in northern Alberta. And here were two young lovers whiling away a university career—at Oxford, no less—with wine and strawberries, trips to the country, silk shirts, and leather-bound first editions. Charles wrote a paper or two, but still informed his pompous cousin Jasper one fine mid-morning that he "customarily" took a glass of champagne at that time of day. Sebastian of course did nothing except spank his teddy bear with a hairbrush and drink. I was hooked; I changed my major to English.

I never did get to Oxford. I went to Edinburgh instead, and was very happy.

My English teacher, a Coleridge scholar, later admitted that *Brideshead* had disappeared from our reading list because he wasn't sure how its homosexual themes would go over in a Catholic boys' school rampant with homophobia. He was right, I think, to worry about that; some of my classmates' obvious hostility to homosexuality was crudely repressed desire, and the rest was crudely repressed uncertainty. But it wasn't until some years later that other dangers became apparent to me.

A linebacker on the varsity football team once pushed me up against my locker and demanded to know why I acted in school plays.

When Waugh wrote *Brideshead* in 1945, nostalgic for an already memory-enhanced time and generation, he was responding to a number of impulses. First and best was his desire to provide some luxury in a world dominated by rationing, ersatz pleasures, and the mundane horrors of war. (Waugh was never much, even in his *Sword of Honour* trilogy, for any other kind of horror.) The insistence on luxury—the silk, the butter, the wines, Charles's chapter-long Paris meal with the boorish Canadian Rex Mottram—makes the novel a giddy feast, almost too rich for palates grown forcibly bland. Its opulence is wonderful.

14

Second, though, Waugh was moved to write a great *Catholic* novel, a story of faith and its loss, the disappearance of tradition and stability. Waugh's longing for cultural permanence, and his sadness at its losing battle with the modern world, is a theme common not only to other seminal British works of this period but also to his other novels. Compare Tony Last, the rather dull country squire of *A Handful of Dust*, a decent landowner overrun by a changing world and ultimately condemned—deservedly, in my view—to enslavement in the jungle. But where Waugh's pre-conversion novels on this theme are bitter and funny, *Brideshead* is instead pious and precious, pointing the finger at decay more in sorrow than in anger.

In this context, religion becomes little more than a socio-cultural weapon. Lady Marchmain's long-suffering grace at Sebastian's waywardness, the priggishness of the young heir Bridey (her good son), and the fervour of their little sister Cordelia are all aspects of the same cloying disapproval. No wonder Sebastian was driven to drink, I find myself thinking. But though the novel is constructed to suggest it, Waugh holds out no genuine sympathy for the fallen blue-eyed boy, the gilded youth of Oxford. Sebastian is, in fact, dissolute; his hinted-at sainthood a bad joke. Even Charles, that weak-willed toy of the family, comes to see it.

More than this, a heavenly "twitch upon the string" will bring them all back into line: in Waugh's eyes, no sinner can escape the hound of heaven. Lord Marchmain, the aged roué estranged from his dreary family in sunny Italy, finally comes home to die. And when "agnostic" Charles falls to his knees at Lord Marchmain's death-bed, we know his corruption by the Flyte family is complete. Only then, after all, can he understand why Sebastian's sister Julia, fallen for Charles in her turn, cannot go on "living in sin" with him. Only then can he appreciate Lady Marchmain's exquisite bitch-out of years before, when Charles, still a boy, failed to stop Sebastian's drinking. "Callously wicked," she called Charles then; "wantonly cruel."

Waugh once wrote to Nancy Mitford, his favourite correspondent, that

To the editor:

"I cannot avoid the conclusion that Mr. Kingwell approaches the book with an unstated but fundamental conviction, common among intellectuals since the Enlightenment, that religion is not a matter to be taken seriously by any person of intelligence."

A correspondent writes:

"I do not know whether or not you are an atheist or at least an agnostic, but I rather hope so. I would then have the pleasure of proving to you the existence and omnipotence of God from the probability curve. I challenge you, for I can do it."

though he was not on Lady Marchmain's side, God was. But the comment was disingenuous. This is Waugh's theology, and it is appalling.

Waugh was always a snob, a climber, from his early years at Lancing School. Before his turn to Catholicism, the snobbery had been social and material, and channelled productively into satire. With *Brideshead* it is social and religious, and remains ambiguous, wavering—as though he had, in converting, lost the ability to tell good from bad, not gained it. He can't resist poking fun at the Flyte family eccentricities, but the tragedy for him is not their destruction of Sebastian (and Charles's naive complicity in it, snobbish in its own right). Instead it is their imminent, and regrettable, departure from the Home Counties.

I used to think that the wistfulness of Charles's revisiting Brideshead during the war lay in his rather distant memories of Sebastian and Julia, the tragic brother and sister so like each other, and so different, whom he had loved in turn. But now I think Charles is less interesting than that. His fatal flaw is not ironic detachment, as we are led to think by the novel's tone, but something far less forgivable: religious hypocrisy.

Antony Blanche, the guru aesthete of Oxford, warns Charles in two separate scenes of the "fatal English charm" of Sebastian and the Flyte family. But the warnings go unheeded, Blanche's honest perception reduced to a campy side-effect. In the end Charles, like Evelyn, is content to be an outsider looking wistfully in. They are two boys with their noses pressed up against the stained glass.

To the editor: "Waugh believed God's grace was available to all, as millions of other people do, and to reduce this belief to 'stained-glass smugness' smacks of both arrogance and hypocrisy."

16

When East of Bay Is a Foreign Land

I turned thirty-five today and, along with the other signs of time's passing that have come to me this long Sunday, I am suddenly conscious that the little one-bedroom Annex apartment I now live in has been my home for longer, seven years, than anywhere else. Itinerant years in graduate school, a childhood spent in tow to a career air force officer on successive three-year postings—these things mean that this single floor of a 1930s brick house near Bathurst and Dupont is my most well-trodden den.

March 1, 1998

I was born in Toronto but didn't live here until my second year in university, seventeen years ago, when I moved into a narrow shared house in Kensington Market. I have lived in three or four places in the city since then, all of them within walking distance of the University of Toronto, which was first my place of education and is now my place of employment—and education.

So my Toronto is small, confined to an area bordered by Dundas on the south, Dupont on the north, and Christie on the west. Almost all my friends occupy the same space and have done so since university. For us, anything east of Bay Street was foreign territory, except maybe for shopping or movie trips. Yonge Street, a-throng with lumber-jacketed thugs in Greb Kodiaks and Gregg Allman haircuts, was out of bounds unless somebody unaccountably had a car, in which case we would go there, ironically cruising, pulling mischievous U-turns in the middle of all that action. Cabbagetown was rumoured to be the home of some of our professors, but Riverdale, on the other side of the Don Valley, might as well have been the moon. I now commute to Scarborough to teach three days a week, but I still feel pretty much the same way. For me, life happens in the Annex, more or less, and southward.

Every now and then I go back to the first house, 17 Wales Street in

The commute is more like an airlift or "Star Trek" transportation, only much slower: I pass the intervening urban landscape underground, on the subway.

17

Kensington, and think of the bunch of us in there, a succession of students, male and female, along with a host of mice and cockroaches—the raucous parties we had, the terrible insulation, the endless disputes over food shopping and bathroom cleaning. Our landlord was a university administrator. I think he rented us the place because we were from St. Mike's, the university's Catholic college. But we weren't very choir-like. My buddy John once dived down the narrow staircase on his stomach, screaming the lyrics to David Bowie's "Heroes," which was blasting out through the open windows from massive speakers. Another friend, now alas dead, used regularly to set the kitchen on fire, cooking hot dogs late at night after returning from a bar. We let an upstairs plumbing leak go on so long the ceiling of the kitchen eventually collapsed in a huge mess of waterlogged plaster.

I think that may have been the year I gave up drinking for Lent, forty days of deprivation that ended with John and me sprinting down the road at midnight on Holy Saturday to catch last call at the Tropicana.

We had no television. Most nights there were long, intense debates in the kitchen about just war theory, the intentional fallacy, the DH rule, or whether the Clash's *London Calling* was the best rock album of all time. (It is.) We swapped books, cooked pasta, drank cheap wine, and argued, always argued. I walked to philosophy class in the morning through the market's fish-laden ice trays and banks of fresh fruit, and came home late at night, hungry and happy, through the piles of stinky garbage and film-set eerieness of the deserted stalls, the streets slick with water and entrails and blood.

I bought navy blue workpants at open-air stalls for ten bucks a pair, brightly dyed second-hand shirts from Courage My Love for five, and wore surplus shoes from one of the surly Portuguese men who lined the northern part of Augusta Street. (I still buy my sneakers there, low-cut Pumas in green and black suede.) There were always great deals on fresh bread, smelly cheese, and thinly sliced hard salami, and we bought all our fruit and vegetables fresh from a truly hideous woman—I mean, a literal crone, shrunken, black-clad, and be-warted—who performed amazing feats of complex addition in her head.

She's still there.

The Jamaican bakery on Kensington provided my first taste of one of life's supreme gastronomic combinations: a beef patty, all hot spice and

18

soft yellow pastry, washed down with sharp Kingston ginger beer. Around the corner, on Spadina, between the art-supply stores that kept the community college students happy, a two-dollar bowl of broth with noodles, beef slices, spring onion, and squirts of hot sauce could set you up for the day. There was a Szechuan place upstairs, next door to the El Mocambo, that served the best garlic chicken in the Western hemisphere.

In the same category as Cockburn '63 and Stilton, raw oysters and Veuve Clicquot, coffee and a Kit Kat.

Later, I moved north to Harbord and shared a tiny hot apartment with some pals with bad study habits and a weakness for illicit chemicals. Night after night we dined on huge pepperoni and mushroom slices from Pizza Gigi, across the street, or just on big hunks of bread from the Harbord Bakery—both still there. Our biggest domestic problem was that the nearest beer store, on Bathurst below College, was so far away.

One of my roommates, Phil, used to carry a two-four of beer on each shoulder on that long walk; we couldn't afford cabs.

Later still, I moved west to Manning Avenue, in College Street's Little Italy, when it was still unfashionably and genuinely Italian, with a few cafés—the Diplomatico, Il Gatto Nero—that were second home to intimidating little men who drank espresso and dissected the Azzuri's World Cup chances. If you were brave enough to walk past them you could get the sustaining panzerotti or mascarpone-stuffed cannoli the cafés specialized in. (Nowadays, College is a bank of hip restaurants and bars, all full of beautiful youngsters in expensive clothes. If you like that sort of thing.)

My current place is about a fifteen-minute walk from there. It's closer to the literary and cultural power points of the city, and I no longer live like a student, but the neighbourhood has a bookish, Bohemian air I find comforting. I walk past Jane Jacobs's place on the way home, sometimes see her distinctive hunched figure, perpetually poncho-clad, pacing ahead of me on Albany. Other writers and academics haunt the cafés and restaurants of the neighbourhood. I buy all my books at Book City, near Bloor and Brunswick, the best (if not the prettiest) bookshop in the city.

Go there. Go there now. Talk to the boys behind the counter. Spend a lot of money.

This stretch of Bloor, from Spadina to Bathurst, anchored at one end by the Jewish Community Centre and at the other by Honest Ed's, the absurdly overlighted discount store, is my favourite block in Toronto.

19

When I returned to this neighbourhood after six years of living abroad, I used to walk back and forth along it on my way to work, thinking how many excellent *freaks* seemed to have made it their special place. There's a hippy-dippy vibe, with all those futon stores and health-food shops, South American craft and incense places. But there's also a string of divey bars, especially the notorious Brunswick House, where I spent many an undergraduate night downing gassy draft from small glasses, listening to Irene, the bar's fat house crooner. Not to mention a scattering of Hungarian restaurants, where you can get bottles of ice-cold Blue and huge plates of wienerschnitzel and dumplings for under ten dollars.

The old Bloor Cinema, near Bathurst, doesn't show rep any more—it's a second-run place now, screening mainstream stuff you missed the first time around—but it's still a funky little theatre with the hardest seats and driest popcorn in the world. I saw a lot of old movies there, classics viewed on the big screen for the first time, at a dollar a pop: *Casablanca, Charade, Miracle on 34th Street, Citizen Kane, The Fountainhead*. I used to sit there, alone in the dark, munching a huge box of that popcorn for dinner, gazing up at the magic glow of the boxy screen. Dreaming of life.

I think I knew, somehow, that I was already living it.

Who gets that kind of casual education in cinema nowadays? Another reason to hate Blockbuster.

Finding Your Way

Scene from KLM flight 947, Amsterdam to Toronto: I'm in coach with the rest of the ruminants, but near the front, ahead of the 747's jet-set circular staircase and through the curtain, I can peer into first class, where they get a choice of six movies, more oxygen, and all the champagne and orange juice they can drink. I, on the other hand, am in the middle seat even though I asked for an aisle when I booked the flight in Stuttgart.

On my right, a Tamil woman in traditional sari, about thirty; she doesn't speak any English. On my left, a Palestinian woman in traditional hijab, about sixty; she doesn't speak any English either. When the flight attendant comes by with the drinks trolley and makes a hoisting motion with her hand, my aisle-mates look up from their respective, presumably clashing, prayers for safety: eyes half-closed, lips moving, hands palm-upward (on the left); eyes half-closed, lips moving, hands clasped together (on the right).

They both stare at the flight attendant for a beat and then say, simultaneously, "Pepsi."

I started to wonder if the prayers might, like meeting waves, cancel each other out: an unforeseen consequence of multiculturalism.

Some random paradoxes and ironies of modern travel: (1) There is nowhere to go, if going somewhere means escaping the reach of MonoGlobal Culture Corp. (2) Therefore, wherever you go, you're already there. (3) Attempts to detour this fact are increasingly desperate and also increasingly doomed. (4) Still, we're going wherever we're going in greater numbers than ever.

How do we go? In what moods? With what expectations?

Perhaps the oldest wisdom about travel is that it broadens the mind,

So-called on the model of Homer Simpson's ambitious but short-lived Internet consulting company, CompuGlobalHyperMegaNet.

makes for liberal ideas. Exposure to other cultures, as Montaigne wrote in the 1580s and Bacon agreed a few decades later, renders us more tolerant and less dogmatic. It chips away the arrogance of the untutored homebody, smooths the rough edges of the go-nowhere galoot who thinks there is only one way of doing anything. It is an indispensable part of education; it makes us better people.

Hence, among other things, the institution of the Grand Tour, which took young European gentlemen through an extended circuit of salons, pensiones, cafés, museums, and spas, from the Uffizi to Florian's to Marienbad, in an effort to give them polish and experience. This was the origin of the been-there, done-that guided tour that today sucks the life out of successive busloads of tourists on every paved road in Europe, joylessly motoring from castle to airport to museum. These high-sided prisons, with their panoramic windows and hectoring, infotainment-spewing Virgils, are the death of curiosity on eight wheels.

For the problem with the Grand Tour was that it first obscured, and then eventually eliminated, the distinction between travelling and touring. The traveller was a sort of adventurer, a person of open and versatile mind. The tourist is a slave to his own expectations—or to those imposed upon him. "A man who has not been to Italy, is always conscious of an inferiority, from his not having seen what it is expected a man should see," Dr. Johnson wrote in 1776, capturing the problem with typical economy. "The grand object of travelling is to see the shores of the Mediterranean."

The point still holds, even if the shores of the Mediterranean have now morphed to (some combination of) Prague in winter, Tiananmen Square, Harajuku, the Leidesplein, Unter den Linden, Chartres, Pamplona, Westminster Abbey, and the Lincoln Memorial. Travelling is all about having been, not going. (Who among us has not smirked at the extensive, and hilariously self-defeating, videotaping of stationary objects that seems to preoccupy so many middle-aged American tourists?) Which means travelling is functionally impossible, because all that's left is tourism.

Edith Wharton, "The Vice of Reading" (1903): Like the reader who reads without comprehension, the tourist is the person "who travels from one 'sight' to another without looking at anything that is not set down in Baedeker."

22

This deepest of the tourist's paradoxes is probably what accounts for the newly inventive attempts to circumvent the hollow character of modern travel: historical recreations at Versailles or Sans Souci, reality-based tours to barrios in Mexico City or Tegucigalpa, non-threatening spiritual pilgrimages to Machu Picchu or Amritsar or Mount Fuji. But these "meaning-driven" tours confess their own failure even as they proclaim escape from the ordinary: pre-packaged, market-ruled and money-heavy, they collapse down into mere tourism as quickly as they articulate their alleged differences. Advertising makes sheep of us all.

What, if anything, is left? Well, there's always disillusion, the favoured mode of smart travellers—at least since Johnson (again) noted in 1778 that the dominant trend in travel writing had become annoyance, boredom, and even anger. This mode of disgruntled travel, whose high priest is probably Evelyn Waugh (see *The Ordeal of Gilbert Pinfold*), is what Paul Fussell once called "post-tourism," but it's really just the logical conclusion of tourism. These people would plainly rather stay home, but they're *expected* to go, so—damn it—they do. But no one can make them enjoy the trip.

A very funny book about—and also by–a very nasty man.

Irony is another option, ranging from the gentle self-mockery of Bill Bryson (a favourite stance of the young literate tourist) to the more biting, sane-man-among-the-nutballs indulgences of David Foster Wallace on the cruise ship or Paul Theroux in Africa. At an extreme, it's travel as high-concept kitsch, undermining every moment as it goes by. Rising levels of self-consciousness attempt to combat the assimilationist power of money and socialization with sheer knowingness. (I can't help thinking, here, of my own honeymoon, spent in an overdecorated motel room in Niagara Falls.)

There is, on the other hand, the alternative of becoming a Great Explainer like Gwynne Dyer, the sort of bombastic scribbler who travels around the world setting the locals straight on the meaning of their culture and history, confident that it all adds up to Progress (or Salvation, or Universal Wisdom) in the end. Or, failing that, the related option of being a hot-spot tourist, a danger junkie like erstwhile Channel Zero

Obviously that's a bit harsh. Sorry.

honcho Stephen Marshall, or Tyler Brûlé, now the editor of *Wallpaper*. Why not travel in order to get stoned or, better still, *shot at* during some minor foreign war? Your career in the media will be guaranteed forever.

These failures to find a comfortable mode of travelling—an authentic tourist stance—are not just a function of capitalism and technology. There's a deeper problem; namely, that you cannot ever escape the extensive socializing and conditioning—the ideology and expectations and prejudices—that reside in your cultural identity. Smirk at the videotaping Ugly American if you like, but remember that you, too, carry around all the material and financial realities of globalization in your well-toned flesh. The hyper-conditioned modern self: don't leave home without it.

Originally a reference not to tourists but to galloping post-war American diplomats; see William Lederer and Eugene Burdick, *The Ugly American* (1958).

We all want authentic experiences as travellers. The trouble is that we can't outpace the conditions of our own comfort, the market aids that come with us on eco-tour, the outrageous First World wealth that is built into our Rough Guides and Lonely Planet itineraries. It sometimes seems that all we have left are the trappings of travel, the snapshots and the prepackaged memories of imperial visitation, the sort of thing we might as well get neurally implanted at a discount, like Arnold Schwarzenegger's character, Douglas Quaid, in *Total Recall*.

But of course the desire to transcend our own expectations is part of what the paradoxes of travel bring to our attention. And there is, finally, wisdom in this. It's not the straightforward expansion of mind Montaigne hoped for, or the liberalizing erudition of the first Grand Tourists, but it's something. Implanted memories would not be enough. Why? Because you have to actually hit the road—even with all its preconditioned features, cultural pitfalls, and projected identities—to put yourself in the way of something unexpected, the little nuggets of insight that might not click until days, weeks, or years later.

You never know how changed you'll be. Small chunks of wisdom come only from the much-scored narrative of near-total recall. Go now; think later.

On Style

Recently, at long last, I achieved a dubious personal goal, one of those markers of urban sophistication that I learned to covet not through experience or direct association but via the altogether more powerful, and more ideal, realm of the movies. A bartender in a downtown hotel lounge knows my "usual" drink.

Yes, it's true. I walk into the bar, which shall remain nameless to avoid any hint of impropriety, and without a word he reaches for the bottle of Bombay Sapphire gin, chunky and blue and multifaceted like its namesake. Soon an icy martini of unwise proportion is standing before me, a triumph of minimalist elegance in lines if not in size: the perfect stemmed triangle of the glass, the dewy condensation on the clear cone of liquid, the curled lemon peel's sole playful colour note. I almost hate to drink it. Almost.

I don't remember when I first started drinking martinis—judgmental people would say this is no accident—but I do know, as anyone today must, that the recent vogue for cocktails has a whiff of retro about it. I like martinis, but I can't help being aware that they are, like so many cultural markers of style today, overdetermined. Or rather, overdetermined and undetermined at once. On the one hand, they have multiple untrustworthy nostalgic associations, the sort of faux Rat Pack posturing that, unless ironically undercut, is the fast road to deep uncoolness. On the other hand, all this ironic undercutting that nimbler hipsters go in for is a kind of style nihilism, cutting culture loose from its moorings, making every marker—every song or suit, every grace note or building façade—a free-floating signifier without history or context.

Take a single but telling example. The Cherry Poppin' Daddies, a young California swing band in the vanguard of the much-touted

I was thinking of those Nick-and-Nora *Thin Man* movies, with William Powell and Myrna Loy, where they line up their martinis in orderly rows for maximally efficient consumption.

Russell Smith, *Noise* (1998): "'Another beautiful mad girl,' said James to no one. He swirled the martini in his oversized glass. The gin on his lips tasted of headache. 'I love martini *glasses*,' he announced."

25

big-band revival, just released an album called *Zoot Suit Riot.* Now, how many people have cultural memories long enough to read that title not as some kind of fashion-dance imperative but as an allusion to racial hostility and immigration politics in 1940s America? Zoot suits, favoured by Latinos, featured billowing high-waisted pegged trousers and exaggerated long jackets: they used a lot of material at a time when material was scarce. Crew-cut Los Angeles white kids took that as an invitation to mix it up; hence the zoot suit riots.

So what does wearing a zoot suit, or listening to swing, mean now, when Mexican-American immigration issues are more tempestuous than ever? Is this blithe freedom from political consciousness really acceptable? Is a suit ever just a suit? (I won't say anything about the band's name, with its vulgar reference to deflowering virgins.)

It's probably a condition of living in these liminal, late-century times that we can't seem to transcend these oppositions of form and matter. And there are many others. Materialism is all the rage, yet a desire for spirituality is stealing across the cultural soul. Technological fetishism has never been more aggressive or more widespread, yet the most discussed new consumer durables are those, like the Volkswagen Beetle or Macintosh iMac, that are technically ordinary but wrapped in a "comfortable" bubble-contour aesthetic apparently borrowed from the toybox.

The modern idea is (as Kant said) that beauty must be "disinterested" to be valid; that in turn suggests that utility is the value of all other things, a sharp departure from the conjoined perfection of form and purpose the ancient Greeks celebrated.

There is of course no simple relationship, still less any necessary opposition, between style and substance, just as there is no necessary conflict between beauty and utility. (The faster car is almost always the more lovely car, and the workaday hammer or knife is, indeed, beautiful.) How we shape the things and experiences of every day in turn shapes us—and speaks volumes about who we are or, more important, wish to be. As style, from the Latin *stylus*, was originally a particular manner of wielding a pen, a way of choosing within the available store of calligraphic and linguistic options, so style is now the attempt to express personality within the grammar of life.

26

That's why the simplest and best definition of style is the title of that classic of post-war sociology, Erving Goffman's *The Presentation of Self in Everyday Life*. Style is the projection of personality upon the canvas of existence, the attempt to impose character on the otherwise undifferentiated—or merely banal—surfaces of eating, drinking, dressing, dancing, perambulating, and dwelling. With the possible exception of how one wears one's hair, all of these style-projects involve, even demand, association with the world of design: the need to be fashioned in particular ways, usually with the help of artisans of some aesthetic accomplishment.

But this is perhaps just to state the obvious. The interesting question is: what is our style today? In terms of design, what will the tag "1990s-style" connote a few decades from now?

I sometimes think the only valid generalization to be made about the 1990s is that, for unsurprising reasons, they have been a time of cultural processing, a restless retro-fitting of design features—in music, in clothing, in architecture—borrowed willy-nilly from the vast lumber-room of twentieth-century invention. Borrowed and, mostly, denatured thereby. Thus, for example, formerly revolutionary bebop is reduced to restaurant background music, aural wallpaper for people eating high-piled pan-Asian confections in a room designed by some tony architecture or design firm.

This recycling is unsurprising because it is typical of milieux on the cusp of something. Whatever you want to say about the much-palavered millennium—and I've said my fair share—it does loom large as a horizon of meaning. We can't get on with things, we can't fashion ourselves anew, until we pass through that arbitrary doorway, hoping all the while that our computers will still function, and therefore begin the compelling business of deciding what it will mean to be twenty-first-century people.

Hence the relentless always-already quality of so much design and style today. It is nothing more than the necessary knuckle-cracking, the nervous arpeggios before the real performance. If we are being charitable

I **don't** know why I made this patently false statement about hair-styling. Perhaps because I wear an extreme crop, what Roland Barthes once called the *zero-degree haircut*.

27

we might call it post-modern, all this cheerful mixing and matching, but maybe it is really no more than the final spin-down of modernism itself, a going-nowhere form of textbook review. There is a genuine 1990s style, in other words, something we might agree to call, with only a little irony, Late Capitalist Pan-modernism. It embraces the contradictions of hard and soft, material and spiritual, and renders them intelligible—even if it doesn't, finally, resolve them. Above all, it says something important about our current obsessions and blind spots.

Genuine not in the sense of "authentic," just definable and up for discussion. Nostalgia for style constitutes a style, if not a very healthy or original one.

I'm writing this in Berlin, where one of the biggest development projects in European history is remodelling the area around Potsdamer Platz, formerly a slab of the Berlin Wall, into what omnipresent posters call *die Stadt von Morgen*, the city of tomorrow. The development, a sky-lifted new downtown, is aggressively, almost parodically modern, mod-elled more on a nightmare vision borrowed from Godard's *Alphaville* than on anything organic to the site: like all "modern" development plans, it is more about what it keeps out and erases than what it inscribes. Construction cranes stretch as far as the eye can see. Cantilevered slabs of steel tubing and massive, hard-edged panes of glass are everywhere. First cousin to concrete brutalism, this emptily "progressive" architectural style now dominates cities from Brussels to Birmingham to Beijing.

Meanwhile, the Euro highways are filled with what Douglas Coup-land once called "bubble-butt cars," bright little blobs of plastic and metal of which the overhyped Beetle is just the latest example. Few have the Noh-mask grille and Noddy-and-Big-Ears charm of the Mazda Miata, a pioneering example; most are just wimpy little squirtmobiles with sewing-machine engines and hopeful "personalizing" decals and sun-screens, the automotive equivalent of homey screen-savers or mouse decorations on your home computer.

He meant, among others, the ubiquitous Ford Taurus, with its prominent rearward bulge. Is this some kind of primate sexuality in play among automotive designers?

But these attempts to individuate—just as with the celebrated excep-tion of a Frank Gehry triumph, say the Bilbao Museum—serve only to underscore the fundamental sameness of this "modern" look across Europe and the world. Style is always about choosing within available limits, but what confronts us is a kind of undifferentiated internationalism, the design fall-out of market globalization. Even the tanklike Mercedes sedans of recent years have been pushed aside by the softer contours of the yummy-looking late-model cars on display outside my hotel room. The room itself is an odd but evidently typical collision of Olde Worlde wood panelling and hunting prints with a bathroom that belongs on board Captain Picard's *Enterprise D*: the squat suction-effect toilet, the cylindrical airlock-tube shower stall with its transparent, rubber-sealed doors. It's all enough to make you long for the shark fins and battleship surface area of a '57 Chevy, the overt militarism of a Ford Bronco or HumVee.

This toilet never failed to remind me of the one David Foster Wallace became obsessed with in his account of a week spent on a Caribbean cruise ship.

What we see, then, despite some doomed rearguard actions, is a generalized modern style that, divorced from particular context, creates its own empty global context. This modernism is arguably also postmodern, not in transcending master narratives but rather in inscribing its nostalgias and selective eclecticism within the same old overarching aspirations of Progress, Freedom, and Commerce. The vertiginous modernist look of such science-fiction films as *Brazil, Gattaca,* or *Dark City,* say, where fountain pens, pneumatic tubes, Avanti sports cars, and hats for men lie alongside featureless mega-buildings and spaceships, is what we seem to be heading towards—only without their warnings of a totalitarianism within.

Likewise in the home, where the sleek pan-modernism of objects from upscale urban-design stores—alien-invader juicers from Italy, neon-green salt cellars from Sweden—cohabits, apparently without rancour, rooms decorated in the Shaker boxes and overstuffed couches of Martha Stewart's notional New England. Newly hip magazines like *Wallpaper,* really just catalogues by other means, celebrate this new urban self-presentation with unabashed self-indulgence combined with a wilful ignorance of the fierce, ongoing struggles for everyday identity that actually dominate urban life.

Obviously I have some kind of hate on for this Tyler Brûlé character.

In fact, this allegedly forward-looking Internationalism for the brand-conscious, jet-set young—Absolut vodka crantinis consumed to the sound of remastered Astrud Gilberto while dressed in a Canali four-button suit—is really no more than a form of lifestyle pornography. Not satisfied with mere conspicuous consumption, this relentless fetishism of style isolates its objects in a loving light whose sheer gorgeousness brooks no refusal. You look because, as with a car accident or erotic movie caught on TV, you just can't help it. And then, presumably, desire takes hold of you: I want those shoes! I can't live without that coffee table!

The pressing political question here no longer concerns the cultural dangers of mass mechanical reproduction, a topic that preoccupied critical theorists of modernism proper, like Walter Benjamin (though these dangers remain, and are still sometimes thematized in the art world and elsewhere). It is rather getting *anyone at all* to see that the ambiguous triumphalism of this new "modernism" is, like jazz gone uptown or R&B rendered by Pat Boone, a drastic diminution of style's political possibilities.

Benjamin, "The Work of Art in an Age of Mechanical Reproduction" (1934).

It is often said that the problem with Marx's critique of capitalism is that it's too forgiving: it doesn't see how good market liberalism is at accommodating and assimilating resistance. (A fact that numerous recent youth-directed ads, with their mock-ironic anti-consumer messages, amply demonstrate.) The same might be said, and for similar reasons, of modernism—at least when it declines to the status of a mere style. The *illusions* of freedom and sophistication are now exported everywhere, often with great aplomb, superb taste, and impressive commercial success. But style no longer seems much to serve its only true purpose, which is to carry forth the uniquely human project of individuating ourselves, of making a claim for personal identity.

Adorno and Horkheimer, "The Culture Industry" (1945): "Hence the style of the culture industry, which no longer has to test itself against any refractory material, is also the negation of style."

And that is deeply sad. We must never mistake the stylish ghosts of modern individuality—however nicely backlit, however well-dressed—for genuine emancipation.

Playing in the Digital Garden:

Getting Inside by Going Outside

1. Think

There is a vantage point in the large kitchen of my almost-Annex apartment from which, looking out the window, I can for a moment obliterate nearly all sense that I live in a city.

You notice I say "almost-Annex"; I didn't mean to imply, in an earlier piece about my part of Toronto, that I lived in the Annex proper. West of Bathurst, okay?

The window gives on to a small back garden cultivated and fostered by my wife, Gail, its uneven patch of lawn rounded off by the bevelled arc of flowerbeds that fill the eye against the stripped paint and genteel decrepitude of a garage with a door and two windows. From this angle, the garage could be a cottage, the garden a well-tended personal adornment, with its variegated rows and clumps of geraniums, pinks, ox-eye daisies, and roses—Baroness de Rothschild, Stanwell Perpetual, John Davis, Blanc Double de Coubert.

There is a purple clematis that climbs in a ragged slash across the peeling wall, and a chunky stone hare who stands in one corner, rising as if startled or, perhaps more likely (he's a burly little bastard), ready to box. There are borders of oregano, allium, Lady's mantle, sweet woodruff, hosta aureo marginata, platycodon, lamb's ears, goat's beard, artemesia, and phlox.

Those names! The charm of plants lies chiefly, for me, in this idiosyncratic ranging over from Latinate specificity to ancient folkloramic homeyness and back again, along the unruled edge between the scientific and the common. Here strict Linnaean precision rubs up against—what?—a sort of pre-modern alchemical Merlinism, which, like the pursuits of those in search of the philosopher's stone, holds in its leaves and roots the same ancient hint of transformative magic.

31

William Boyd,

Armadillo (1998).

"Lorimer had a view of the small garden from his bathroom," the novelist William Boyd writes of an inhabitant of London, in the same mood, "and he had to admit that, when the acacia was in leaf and the clematis was out, and the hydrangeas, and the sun angled down to strike the green turf, Lady Haigh's little verdant rectangle did possess a form of wild invitation that, like all green things growing in the city, did console and modestly enchant."

Just so. My apartment, and the garden, are just a block away from the busy intersection of Bathurst and Dupont, with its diesely bus lanes and truck traffic, but, barring an emergency-vehicle siren or an atypical outbreak of energy from the body-shop workers across the alley, the garden is calm, even meditative. It ever preserves the illusion of its own country-ness, but especially from inside the kitchen, where it seems to beckon the weary urbanite—i.e., me, often enough demonstrably weary, and certainly an urbanite—with its promises of rest and rehabilitation, of restorative food and drink. It speaks of crustless sandwiches of cucumber and cress, of pint glasses of Pimm's or big tumblers of gin and tonic, of more elaborate and yet less mannered al fresco meals of garlicky plum-tomato salad, cold asparagus, grilled flank steak, and cellar-cool bottles of

This is perhaps more than

you wanted to know about my

eating and drinking habits.

Beaujolais—all of which, to be fair, and more, have been consumed within its tiny green circle now and then.

But somehow falsely. Or rather, not so much falsely as self-consciously, knowingly, in the manner of a mild social performance, an acting-out of expectations in a way that layers genuine enjoyment—I actually *do* like a glass of Pimm's on a sweltering, wet-cotton Toronto afternoon—with a sense of affectedness. That affectedness is exactly, minutely, counter-balanced all the while by another kind of awareness that can only be called intellectual, of the way such affectedness is, must be, undercut by precisely the act of cultivating such awareness. In other words, the garden acts on me not so much falsely as ironically.

And yet that ubiquitous description of how we ubiquitously comport ourselves in this world—which, okay fine, I'll bust a gut and call post-modern, this post-modern world—that description, I mean that

32

description *ironically*, somehow just fail, to capture the range of nuances and pleasures of the kind of falseness I'm talking about. It fails to embrace those pleasures mainly, I think, because the sense of irreverence associated with the operative stance of certain forms of irony (which irreverence has, according to David Foster Wallace, lately devolved into a kind of empty reverence—the cheap irony of a self-referential television ad for 7-Up or the smug post-modern fiction of a Mark Leyner) does not speak to the *enjoyment* of the layering, the playfulness of noticing, even while crossing, the gaps between implied and meant.

David Foster Wallace, "E Unibus Pluram: Television and U.S. Fiction," in *A Supposedly Fun Thing I'll Never Do Again* (1997).

Ironically, Wallace says, irony's success as a critical attitude has made it empty as criticism: the more widely practised it is, especially in places like television, where it was formerly present only as the outside force, the hunter moving in for the kill, the less it is able to make a useful point. Pervasive self-consciousness obviates the power of self-consciousness. But, equally ironically, that success has obscured the deep happiness of simultaneously meaning something and not meaning it, which form of happiness is not critical, in the end, but actually sincere: that is, a form of unsophisticated (because meant) sophistication.

Or, as they say in *This Is Spinal Tap* (1984): "Such a fine line between clever and stupid." Like one or two of these sentences.

That is the happiness which the garden, for me, makes possible. A friend of mine has a decorative magnet on her fridge that depicts a beaming, ladies-magazine-style, well-coiffed Fifties housewife, complete with perfect dimples and some kind of frilly apron adorning her tight-waisted body. The colours are garish primaries, the familiar four-ink dot-screen separations of a comic book or a newspaper cartoon. "I'm happy," her thought-bubble says, "yet I'm aware of the ironic ramifications of my happiness." Precisely. In the garden, I am indeed happy—yet I am aware of the ironic ramifications of my happiness. (Not the least of which is, perhaps, the fact that I can, apparently without irony, use the phrase "ironic ramifications" with respect to anyone's happiness, even—or especially—my own. But let that pass for the moment.)

I wish I had had this image, and the sentiment, available to me when I wrote about the ironic ramifications of happiness in my book *Better Living* (1998).

The garden makes this layered form of happiness possible, I want to suggest, because of its own inescapable structural tensions, its in-built tendencies—which are really more than tendencies, are in fact imperatives—to play with the layers of meaning that accrue to all of the most diverting human activities. Gardens are threshold spaces, liminal playgrounds, portals of possibility. While seeming to enclose us in their greenery and lushness, they instead split us open like expertly gutted fish, making us suddenly alive to the dialectic potentials of life and art, nature and civilization, fact and value, wild and tame, public and private. We spill out of the drawing-room comedies of our enclosed lives, through the French windows of resented restraint, and into the nooks and wild-seeming garden spaces of the not-quite-public—where we try, perhaps more in the manner of Bertie Wooster at Blandings than of Laclos's evil chevalier in pursuit of *une liaison dangereuse*, to steal the sweet kisses of self-transcendence.

It is a commonplace, but an illuminating one, that the garden is a living oxymoron, an artificial wilderness that stands awkwardly astride the natural and the man-made, an uneasy *via tertia* of human existence poised between the solitary/poor/nasty/brutish/short tendencies of life without, and the warmly lit, hearth-centred *Heimlichkeit* of life within. "Awkwardly" because, as various let's call them philosophical disputes evolve and swirl within the history of gardening—when we try, or try not, to keep up with the (Inigo) Joneses, or worry about the (Gertrude) Jekyll-and-Hyde tendencies of our own little plots, sliding from too-rigid formality to artful dishevelment and back again—the question is always one of *appropriate degree of mediation*.

> **Literally, homeliness:** the feeling of familiarity that comes from being near the hearth, the centre of home.

There are Edenic resonances here, of course, of innocence and temptation and expulsion and loss; there are, too, academic ones, of *peripateia* and *theoria*, of walking through the groves and seeing the world reflected. There are gardens of wildness and gardens of order, public ones (like the famous one in Boston where Newland Archer makes risky love to Madame Olenska) and private. In these and countless other ways, playing with cultural associations even while putting the idea of the cultural into question via exposure to the cultivated natural, the garden is to the home what the convertible is to the car: exposed yet enclosed, open

> **In Edith Wharton's** *The Age of Innocence* (1920).

to the outside yet firmly linked to the inner. Allan Hepburn has argued that the pleasures of the convertible include the borderline fear of being pulled outside, of extending ourselves too far into the rush of warm air, into the elements—a fear synecdochized by the piece of paper or other small object that flies out of the glove box or off the dash and into the wind. Likewise, then, on a larger and yet subtler scale, with the garden.

Allan Hepburn, "Driving: Fifteen Lessons in Destiny and Despair," *Journal X* (1998).

The garden, therefore, while necessarily seeming calm, is in fact seething with contingency and antithetical energy, is indeed a roiling cauldron of the conceivable. The awkwardness of its threshold status is what we cherish about the garden—what, oddly, makes us calm. And perhaps that is precisely, paradoxically why—as with, say, the necessary oneiric-noctivagant brain-repair of REM sleep, during which blood pressure and rates of synaptic exchange rise to levels higher than most of waking life, even as the body is paralytic in its motionlessness—that is why the throbbing garden proves the site of so much complicated pleasure, and insight.

Slavoj Žižek, *Looking Awry* (1991): "To those sitting inside a car, outside reality appears slightly distant, the other side of a barrier or screen materialized by the glass. We perceive external reality, the world outside the car, as 'another reality,' another mode of reality, not immediately continuous with the reality inside the car."

2. Think Again

Now, from the very same place where I have this view of the garden, I am, habitually, seated to watch television. This I do almost every day, sometimes for extended periods. I'm embarrassed to say how extended: I may be fiddling with my laptop or grading papers or reading magazines or eating, but I do so from the same position on the little flower-patterned couch, and the television is invariably on. In fact, I probably spend more waking hours in this particular position than in any other single one—a situation that has only been exacerbated by the recent absence of Gail, the cultivator of our little garden, who for the moment lives elsewhere and who, therefore, must be replaced, or anyway exchanged, with some kind of ersatz company, the illusion of fullness in the room that comes from the electronic voices and pixellated faces.

Everyone says it's a digital culture, and who am I to disagree, writing this on my computer and preparing to e-mail and fax-file it to the editors of the journal that will publish it, checking my voicemail every fifteen minutes and taking calls even as I edit by using a headset-equipped portable phone? Nobody needs reminding of the facts of the digital case, especially since that would risk committing the cardinal sin of the times, namely, being boring, and thereby subverting the dominant imperatives of speed and neural stimulation—than which there is, apparently, no greater crime today. More than that, to rehearse the reasons why this time and place of ours is so immersed in technology, especially computer and television technology, would be as superfluous and meaningless as pointing out to a fish that water is wet: we all know it's true, we all behave exactly according to that knowledge, but knowing all this just doesn't help us very much.

See "Fast Forward" (Section IV) and "Warning: The Topic Today Is Boredom" (Section V).

So never mind that. What may be illuminating, instead, is to think about the interface of gardens with this consensually technological culture of ours. A 1996 exhibition of artworks at the Power Plant Gallery in Toronto's Harbourfront Centre, "Digital Gardens: A World in Mutation," attempted to do just that, with varying degrees of success. I was invited, along with several other people, none of us art experts, to offer personal commentaries on this exhibition, little running monologues that were used to shepherd people through a protracted exposure to the works, sort of weird, uninformed (if not, I hope, unintelligent) guided tours.

I was nevertheless chided by some people in the audience for not making reference to Martin Heidegger's essay on ontology's distortion by modern machines, *Die Frage nach Technik* (1977). I hereby apologize.

All of the works included in "Digital Gardens" involved some kind of play with the ideas of technology and the garden, information and nature. There were elaborate, Rube-Goldbergesque machines, constructed of discarded parts, that sow and water seeds, sprouting grass (Doug Buis); painted scenes of bucolic innocence that included blurred but intrusive reminders of human tools and their human damage (Gregory Crewdson); photographed scenes of industrial or high-tech success, captured in such a way as to emphasize the meditative greenery of a strip of parkland or infield grass (Rosemary Laing); and immersive game-like environments that were like Nintendo's or Sega's vision of the garden's spiritual refreshment (Janine Cirincione and Michael Ferraro).

The best of all these works were Rosemary Laing's time-lapse photographs of airstrips and highways, with their muted and lovely juxtapositions of planes and verdant spaces, of diesel conduits and lush channels of greenery, of the made and the grown. Here the shiny surfaces and hard edges of an aluminum wing or fuselage were softened to a supple greyness that complemented the bright greens of grass and leaf even while being held apart from them.

The wisdom here, it seemed to me, was to find the garden-like elements even in the most technologically hostile sites of transportation—the airport, the multi-lane highway—so that the energy of travel, ruled more by speed's insistent longing than almost any other aspect of modern life, could be isolated and refocused. The images captured, or rather created, gardens of beauty and philosophical reflection against the most antipathetic, least promising, backgrounds. They planted gardens where there were none before.

And because these works, like the others in the exhibition, were offered within a context of assumed hostility between technology and the natural, a hostility emblematic of the larger, indeed dominating, cultural dichotomy of technophilia and technophobia—a dichotomy that, like all binary oppositions, is associated with the deep structure of instrumental reason itself, not least in the digital 1-0 logic of computer code, which effectively reduces all meaning, if not the world itself, to long strings of on-off switches—their blending of the machined and the natural was potentially provocative and illuminating. (Not all the works, unfortunately, were as interesting in this regard as Laing's photographs.)

How is that? Well, in keeping with this binary dominance of the world, there is great pressure, in most contemporary thought and writing, to form up attitudes to technology into two opposing camps, the optimists versus the pessimists; and it is difficult, if not impossible, to resist that structure—as I have found, now and then, when speaking of these issues on television or radio. Which is why the notion of the "digital garden" is so cool, and Laing's photographs of jetliners blurred

This tendency to dichotomize is a favourite target of post-modern critics—although that criticism often falls prey to its own dichotomy, the binary opposition between those who favour binary oppositions and those who don't.

to vector slashes of silver so compelling and beautiful. Here the through-and-through technological is revealed in its beauty, not as *opposed* to beauty. This is not quite the beauty of the machine itself, the sort of mechanical sexiness that excited a Futurist like Marinetti or, in our day, calls forth the fine aesthetic sensibilities of someone like David Gelernter. But it is related, and as much to the point in getting us to see beyond the categories of thinking that currently dominate our projects of world-construction.

Gelernter, a Yale University computer-science professor, has lately articulated with some success the eroticism of the sleek and curvaceous machine, an eroticism that most of us, if we are being honest, will acknowledge we find fetching, sometimes deeply so. This is not simply a matter of our accepting that a given tool, a frozen chunk of instrumental rationality, is capable of supporting rich aesthetic as well as use values: an Italian juicer that has the brushed-metal smoothness of a miniature invading spaceship, say, or a vacuum cleaner that sports the supervenient racing-car scarlet and sweeping French curves of a design by Enzo Ferrari.

No, at some level the matter is more complicated than this old rigid structure in which we presume that a surcharge of (value-added) beauty illicitly rides atop the (basic) instrumentality of a machine. There is a closer marriage than that in the flowing lines of the B-1's delta wing or the Maserati's smartly swept bonnet, even in the bicycle frame's minimalist triple-triangle or the hammer's snub nose and flared neck. For here the instrumental and the aesthetic are not even opposed, let alone separable. The sleeker machine actually goes faster, performs better: it is superior *as a machine* to the ugly one. The deep beauty of machines is never a matter of overcoming a basic opposition of efficiency and beauty by adding the latter to the former; it is rather that, at some fundamental level, beauty and efficiency are one thing, a single value pursued singly.

It was insights like these, of course, that made Gelernter a target for the urban-terrorist serial killer known as the Unabomber, whose 1993

David Gelernter, *Machine Beauty: Elegance and the Heart of Technology* (1998). For an altogether funnier and more enchanting perspective, from a front-line hacker of code, see Ellen Ullman, *Close to the Machine: Technophilia and Its Discontents* (1997).

mail-bomb attack on the computer scientist resulted in the loss of his right hand and right eye. Gelernter opened what he thought was an unsolicited doctoral dissertation, only to have it blow up in his face, damaging most of the right side of his upper body.

Blinded and bleeding but still, amazingly, conscious and able to move, he staggered to nearby Yale New Haven Hospital, humming a Zionist marching song "with a good strong beat" to himself the whole way, and collapsed in the emergency room with a recorded blood pressure of zero. Doctors thought he had lost so much blood that he would certainly die, but some of those beautiful machines saved him. Gelernter is a conservative of the moral-tradition sort, a guy who thinks "the liberal elite" is draining America of its lifeblood; but he's also a subtle and original thinker whose views on technology are far from monolithic. (He also has a fondness, which I share, for the user-friendly Macintosh desktop interface.)

All of which is by way of saying that, whatever else may be true of the Unabomber, he shows a distressing lack of imagination in thinking that someone like David Gelernter is the enemy. At heart the Unabomber is an essentialist, a prisoner of his own critique (as well as, now, of the federal authorities). He succumbs to the binary logic of the oppositional thinking he claims to oppose, constructing along the way a violent either/or universe in which, if you're not part of his manifesto-defended solution of small-scale communities and face-to-face communication, you're part of the problem—and hence fair game for the destruction of your face.

If there is, as I believe, a little of the Unabomber in all of us, the Neo-Luddite Within who fears and hates the apparently heedless "advance" of technology across our culture and our lives, it is equally true that such fear and hatred only solidifies the conviction of those who would naturalize technology, make of it an inexorable juggernaut that cannot be resisted, cannot even be slowed. If, in other words, we don't acknowledge the attraction of technology along with our fear of it—and perhaps the two are not unrelated, just as the fiercest kind of erotic attraction can be

Gelernter, *Drawing Life: Surviving the Unabomber* (1997). You might wonder why nobody balked at this sight, but the neighbourhood around the hospital is the kind of place where auto-body shops offer a two-for-one bullet-hole special.

Theodore Kaczynski, the former mathematics professor who was the Unabomber, is now serving the four life terms he was sentenced to in May 1998.

Jim Dixon in Kingsley Amis's *Lucky Jim* (1954) finds that the sight of his beloved makes him want to "pull the collar of his dinner jacket over his head and run out into the street." Says the narrator: "He'd read somewhere, or been told, that somebody like Aristotle or I.A. Richards had said that the sight of beauty makes us want to move towards it. Aristotle or I.A. Richards had been wrong about that, hadn't he?"

felt, sometimes, as a strange form of revulsion, an inability to be comfortably near the object of intense desire—we will never understand the possibilities of transcendence that lie within our grasp. It is not so much a question of "what to do with technology" as it is a matter of how to understand ourselves as people who are everywhere shaped by our own capacity to make and use tools.

The beauty created in the digital gardens may have this virtue, then: it makes us aware of the complexities in thinking through the relationship between art and nature, between elegance and efficiency, between machined and cultured. It makes us see two sides of ourselves, and therefore makes us see that we are more than two-sided.

3. Think Twice

That interplay is but one reason why the currently fashionable flight from the digital world, the refusal of technology embodied in the gentler neo-Luddism of the "voluntary simplicity" movement, which lays so much emphasis on gardening and home-baking, is self-defeating. Another prominent reason: this new simplicity is a form of luxury good, a lifestyle option, often pursued moralistically, that is open only to the privileged few. Genuinely oppressed people typically want more, not less, technology in their lives, cars and running water and telephones.

The digital garden reminds us that gardens, even when they are not digital, are always already sites of high-level technological success, the imposition of human will on alien landscapes. They are cultural creations, the result of sustained and careful human intervention. Not nature at all, in short, but our idea, often enough excessively pretty or distorted or simply banal, of what nature ought to be. If we fail to see that, then we fail to understand the insights about ourselves and our desires that make the garden so interesting a place to visit—or just to look upon.

But, more than that, nature itself is likewise implicated in the far-flung influences of human concept-construction. "Nothing is natural until we make it so," a philosopher once wrote, and he was right. Nature as something set off against us, whether it is seen as threatening (red in tooth and claw) or as comforting (the spiritual refreshment of the bird-watcher or hill-walker), is not the straightforward natural category we usually take it to be. Indeed, the concept or category "natural" makes sense only against the presumed background of another concept or category we call the "artificial," and both of these can make sense only as part of an even more basic epistemological commitment to dichotomizing thought, a misleading, if enormously powerful, anti-holism. That commitment is so basic, indeed, that it goes largely unquestioned—until we begin to consider how our expectations and notions of nature have been conditioned in countless social and cultural ways, from the sunsets of Turner to the lyricism of Whitman.

As a habit of thought, the fundamental presupposition of oppositional reason is, as we say, so effectively naturalized as to appear not just beyond question as a matter of fact, but unintelligible to question as a matter of principle. But that is not so. The exclusive logic of A or not-A, however useful it is for all manner of purposes, is not woven inextricably into the fabric of the universe, or anyway is not necessarily the limit of what can be thought in this universe—as you and I are proving right now, as we engage in the mysterious act of communicating our suspension of the very presumptions that made much of this communication possible. *Play* is not A and it is not not-A. To play is therefore, as before, to make sophistication unsophisticated. And once again we can thank the garden, digital or otherwise, for being one of those human things that make such play possible.

If the natural is always artificial, it is likewise true that the artificial is always natural. We are culture-making creatures of this natural world too, with our thoughts and our dreams and our sometimes violent plans. We should go into the garden not to flee that unsettling, multivalent knowledge, but to find it and revel in it.

Francis Bacon, *On Gardens* (1625): "God Almighty first planted a garden. And indeed it is the purest of human pleasures. It is the greatest refreshment to the spirits of man; without which, buildings and palaces are but gross handiworks; and a man shall ever see, that when ages grow to civility and elegancy, men come to build stately sooner than to garden finely; as if gardening were the greater perfection."

41

Politics

Voices, Images, Reflections

....

Politics is my abiding passion, and political philosophy my professional
turf—though some, notably Plato, would say that this is an untenable
combination. The pieces in this section do not attempt to resolve that issue.
They are concerned, instead, with the relation between surface and
substance in the world of the political. The way spin and mediation sometimes
threaten to steal our citizenship from us. The way depth is sometimes
sacrificed for image. The way we can, perhaps, battle these tendencies with
a more robust and thoughtful commitment to the public good.

   None of this amounts, in itself, to a political theory. But all of it is necessary
to begin the process of clearing our minds, that crucial enabling condition of
all worthwhile political activity. And so we discover some important things. For
instance, that not all images are false, or all reflections empty. And that, in
the end, there is no unmediated political sphere, because politics begins in the
original act of human mediation: trying to say something to someone else.
That is where we can always, must always, begin.

Insanity Lurks on the Campaign Trail

I think it was Salman Rushdie who said that a writer should re-read George Orwell's essay "Politics and the English Language" at least once a year. In general, this is good advice. There is no more brilliant, and brief, dissection than Orwell's of flabby euphemism and rhetorical wheeziness in the writing of English.

But there are dangers. A minor one at any time is that the brisk vigilance counselled by Orwell will render a lot of what you commonly write unconscionable. You will find yourself with your hands tied, more or less unable to write a word that does not offend. This is the linguistic equivalent of being a shortstop who thinks too much.

The condition probably won't last long. In a U.S. presidential election year, however, there is an even greater danger. Put baldly: if you take Orwell's counsel to heart as you listen to the campaign speeches written for the candidates, *you will go mad.*

The reason is that Orwell is too right. His view of the dodges and shortcomings of political language is just too clear-eyed, too exacting. While listening to the kind of political speech-making that will carry George Bush or Bill Clinton into the White House this November, it's possible that the awful truth of Orwell's demythologizing will expose you to the cold chill of metaphysical loneliness. We can take only so much of this; then we go bonkers.

I don't mean to imply that we would prefer it otherwise. Most people who force themselves to listen to that speech-making will realize, in some far reach of their souls, that it is all nonsense, self-serving sham. They will. They just won't want to face up to the implications of the realization. And who can blame them? The truth is a cold, hard thing. It's unsettling.

This is truer than ever in the wake of Bill Clinton's 1998 grand jury testimony, which took linguistic distortion and lawyerly casuistry to new cynical heights.

44

"When one watches some tired hack on the platform mechanically repeating the familiar phrases—*bestial atrocities, iron heel, bloodstained tyranny, free peoples of the world, stand shoulder to shoulder,*" Orwell says, "one often has a curious feeling that one is not watching a live human being but some kind of dummy: a feeling which suddenly becomes stronger when the light catches the speaker's spectacles and turns them into blank discs which seem to have no eyes behind them."

I experience this vertiginous feeling all the time, maybe twice a day during the Republican convention. And I was reminded of this passage when I looked at an article in the August *Atlantic Monthly* called "A Visit with George Bush." The article was illustrated by a drawing of Bush, his trademark wire-rims turned, indeed, into "blank discs." The hook-line for the article was a simple question: Can George Bush Think? The answer was unsurprising. "Can he think in an organized, linear way about problems?" a former presidential staffer asked rhetorically. "Can he pose the thesis and antithesis, and draw a synthesis? No. He's the least contemplative man I've ever met."

Now, is Bush an execrable speaker because he can't think, or does it work the other way around? Or does it matter? Orwell said no. English "becomes ugly and inaccurate because our thoughts are foolish, but the slovenliness of our language makes it easier for us to have foolish thoughts." We all get into bad habits, the laziness and vagueness Orwell minutely examines. The point is that "[i]f one gets rid of these habits one can think more clearly, and to think clearly is a necessary first step towards political regeneration."

> **Orwell shows** up the feebleness of the common view that an idea can be clear in mind but somehow not make it clearly to the page. Nonsense. Until you *write* it, it doesn't exist.

So don't blame George Bush for his laughable mangling of sense and syntax. But don't look to him for Orwell's revolution either. Oh, no. Logic demands that only a person who can think can think *more clearly*. Leave Bush out of it.

Orwell detailed many bad habits of writing and speaking that are still with us today, but his greatest scorn is reserved for euphemism. Pretentious diction, dying metaphors, passive-voice constructions, and other carbuncles on the body of the language—the habits of the bureaucratic

45

Or, perhaps even more so, the academic.

mind—obscure meaning with great efficiency; but only euphemism actively subverts it. Only euphemism substitutes false for real meaning.

"The great enemy of clear language is insincerity," Orwell therefore concluded. "When there is a gap between one's real and one's declared aims, one turns as it were instinctively to long words and exhausted idioms, like a cuttlefish squirting out ink." The simple reason is that, in politics, most of one's real aims are too cruel, nasty, or self-serving to be publicly aired.

Can anyone speak sincerely in the political forum? I don't know. What I do know is that another Orwellian vision, Doublethink, appears to be dominant in political rhetoric. The problem, in other words, isn't insincerity itself, but insincerity that the speaker actually comes to believe: the obliteration of the distinction between false and real. George Bush saw no gap between his real and declared intentions when he gave the "Read my lips" speech. I think he probably does consider himself "the Education President."

What this means, ultimately, is that nobody can appeal to sincerity and make any headway. Consider Al Gore, speaking to an Israeli political action committee during the run-up to the recent Democratic National Convention. "I don't want you to think that I'm saying this as part of . . . some kind of . . . political rhetoric," Gore said, the pauses acting as marks of sincerity, as if he were groping for the right word. "I say it because . . . I believe it . . . from the bottom of my heart."

I'm overselling this argument. As Lionel Trilling noted, only in a modern state of dissociation do we put so much emphasis on *sincerity* as a virtue. What's so great about sincerity anyway? I may sincerely believe the most atrocious things.

When sincerity has lost the ability to speak in anything other than clichés like these, we know the battle is lost. Worse, contrary to Orwell's hope, thinking doesn't necessarily help. The trade secrets revealed by a panel of political masterminds in a recent *Harper's* magazine forum on campaign advertising showed what we long suspected: the best lack all conviction. Clever, happy people they were, these ad execs, pushing our buttons to make a mockery of the very notion of sincerity in political life.

So, as you watch the candidates this fall, gasping with feigned (or is it real?) horror at the low tactics of their opponents, making promises they know they won't keep (or do they?), it's best not to dwell on the fact that sincerity and thought aren't meaningful notions in political rhetoric. Any sense that things are actually *worse* than Orwell imagined—no mean feat—is to be avoided. You want to stay sane until at least Thanksgiving.

Sigh. I have to say that, ten years on, plain language is no easier to find in politics than it ever was. But now that fact makes me merely depressed, not insane.

The Voice of the Pundit

Is Heard in the Land

What is it that makes someone an expert? Ours is, after all, a society more of experts than of leaders. If you doubt this, I invite you to observe closely the conduct of our elected federal politicians in the approaching national election.

They will not make their decisions on the basis of vision or instinct or principle. They will be listening to experts—experts on policy, experts on tactics, and above all, experts on how to generate and interpret poll results. Their actions and speeches will be commented on by other experts, academics, and journalists, who will loom large in television screens and Focus sections, offering the polished phrases of punditry. All of these people will speak with conviction and evident authority. Some of them will sport titles and formal qualifications. They will be exemplars of a peculiarly modern political phenomenon: the expert as pundit.

Now, not all experts are pundits. Pundits are just a highly visible subset of the expert class, a particularly virulent strain, especially around election time. They are also the kind of expert most people long to become. This is mainly because punditry is not really expertise in the genuine sense. The dictionary defines an expert as "someone possessing special skill or knowledge." It also tells us that "pundit" is a Hindu word that originally meant someone learned in Sanskrit.

Okay, I appreciate the irony of my now being something of a pundit myself. But believe me when I say this article was not written out of envy. Really.

Today's pundits are not really experts, let alone experts in Sanskrit. Being a pundit does not depend on systematic or long-term training. It does not imply mastery of a complex body of information and theory. It just means saying obvious and/or opinionated things *with an air of unshakeable authority.* The *Globe and Mail* displayed disarming honesty when it headed its recent election preview with the tag-line "Punditry."

So you don't really have to know anything in particular to be a pundit. You can also be wrong lots of the time without affecting your anointed status. Nobody keeps track except a few wacko nit-pickers, and anyway, who cares? If you give good pundit-value before an election, nobody who's anybody is going to check, afterwards, to see if you accurately predicted the number of NDP seats in the new Parliament. Bad picks won't get you taken off that producer's Rolodex or out of that editor's Filofax.

Eric Alterman, whose book *Sound and Fury: The Washington Punditocracy and the Collapse of American Politics* is the best analysis of these matters, offers these five rules on the golden road to punditry:

1. Accumulate national prestige.
2. Remember that it is better to look right than to be right.
3. Write a book that transforms the entire debate on a subject of major importance.
4. Blanket the media with a contrarian view about an argument already in progress.

This is widely known as the Andrew Coyne Manoeuvre.

5. Quit your job at Harvard, get yourself appointed National Security Adviser, then Secretary of State, bomb a small Indochinese nation into oblivion, lie about it, wiretap your staff, win the Nobel Peace Prize in spite of all this, speak with a heavy German accent, and appear on "Nightline" in a tuxedo whenever possible, as if you have just left someplace terribly important.

For what it's worth, I don't own a tuxedo.

As Alterman says, punditry is not for everyone. Rules 1 and 3 mean you actually have to do something to become a pundit; people have to know who you are. But "national prestige" can mean a lot of things, and I sense a trend in which Rule 3 is becoming ever more dispensable. Rules 2 and 4 are the ones that really stick out. They demonstrate that punditry is more appearance than reality, and that it depends on the media's insatiable appetite for oppositional issues. Every producer knows it's better to have two people with wildly different positions than to have two people—or God forbid, one—expressing subtle shadings of difference.

49

In fact, because the distinction between pundit and expert has been effaced, being expert is nowadays precisely the opposite of what it used to be. You're not expected to know the fine points of a debate, let alone care about them. You're expected to hold, or at least pretend to, a stiff-necked and easily stated position. If that position can be caricatured breezily by your host or opponent, so much the better. The battle of the pundits is on. Is there a more satisfying spectacle anywhere than two experts, each convinced of his utter correctness, slugging it out on network television?

The mistake most of us make is that we worry about this. People bemoan the rise of the culture of expertise, its allegedly pernicious effect on public discourse and decision-making. They think it undermines the claims of "ordinary" citizens.

Nonsense. The battling "experts" merely cancel each other out in a flurry of claim and counter-claim. To be sure, this leaves an authority vacuum at the centre of our national life. But far from being a disaster, this is a prime democratic opportunity. We can *all* be experts now. Start writing your op-ed columns. Begin polishing your radio delivery. Trim those nosehairs for TV.

This is of course as true as ever. I'm still waiting for the democratic possibilities to begin.

And then, when we have finally flattened out the notion of expertise, when everyone's claim is superficially as good as everyone else's—when, in short, everyone is a pundit—we can get down to the real work of citizenship: making sense of arguments on their own merits, not on the basis of who offers them. Maybe then, as we go along, some genuine experts will emerge.

Graven Images

Near the beginning of *Palimpsest* (Random House, 1995), his bitchy, rollicking memoir of a remarkable, well-connected life, Gore Vidal sketches a scene that holds fast in the memory.

It is 1957 and he is at a wedding reception for his half-sister, Nini. Her maid of honour is a resplendent Jackie Kennedy, who, in the posed photographs of the event, seems to draw the eye more insistently than the begowned bride. Jackie and Vidal, related by parental marriage—they had the same step-father, Hugh Auchincloss, at different times of his much-married life—are avoiding the dullness of the party and prowling around the Washington, D.C., house both had known for a time. They find themselves in the small bedroom each had slept in, a room Vidal describes as "little larger than a closet."

"When I first moved in here, I found some old shirts of yours," Jackie tells him. "With name tags. I used to wear them, riding. Then Jack and I stayed in here, after the honeymoon. I must say he suffered quite a lot in this house, from Mother."

Skip ahead four years, and three hundred pages in this palimpsest, Vidal's much-scored tablet of writings and erasings. The author is now in Provincetown, the popular gay resort town on Cape Cod, "losing weight." Jackie calls to invite him down to Hyannisport for dinner, where she, Jack, Bobby, and their various retainers are spending the weekend. "House unchanged since before election," Vidal's notes from the time read. "Jackie at bar in pair of Capri pants and windbreaker from water-skiing. She is making daiquiris. Embrace. Into the living room from porch bar. JFK in chinos, blue shirt, looking trim."

A new perception from the distance of 1995: "It is always a delicate matter when a friend or acquaintance becomes president. Ease must

> **Jackie's mother**, Mrs. Bouvier, was a notorious harridan.

> **Now isn't** that a scene any-body would want to be part of? *Pass the daiquiris, Jackie! More chips over here, Jack!*

51

be maintained, yet one may not call him by his first name or walk ahead of him into a room." Before dinner, Vidal listens as Jack and Bobby, lounging in easy chairs, discuss affairs of state—Cuba, Berlin, the Soviets—in telegraphic family shorthand. During dinner Jack wants to talk about movies, not politics. Vidal invites Jackie to Provincetown for a night of drinking. She turns eagerly to the president: "Can I, Jack? Can I?"

They went, though Jackie, self-consciously incognito in sunglasses and scarf, did not enjoy it very much: the beginning of the iconic tragic persona she later perfected.

Gore Vidal was never so close to the world's power centres as when his friend Jack Kennedy complicated social niceties by becoming president. But from its beginnings in 1925 his life has been very much at the centre of this American century. His grandfather, Senator T. P. Gore of Oklahoma, was a blind lawmaker of famous probity; he is related, on the Gore side, to the person Vidal calls "our young cousin who currently lives in vice-presidential obscurity, a sort of family ghost flickering dimly on prime-time television." His father, Gene Vidal, was an outstanding West Point football player, the academy's first flight instructor, and later started Eastern Airlines.

His mother, Nina, spun young Gore even farther into the complex webs of Eastern Corridor power when she married Auchincloss, a long-time Washington money-man. He attended fashionable St. Albans school in Washington, where he met the love of his life, a boy called Jimmie Trimble, killed very soon after on Iwo Jima; then Exeter prep school, where he learned how to write and how to be a pain in the ass— two skills that would carry him in life.

Allan Gotlieb, patron of the arts, publisher, and former diplomat, once commented to me on the charms of Gore Vidal as encountered in Washington society. "You know," he said, "he was an asshole."

By Vidal's own account, Nina wasn't much of a mother. Indeed, she is depicted here as a self-obsessed gorgon who resented her husbands and her children even while claiming credit for their achievements. When Gene Vidal's picture was on the cover of *Time* magazine for his work in commercial air regulation, she flung the issue in his face. When, years later, the younger Vidal earned the same distinction, she wrote a long denunciation to the editors, accusing them of plotting against her.

She was, in short, a bitch. Yet Vidal himself can be gratuitous in paying back this longest of long-term debts. Below a picture of Nina wearing a peculiar high-crowned hat he writes: "Nina's defiantly phallic hat betrays her inner need."

The main purpose of any good memoir is settling old scores, and Vidal lays about with a will. His scathing judgments leave no one untouched, with particular attention reserved for a few choice subjects. Vidal on the mendacity of Truman Capote: "A famous name would be mentioned. The round pale fetus face would suddenly register a sort of tic, as if a switch had been thrown. 'Eleanor Roosevelt. Oh, I know her *intimately!*'" On the low wattage of the Duke of Windsor: "he always had something of such riveting stupidity to say on any subject that I clung to his words like the most avid courtier of the ancien regime." And on the hypocrisy of Bobby Kennedy: "Between [his] primitive religion and his family's ardent struggle ever upward from the Irish bog, he was more than usually skewed, not least by his own homosexual impulses."

Compare Kingsley Amis, *Memoirs* (1991): "I grieve at the non-flowering of that talent . . . and find it a sad come-down that James should be doing the *Spectator* literary competition every week." Or: "Given a touch of malice, not inappropriate in his case, it would be easy to present Malcolm Muggeridge in an unflattering light."

In fact Vidal spares nobody. To the age of roughly forty, when this memoir breaks off, Vidal pursued successive (and sometimes simultaneous) careers in letters and public affairs that brought him into close contact with the famous and the powerful. Never has one person known so many for so long—and kept such good notes.

First he wrote novels, publishing his first book at age twenty and a "notorious" tale of homosexual love, *The City and the Pillar*, a few years later. ("You can't be a good writer," the poet Charles Henri Ford said to the young Vidal in 1946, "because you have such lovely legs!") Soon after, desperate for money, he wrote drama for stage, television, and film—producing in the end one of the best American films ever made about politics, *The Best Man* (1964). "Outside political Washington," he says of his Tinseltown adventure, "I have never known a world so completely obsessed with itself as Hollywood, making the marriage between movies and politics inevitable."

Starring Henry Fonda and Cliff Robertson, in a battle between an intellectual gentleman and a ruthless climber.

Vidal even sought political office—once—but lost, dragged down, he says, by his Kennedy connections. Later he crafted razor-sharp political journalism and even, recently, began acting in films, turning in one brilliant performance as a cynical old pol in the 1992 election satire

Bob Roberts. Vidal was also sexually promiscuous in his youth, leading to a memorable seduction of Jack Kerouac in 1950, not to mention hilarious scenes of joint, sometimes competitive, boy-hunting with the likes of Anaïs Nin, Leonard Bernstein, and longtime friend Tennessee Williams.

All that is diverting, but the key to Vidal's success as a *political* commentator, evident in numerous wickedly accurate assessments here, and equally in his collection of essays, *United States,* published last year, is a fierce independence of mind. He hews to no party line and his politics, a mixture of sexual licentiousness, ingrained social-democratic belief, and the successful writer's disdain of both taxes and arts subsidies, are *sui generis.* He was, for example, no fan of Kennedy's presidency: "I thought him something of a lightweight politically, since he was pretty much what the sheltered and unadventurous son of a rich right-winger would be." And yet the objection is not especially deep. "For me," he says, "politics had been the family business and I regarded it more as a process than as a matter of theory, much less ideology."

Vidal can be vicious, but mainly because, having been raised in its embrace, he has an unerring instinct for the foibles of privilege. He takes great pleasure in exposing venality and that, more than all the salacious gossip, is what makes the book so enjoyable. Once, a friend congratulated Gene Vidal on his son's evident courage in speaking his mind before the powerful. "What's courageous about it?" Gene wanted to know. "He just doesn't give a damn what anybody thinks."

Good for him. And, with this entertaining and unexpectedly moving memoir in hand, good for us too.

I found the Bernstein material a little hard to credit at the time; but then, who knows?

Some might call this hypocrisy, of course.

Six Scenes of Separation:

Confessions of a

Post-Facto Trudeaumaniac

1. CFB Summerside, 1973

She could touch her nose with the tip of her tongue, this girl. She didn't
like to do it, because she felt like a freak, but now and then she would, to
impress a boy or a crowd. Her name was Alison Gaudet. They were all
called Gaudet or Arsenault or Beamon or McIntosh, it seemed. She was a
bit cross-eyed, her face covered in freckles, her hair a hand-cut brown
helmet. Like the rest of us, she always wore baggy sweaters and worn
corduroys to school. It was Grade Five, we were ten or eleven, and we
lived on a grubby air force base. We had good clothes for church—I had
my First Communion outfit, a purple leisure suit in itchy polyester, tight
bell-bottom trousers and a sleeveless tunic that went over a matching
purple-and-white paisley shirt with huge wing collar and five snap buttons at each wrist—but on the whole we dressed like slobs. This was
before ski clothes went neon, before the NFL and NBA annexed the playgrounds of the continent, before clothes became billboards. We were
genderless, indiscriminate, anonymous.

Even for 1973, purple
paisley was pretty daring;
hence also my possible future
manifestation as the Writer
Formerly Known as Kingwell.

One day Alison Gaudet showed up wearing *it*. The bright red oblong
popped out of the brown-and-grey visual field of the concrete schoolyard, otherwise brightened only by the twined-together rubber bands we
used to jump over in a modified hopscotch game. It felt like the whole
playground suddenly went into glacial stop-action, zooming in frame by
frame to the dab of colour she sported with studied casualness. The patch
was made of thin, shiny fabric with a sticky back, and it adorned Alison's
brown jacket like a gaudy military decoration or badge of rank. In the

55

middle there was a stylized *L* and a small maple leaf. Alison had joined the Great Man's army. She was a Liberal.

Alison brought more patches to school the next day and she was, without warning, the most popular girl in Grade Five. We all wanted the L-patch for ourselves, craved the obscure identification with the great events, and especially the Great Man, whose talisman it was. We knew his face well enough, the famously simian features, the curved lips of that slight smile. Vaguely we recalled the tossed Frisbee, the trampoline escapade, the screaming crowds, the flashy sports jackets—images imprinted not from television, as they would be now, but black-and-white stills from the front pages of the newspapers left on the living-room floor, glimpsed as we lay on our stomachs looking at the cartoons. He was the first media icon, the first Personality, I ingested almost entirely by osmosis, soaking up the snapshots and judgments and alleged character traits without full consciousness. I had seen cartoons and T-shirts of him saying "Fuddle Duddle" and I thought that was funny, though I didn't know what it meant. I heard people talking about the rose in his lapel, the rumours of sexual escapades, the ability to make young women swoon, and the subtle promise of sexual and political liberation from our bleak northern lives. He seemed sophisticated, urban, impossibly far away—yet somehow mine too, my leader, my beacon. I was ten.

Before long there was a war on the playground because somebody's brother had obtained a small supply of Conservative patches—red, blue, and white rivals for our attention. Running battles broke out, with little gangs of us ostracizing each other for wearing the wrong patch, or making sudden runs at one unlucky girl to tear the sticky thing from her jacket. We had debates about the relative merits of the two parties: which looked friendlier, or cooler. The Conservative patches appeared to fly the American colours (very bad), while the Liberal ones were reminiscent of Team Canada (very good), which we had watched beat the Russians the year before on a big cabinet-style TV rolled into the portable. The word "conservative" sounded dull, boring, parental. "Liberal" seemed, by contrast, full of possibility, a tiny squeak of adolescent rebelliousness still audible in its etymology.

I decided to expand the scope of my enthusiasm. I asked my mother about the leader, the Liberal, the Great Man, the Personality. She twisted her mouth in disapproval. "Arrogant," she said. It was the first time I had heard this word. "What does that mean?" I replied. "Ask your father."

But my father was non-committal, contenting himself with hinting darkly at past sins and future punishments, all beyond my ken. The Great Man, he suggested, was on the verge of something disastrous. "Pride comes before a fall," he said, like a fire-and-brimstone preacher. The grisly and incongruous events of 1970—the Cross abduction, the Laporte murder, the military occupation—were still fresh in many minds, though not my own. My father, who had grown up on the hardscrabble streets of Quebec City, entered a religious order, left to join the air force, and studied political science in Ontario, perhaps felt some proprietary interest in the case: the deep pull of righteous political violence in general and Quebec nationalism in particular, the countervailing prickly dangers of statism, the sick logic of the crackdown. On the whole, he seemed to think the Great Man had done more harm than good with his treatment of the October Crisis. The journalist Walter Stewart was of the same mind; already, in 1971, he had written a book called *Shrug: Trudeau in Power*, the first sustained critique of the Great Man's loose-cannon approach to political leadership.

Understanding came to me only later. At the time, the suggestion of these big events, all this passion and violence, just made me wish, as no Grand Funk Railroad or Edgar Winter record in my brother's collection could, that I had been born a few years earlier, so I would be old enough to understand the pull of the shadowy Great Man, this political magician who had such power to inspire strong feeling. So I could make sense of the excitement. So I would know why people found the phrase "fuddle duddle" worthy of wearing on a T-shirt. What could it mean?

My brother's collection, to which I contributed a couple of Alice Cooper albums and Jackson Five singles, was full of quintessential early-Seventies dinosaurs like Deep Purple, as well as the complete Creedence Clearwater Revival *oeuvre*.

57

2. Winnipeg, 1977

It meant he *was* arrogant, I realized from the relative wisdom and world-liness of high school. In February 1971, it turns out, the Great Man had, in a stormy Commons debate on unemployment rates, told two Conservative MPs to fuck off, mouthing the words to keep them out of Hansard. Challenged by an opposition backbencher, Lincoln Alexander, to repeat the words, the Great Man did so—silently again. "Mr. Speaker," he then said to the House, "I challenge any member opposite to say that they heard me utter a single sound." Asked by the press scrum later what he had said, he uttered the immortal phrase, the keynote words of early 1970s Canadian politics. South of the border, at around the same time, the Americans were having their own go at a troubling leader with aspi-rations beyond democratic accountability—Nixon's downfall was a process we all watched unfold between doses of Saturday morning car-toons—but here we had mostly made a joke of it: Fuddle Duddle, for God's sake. It was ridiculous.

But the Great Man loved the absurdity of it all, and now looking back at it from the perspective of high school, I was impressed, though not entirely in a good way. I found it tempting to read Fuddle Duddle as a kind of mythical midnight for Canada's celebrated civility, the old cul-ture of diplomatic politeness I associated as much with Lester Pearson as with my parents' moral strictures. This seemed exciting, daring, even counter-cultural. It was easy for me to imagine the Great Man swearing with inventiveness and abandon, and indulging in other profane pleas-ures like sex and strong drink—things that appealed to me at a pretty deep (if unrealized) level in Grade Nine. He was a man; more than that, he was a *mensch*.

In fact, this judgment of the Fuddle Duddle episode's cultural weight was entirely in keeping with the new image of the Great Man that I now began to construct. This new version of the Personality had been there all along, but it was new to me, distilled not from the overheated chemicals of late-1960s mania but from older materials, nostalgia about the heady Sixties days at *Cité libre* (which I had never read), intense

A reporter writes: "Trudeau appeared to tell Conservative MPs to 'fuck off.' There are various accounts of what happened later in the media scrum and I think Kingwell has it slightly wrong, but in essence Trudeau claimed he had said nothing and merely mouthed the sentiments."

discussions on the streets of Quebec City (which I had never visited). This new Great Man was more intellectual, less frivolous, than the leader of the red-L playground faction: brainy, reflective, more *il penseroso* than *l'allegro*.

I often found myself looking through one of Don Harron's satirical Charlie Farquharson books, somebody's Christmas present to my father, which featured pictures of the Great Man in compromising poses, under captions that mocked him and his carefully maintained Personality as the philosopher-king. It was meant to be dismissive, but somehow, though I did not then know anything about Plato, I found myself thinking, Yes, that's it. The mythical leader, the politician as worldly sage— the ruler greater than the man, the leader larger than life. I read the biographies, soaked up the details of his bicultural upbringing, the Jesuit education, his sense of manifest destiny, especially the celebrated *citoyen du monde* period, in which the Great Man travelled the globe, deciding at leisure where he would make his historical mark. I was, let it be said, in a Jesuit school myself.

Arrogant—I knew exactly what it meant now, the twin edges of a personality admirably certain of itself and distressingly convinced of its own utter superiority to everyone else. I also knew that nobody was more so than the Great Man, that he was a genius with it, a virtuoso, especially when you factored in the faux modesty, the boyish charm, with which he had fended off suggestions of a design on the highest elected office in the land. "I just want to go on being justice minister," he had said, smiling bashfully, not looking at the cameras. The same way he had said a year before, with a sense of knowing what he was talking about, that "the state has no place in the bedrooms of the nation."

What did it all add up to, what did it mean? It meant he was a star, maybe the first and last one Canadian politics has produced, his status as Personality stronger by the year almost despite the realities of policy or budget plan. Things had moved on even in the Personality, of course, and the mania was fading quickly, all but gone. But I was looking backwards and there were facts that could not be denied, even if they could be

John Milton, *Il Penseroso* (1632): "But let my due feet never fail / To walk the studious Cloister's pale, / And love the high embowed Roof, / With antic Pillars massy proof, / And storied Windows richly dight, / Casting a dim religious light."

obscured. Bedrooms, roses, intellectual passion, that wiry athleticism—still all there. And then there was Margaret, the hippie the Great Man had wed in 1971, when she was just twenty-two—her own mother only two years younger than the groom himself. Even when they split apart, even when she was spotted partying with Mick and the Rolling Stones at Studio 54, it somehow reflected well on the Great Man. "If this gorgeous, free-spirited flower child could go for the PM—despite the chasm of age, experience, intellect and inclination that yawned between them," one spectator wrote, "then we must indeed have the coolest and sexiest leader on the face of God's earth." Oh yeah, baby.

"Just watch me!" he had said of his decision to invoke the War Measures Act in 1970. Who could resist watching his every move? Not I, looking wilfully backwards, at fourteen.

From **Greig Dymond** and Geoff Pevere, *Mondo Canuck* (1996), a very funny book that contains the best analysis I know of Trudeau's pop-star status; I have relied on it throughout for various details.

3. St. Michael's College, University of Toronto, 1980

I learned what a philosopher-king really was in my first semester, in a philosophy class taught with truly extraordinary ineptness. In a year-long course that was supposed to span the centuries of the Western tradition, we barely made it past the pre-Socratic philosophers Heraclitus and Parmenides. But we did read *The Republic* cover to cover, or I did, and it is still the most illuminating book I have ever read on the snaky temptations of political power, the harsh demands and occasionally soul-destroying imperatives of ruling. Only those who had glimpsed the Form of the Good, says Plato, the ultimate truth, were suitable to rule, because only they could be trusted to orient the state to proper ends with the necessary mixture of wisdom and deft deception of the philosophically less able. The philosophers would not want to get their hands dirty in this fashion, of course, preferring the tidy pleasures of abstract contemplation of geometrical figures, mathematical axioms, and philosophical essences. But devotion to wisdom would demand it of them: reluctant kings, condescending to lead the rest of us out of our dark ignorance. "Cities will have no respite from evil, my dear Glaucon," Socrates says to his young friend at the crucial point in this argument, "nor will the human race, I think, unless philosophers rule as kings in the cities, or those we now call kings and rulers genuinely and adequately study philosophy—until, that is, political power and philosophy coalesce, and the various natures of those who now pursue the one to the exclusion of the other are forcibly debarred from doing so."

That's an inspirational thought to some—a terrifying one to others. But it seemed to me that the Great Man was not quite what Plato had in mind. For one thing, his reluctance to rule—a paradoxical sign, Plato suggests, of someone's suitability to take up the job—was always more feigned than real. The Great Man actually craved power, felt the need of it in every bone of his small frame. In Platonic terms he was not so much philosopher as *timocrat*, the honour-lover or guru who seeks self-aggrandizement in the form of political power; the man devoted not so much to wisdom as to himself. And there was of course no mention in *The Republic* of the singular portentous talent for siring children born on Christmas. At the same time, the haughty style of the philosopher-king, the unwillingness to suffer fools, the sense of superior knowledge, were all there.

As was much else too, always depending on the moment and the audience. That same year, on New Year's Eve, Marshall McLuhan, the college's resident sage and media darling, died at the age of sixty-nine. There was a long obituary of him in the college newspaper. McLuhan, I discovered later, had been a fan of the Great Man, or of his media phenomenon, of his Personality; they had corresponded and dined together regularly. McLuhan had famously called the Great Man a pure creation of the television age, certainly the first one in Canadian history, a persona-projecting actor admirably suited to the demands of media-saturated politics. A politician who expertly practised the truncated discipline of the sound bite, before the term was invented, and made his personality more important than his policies. A prime minister who thrusted and parried with members of the press, mocking their inadequacies, demolishing their lines of reasoning with an alchemical

Plato, *Republic,* Book V, 473d–e: "Otherwise the city we have been describing will never grow into a possibility or see the light of day. It is because I saw how very paradoxical this statement would be that I have for some time hesitated to make it. It is hard to realize that there can be no happiness, public or private, in any other city."

61

Michael Ignatieff, a worker on the first campaign, told me that Trudeau was actually extremely uncomfortable in front of the camera and the microphone in the early stages of his political career.

compound of witty deflection, exaggerated Gallic shrugs, and shrewd insult. "The medium can't take a real face," McLuhan had famously said of the Great Man's televisual triumphs. "It has to have a mask."

Also that fall I actually heard, for the first time, the phrase "cult of personality." It was used, pejoratively, to describe an editor of the main undergraduate newspaper who possessed qualities of wit and bravado sufficient to motivate his skeptical peers. He made himself and his moods the subject of editorials, wrote incessantly in a style borrowed from comic books and tabloid newspapers, and did wickedly accurate imitations of everyone he knew. His merest utterance was listened to with a mixture of devotion, fear, and dislike. He was hated, respected, and—in an odd way—loved. You felt you wanted to resist the influence of that carefully crafted persona, that whiff of self-cancelling energy in the inability to be natural, but you were drawn to it anyway. So with the Great Man, and for the same reasons. He was still, at this comparatively late date, an obscure object of our love: a complicated and much-scored devotion that prized, even while mistrusting, the fact that he could be charming or statesmanlike or cool, whenever the occasion demanded it. Robert Fulford has said, accurately enough, that Canada was a much less provincial place in the late 1960s and early 1970s than it became in the 1980s, when we bogged down in constitutional bickering and intramural dither. In 1969, for instance, John Lennon and Yoko Ono came north to visit both McLuhan and the Great Man, a politico-media pilgrimage of almost unmeasurable cool. The latter meeting, in Ottawa, has been sagely described by one analyst as "the politician as pop star welcoming the pop star as politician." Yes, indeed.

But by 1980, with McLuhan dead and the Great Man apparently not long for the political world, Fulford's judgment seemed all too accurate—and depressing. Once again I felt deprived of something dangerous and challenging but highly desirable, like a boy who turns eighteen the day armistice is declared. "Trudeaumania" had by this time become almost a joke word, as diminished and tarnished with time as the word "groovy," as risible as platform shoes or bell bottoms. People who had

Of course, platform shoes, bell bottoms, and the word

been drawn into politics by the mania, seduced by the madness and aura of the 1968 campaign, the Great Man's pop-star ascension to the highest elected office in the land, now looked back on their youthful foolishness with a kind of detached disapproval. How very young we were! How impressionable! How desperate in our longing for something sexy . . . modern . . . world-historical! But I didn't want to go to that middle-aged, self-abnegating place, that region of what I now recognize as Boomer revisionism. I was seventeen and I wanted the cool party, the celebration of the politician as hipper-than-thou Personality, to keep going and going. I wanted my political optimism, my sense of Canada as a player on the world stage, my suspicion that power really is sexy—and I wanted them free of the cheap editorial cynicism of hindsight.

So in some quarters, notably among the newly politicized left-liberal university students of my acquaintance, the cult itself continued, even intensified—modulating now away from sheer pop-star hysteria and gradually taking on the quality of a religious or spiritual gathering, a focusing of hope and aspiration on a central point that seemed to possess position but not dimension. The very idea of the Great Man alone remained now, the politician as wise patriarch, dutifully supporting the three children Margaret had borne him, a father to us all. She was long gone, a dim reminder of the lesson of 1967—that Canada could be genuinely world-class without having to resort to actually saying so. But the surface cool had deepened to a richer and more lustrous appeal, a mature charisma, and in this way, as Larry Zolf said so accurately in 1984, the Great Man became "our permanent Expo," aging patchily along with Habitat and the rest of the Montreal site but reminding us, despite the cracks and stress spots, of future possibilities as well as former glories.

In 1982, finally, the Constitution Act patriated the founding documents of Canadian politics. The Great Man was fading, the mania a thing of the past, but his legacy was going to be glorious. I bought a copy of the act, which I still have somewhere. In first-year politics class, the shadow he cast over all of us was long, if also rarely mentioned. We didn't bandy his name about because we didn't have to; it was in the very air,

"groovy" are all back in style. Personally, I pride myself on never having stopped using the word "groovy."

The professor was Stephan Dupré; his POL100 course, which explained Canadian politics to semi-conscious neophytes like me, was known as "The Jeanne Sauvé Show."

63

even if not on the cover of the act itself. We were his children, three hundred of us in a giant lecture theatre every Monday, Wednesday, and Friday at ten, the former patch-wearing kids from the playgrounds of the nation. When we thought about what it meant to be Canadian—when I think about it even now—he came inevitably to mind.

4. Convocation Hall, University of Toronto, 1984

It was his last speech as prime minister, part of what can only be called the farewell tour. Like an aging rock musician or clapped-out tenor, he took to the road to call in on the little people and thank them, one last time, for the glory days of old, the bright promises and high hopes of two decades of public service. Not mania again, even now at the end, but a muted hint of that madness, a willing suspension of the accreted disbelief and misgivings, for the sake of the moment. The 1983–84 global peace initiative had been a bust, the scope of the Great Man's ambition for the first time openly mocked: Here, after all, was the same man who, in 1970, had sent tanks into the streets of Montreal with a dismissive shrug. But still we could not resist watching him, cheering him. As editor of the university newspaper, I had a ticket. With a mixture of awe and irony I joined the expectant crowd, aware that my younger selves—and those I had not been, but only imagined—were all along for the ride.

There was, too, a mythological aspect to the story of the Great Man's stepping down—his famous midnight walk in an Ottawa snowstorm, his striking out on foot, game as always for exercise even at sixty-four, to ponder his future and his calling: a piece of self-dramatization so perfect, so Byronesque in its romanticism, that if it had not happened we would have had to invent it. The dark sky, the snow falling, the hard choices: it was like a scene from a dream or a film. It was both fake and utterly right; and why not? On such moments as this the Great Man's entire image depended, a cult that had been artfully, lovingly constructed.

I saw him, before the speech, striding manfully around King's College Circle on the front campus with the president of the university. The

64

Great Man was wearing a big fur hat to keep the cold away from the famous bald head, now considered thoroughly chic, a sign of mature virility. The two of them, swinging their arms and taking bold steps through the scattered, awestruck undergraduates, looked like they were having some kind of race. The Great Man, smiling impishly, was of course winning. I came within perhaps ten feet of them. He seemed happy, enjoying himself thoroughly, making even this little convivial stroll into a fierce competition. That spoke easily of the man's mercurial personality, the ingrained vigour and charisma, but I saw, too, an eerie analogue of the midnight walk, a kind of Russian-poet-turned-double-agent effect now, a low-pitched John le Carré echo.

The president would have been George Connell, who was a lot taller and longer-legged than Trudeau. Could the Great Man really have beaten him in a foot race?

The speech itself was not memorable. He was going. He was gone. And all those who followed him must be, by comparison, as dwarfs milling round the legs of a titan. Looking on benignly, from above, he would watch them bury themselves. Some acts really are too hard to follow, he said, without having to shape the words. I sat in the stuffy hall, slush melting off my boots, and believed him.

5. Bora Laskin Law Library, University of Toronto, 1987

The last time I saw the Great Man in the flesh was in the fall of 1987, when I returned to Toronto for a visit from Yale. I was twenty-four, and had just started to grapple again with the idea of justice and the philosopher-king. By a delicious coincidence, the October edition of *Saturday Night* magazine placed a reprinted 1960 profile of Pearson, written by the pundit-on-the-rise and future Trudeau biographer Richard Gwyn, next to a subtle new analysis of the Great Man's legacy by the historian and novelist Michael Ignatieff, the son of George, a diplomatic colleague of Pearson. "He lacks a capacity for ruthlessness," Gwyn wrote of Smiling Mike, then leader of the Opposition, "and will go out of his way not to hurt people's feelings. . . . His success at the UN did not come about through grandstand plays but through patient negotiations in back rooms to bring about commonsense compromises." In contrast, Ignatieff

65

had a different take on the Northern Magus: "In political warfare he never had any patience for niceties. No-one played harder or rougher than he, and he would claim that the constitutional issues at stake demanded the knockout punch rather than the polite rebuke."

The more I thought about it, the more I was convinced that Fuddle Duddle had indeed been the death knell for the old Canadian culture. It signalled the beginning of a long decline into political manipulation and braggadocio, the unquestioned preference among subsequent generations of pols for hardball and, on the flip side, the voters' penchant for cynicism about lawmakers. Fuddle Duddle *was* Canada's Watergate, the first significant breach in the old bargain of good faith between governors and governed. The Great Man had, perforce, been at the centre of it, cementing his status as the most notorious politician of his country's young existence. His arrogance had extended not only to his parliamentary colleagues, but also to the conventions of Parliament themselves, even—taking the statism of the October Crisis into account—to the rule of law itself. Not even high stakes could justify such contempt for citizens' rights, I thought. The glow of adulation faded in me, as in so many others, though I have to admit to a certain delayed reaction. I saw it all, clearly, for the first time. And for me, the bloom was finally off the rose in his lapel.

Or was it? Once again I sat in Convocation Hall and listened to the Great Man speechify about the nature of politics. Not a firebrand address this time, nor even a wistful one, but, instead, he presented a reasoned legal brief, heavy with casebook references that I could not imagine he had chased down himself. He reviewed the growing body of Charter decisions, speaking dispassionately but still somehow like the proud father of that document. Carefully, and in detail, he assessed the judgments of Chief Justice Brian Dickson, who was sitting in the front row, gazing awkwardly up. It was eerie: a thoroughly academic performance, but set against a background of history and personality, a strangely moving drama of nation-building people pausing to reflect on their work.

The occasion was the opening of the Bora Laskin Law Library. The reception after the speech was picketed by striking library workers and, though I have never crossed a picket line before or since, I decided to squeeze through the gate in order to get closer to the Great Man, to feel the dying heat from the embers of his Personality. There was a crowd. I tried going to a smaller gate, reasoning, incorrectly as it turned out, that there would be no pickets there. With no other visitors around, I was singled out for special attention and called a scab. I didn't feel much better when, glass of wine and cheese-and-cracker in hand, I watched the Great Man stroll by. He swam through the crowd expertly, smiling and greeting like a royal, and I caught his eye and smiled at him. His gaze didn't linger. I was left standing. I took a sip of my lukewarm wine.

6. The Annex, Toronto, 1997

I have never met him, certainly never had the opportunity to test the limits of the Personality, in its various forms, against the reality of the person. I have been close, in spirit and in body, only these few crucial times—close enough to reach out and touch him, close enough (in another mood) to spit on him. In 1993 the television series images of him slowly paddling across a glassy lake, resplendent in buckskin and seventy-three years of hard-won experience, struck me as ridiculous, especially when he J-stroked past the camera to reveal the cheesy "Canada" logo embroidered on his back. The famous arrogance was revealed again—Canada personified, no less, the philosopher-king as a soulful combination of hardy woodsman and Emersonian nature poet. Less interesting, and less forgivable, was the cynical fact that the television series was aired to coincide with the publication of the Great Man's gruel-thin memoirs. Still, both the series and book enjoyed great commercial success—proof of the Great Man's continuing hold on the Canadian people.

These days I live a few blocks from the home of the young love-child, the product of a late-life romance, the celebrated case. The Great Man has been spotted in the neighbourhood, an unmistakably old man now,

Why, I wonder? Perhaps, as Stephen Clarkson and Christina McCall put it, it's a kind of spectral visitation–a haunting– we just can't shake off.

trundling the love-child up and down the streets, pushing her idly on a swing in tiny Sibelius Park. I figure a meeting is only a matter of time.

I like to imagine it as I stroll through the neighbourhood on my way to class or to the bookstore. I will be cool, of course, because we are after all Canadians, and he is a private citizen now, and anyway the love-child has enough burdens already without having to grow up as the object of prurient interest from fans (or otherwise) of her unlikely, aged father. But I will stop to pass the time of day, chat about the weather, compliment the child on her complexion. I might allow that I know who he is, that his Personality has had some impact on me, and that his presence has shaped my views both of politics and somehow of life itself. I might even tell him the ups and downs I lived through as an heir of his vision, a fan, a critic, a disciple, in the original meaning of that word, which our Jesuit masters would have understood well.

He will be old, wizened, maybe a little weary, his sharp eyes a bit bleary now, and too many lines of battle and aspiration etched on the waxy skin of his face. He will be past it, in short, a cult leader without a following, living out this chosen retirement, an elder statesman and his incongruously young daughter, herself a kind of emblem of the old days, the Great Man's virile legacy.

I will ask him to shake my hand.

This essay was written and published before the shocking death of Michel Trudeau in 1998. Now a much sadder image of the former prime minister must be forever etched in our minds: the terrible, moving sight of him and Margaret grieving at their son's untimely funeral.

The Mirror Stage: Infinite

Reflections on the Public Good

Socrates, that great hero of public discourse, remarks somewhere in one of Plato's dialogues that "an excess of precision is a mark of ill-breeding." Maybe it's in the *Theaetetus*. Or maybe in one of those works nobody actually reads, like the *Charmides* or the *Lesser Hippias*. I could tell you, but I won't: bad manners.

And of course it's possible Socrates was just kidding anyway. Precision is God's gift to philosophers, after all, and if a taste for it, once acquired, occasionally leads them to spend whole afternoons discussing the logically modal differences between the ordinary-language conditionals "if it was" and "if it were," well, then so be it. It keeps them happy and off the streets, where they might do damage to somebody innocent. I could begin by suggesting that more philosophers should get back on the streets, and that people on the streets should perhaps get more philosophy, but I want to begin instead by applying what I trust is only a well-bred modicum of precision to our chosen topic.

I **stole** this line from Martin Amis, *Night Train* (1998), where it's used to describe a philosophy professor who is suspected of murdering his wife.

Before we can say what *the* public good is, or even whether there is one, we have to ask what *a* public good might be. And before we can talk about *public* goods, it's probably a good idea for us to specify the class of things we are modifying with that adjective. That is, before there can be public goods, there must be goods in general. What are they?

A good is, first of all, something both desirable and worth desiring, something (as we say) that is choiceworthy. In the early parts of Plato's *Republic*, Socrates remarks that goods come in basically three flavours, which he rank-orders from lowest to highest: those desired because, although not necessarily pleasant in themselves, they achieve an end we wish for (think of going to the dentist or working out); those desired not because they realize any end at all but are inherently pleasant (like taking a stroll or whistling a tune); and those desired because they are both good in themselves and contribute to something beyond themselves. His paradigm example of the last kind of good is personal integrity, the sort of harmony in the soul that is both intrinsically enjoyable and directed towards the greater ends of justice.

Now, of course Plato was able to think this way in part because he was convinced that there was really one Good, with a capital G, that structured all of reality. Good acts and good people, good qualities and good thoughts—not to mention good knives and good horses and good looks—were all related to this Form of the Good as reflections are related to that which they reflect. The Form of the Good is eternal and unchanging; any actually experienced good thing or person is but a pale imitation of that divine reality.

For various compelling reasons, we have abandoned this robustly metaphysical notion of the Good. Aristotle, Plato's otherwise devoted pupil, advanced ten separate arguments against the theory of the Forms in his *Nicomachean Ethics*. We cannot actually demonstrate that all things we call good share in some single property of Goodness. Things are good in different ways, for different purposes, and it's not simply a matter of people disagreeing in particular cases: to judge meaningfully what makes a good society, it just doesn't help us much to know what makes a good knife. We may speak of functionality and the virtues that make for it, as Plato did—as sharpness is to the knife, so justice is to the city, the excellence that makes an activity possible—but beyond a certain elementary kind of analogical generality, we are in murky waters. And putting capital letters on the words does not help.

Goods are choiceworthy, then, but probably not because they all share some overarching quality; or, anyway, this is not a quality we can expect to get our hands on in general or before-the-fact terms. Goods are choiceworthy, rather, because they serve some local or contingent end, like cutting the bread or riding into town.

Where does that leave us with respect to the subset of goods we choose to call public? What, exactly, makes a good a public one? Well, we have to say what a public undertaking is for, what purpose it has. The roots of the word provide one kind of clue here. "Public" comes from the Latin *publicus*, which in turn is rooted in *pubes*, or adult. Thus Cicero's famous work *de Re publica* is not best translated as "of the shared thing" but rather as "of the grown-up thing." (Who would have thought that the old typographical joke, keying in "pubic" when you mean "public," was actually a sign of deeper meaning?) If the public is the community of adults, then public goods are presumably ones that serve that community's interests.

Fine: in public we're all supposed to be grown-ups. But leaving behind Plato's Forms—or any other lofty account of higher-order goodness, for that matter—saddles us with a special problem with respect to the idea of public goods. We can say, perhaps, that public goods are those that contribute to the functional success of the society, but how do we conceive and measure that success? Where do we base our judgments that a whole *society* is good or not?

The modern answer has been that the source of public goods is the democratic will of the people, and the point of public goods is, by the same token, their happiness—even if their happiness is, in the event, much confused and subject to distortions or manipulations that only a very reckless philosopher would try to untangle in, say, a 400-page book called, of all things, *Better Living*. I will not try to assess, here, whether this modern democratic answer is the best one possible because it is, like it or not, the answer we now have. And as with most modern things, it's been a mixed blessing, but one that on the whole we rightly celebrate.

One immediate consequence of the democratic answer is that we can no longer continue to speak of "*the* public good," as if there were one, even a very complex one, which could embrace all the needs, desires, and wills of the people in a society. In other words, a primary cost of surrendering the Platonic metanarrative, or any other grand story of capital-R

Just how reckless I leave as an exercise for the reader's imagination. Suffice to say the question "So, are you *happy*?" can be asked in many different tones of voice.

reality, capital-T truth, is accepting that there is a multiplicity of goods, and no possibility of final agreement on the nature of them. No metalanguage of philosophy or politics can translate all our individual claims into a smooth transcript—not even, as some philosophers still maintain, the allegedly pure language of reason itself.

This notion of reason's triumph is an intoxicating dream, to be sure, and one rooted not in the eternal ether but in ourselves. Yet we must recognize that any ideal of perfect rational consensus, realized via an extraordinary public discourse in which fractious citizens hammer all their differences into a kind of uniform political purée, a single ringing language of legitimation, is a fiction. Such transcendental consensus may be an intermittently useful fiction, as ideals sometimes are when they serve to regulate and direct our less-than-ideal actions; but, taken too literally, it has as many dangers as the frankly other-worldly metaphysics of the Forms. It denies the deep otherness that marks genuine political encounters, the face-to-face confrontation of stranger with stranger that is the moment of truth in any social web of relations. It denies, too, the residue of otherness that must persist in democratic societies even after all our best efforts at reconciliation.

It is in the nature of politics today, then—and I mean by "today," as philosophers usually do, roughly since the democratic revolutions, in thought and deed, of the seventeenth and eighteenth centuries—that we can no longer be seduced by the idea of a unitary public good. The multiplicity of goods is a fact that politics must address, not with some kind of final settlement, but with a flexibility and tolerance that forever postpones the impossible task of reconciling all competing claims. In social life conflict is endemic; more than that, it is ineliminable.

This may sound worse than it is. Many of the goods we pursue are not public ones at all, and therefore potential conflicts simply do not arise as actual problems. Suppose I privately despise opera, while you spend thousands of hours and dollars on your unhealthy obsession with the

Which hasn't stopped plenty of philosophers, and of course politicians too, from continuing to seek such a metalanguage: of happiness, of market preferences, of voting patterns. Whenever they do that, count the spoons.

See Michael Ignatieff, *The Needs of Strangers* (1984), the best book I know on this deep fact of social life.

up-and-down career of the troubled diva Anna Moffo. Well, who cares? We agree to disagree, or we simply don't speak of it. Now, music may seem a trivial matter—though I confess it is not to me—but could we imagine performing the same abstraction on more serious matters, like sexual mores or the work ethic? This, indeed, is the aspiration of some forms of liberalism: that all deep conflicts should be placed somewhere off the public agenda, leaving just a basic agreement about fundamental social and economic structures that allows us individuals to go about our private business in peace.

We know, however, that this vision of a bright line between public and private cannot be so easily realized: it is itself a source of deep conflict. Is child-rearing a public or a private undertaking? What about work? Or marriage? Or death? Is what you do with your garbage a merely private affair? Is a lack of literacy skills? In fact, the distinction between public and private realms is one that must be publicly debated. And that means that the most important of the specifically public goods, the thing that serves the ends of society as a key enabling condition, is the public discussion of where, if anywhere, a line can be drawn separating public from private.

This idea not only emphasizes the discursive elements of public life for us democrats—the incessant political debate that is our birthright and our burden—but also begins from the important assumption that no claim to privacy can be made except in public. It is never enough to say to a fellow citizen, "It's a private thing. You wouldn't understand." We have to justify claims to privacy, not simply assert them. All claims, if they are really claims, are made on the basis of reasons; and a reason is only truly a reason if it can be publicly defended. You may not always actually articulate your justifications to somebody else; but it is essential that you should be *able* to do so, if called upon. That requires wit and goodwill, civility and tolerance, forthrightness and sensitivity—all the workaday virtues of citizens.

Or at least, it is essential that you should *try* to articulate them.

I should jump in right here and forestall some obvious, if misdirected, criticism of this position. I am not suggesting that there is no privacy, that everything is public, that society should be dedicated to panoptic surveil-lance, or any of the other bugbears that haunt the febrile imaginations of various right-wing libertarians (and some left-wing ones). For one thing, as much as our bland, arrogant elected leaders appear lately to think so, the public sphere cannot simply be reduced to the state, nor the public good to the will of the state. The state, if it is legitimate, serves the public good; it never determines it. Nor is it the case that there is no private realm remaining merely because, as we sometimes say on the left, every-thing is political. Everything is political because every piece of private property, every lawsuit, every relatively secure personal space, is the result of an ongoing negotiation that must be seen as always provisional, fractious, and open-ended. Social relations and the distribution of goods are—must be—always up for grabs. Those of us who enjoy privileges in this world do so not by any divine grace or natural right but per conven-tion, as the result of a complex history of argument and settlement, of challenge and reply.

That does not mean, however, that the public good is always somehow over against us, or just something we confront passively. Rather, a gen-uine public sphere of goods demands active participation. Some public goods, like clean water or fresh air, call for no particular degree of partic-ipation to be real, as long as we don't hamper their availability for others. But others, like the maintenance of vibrant public discourse or having a distinct civic culture, are participatory as well as public. That is, they are goods which, as my colleague Denise Réaume once put it, "involve activ-ities that not only require many in order to produce the good, but are valuable only because of the joint involvement of many." Even if goods are only ever enjoyed by individuals, in other words, it is not the case that all goods are enjoyed individually. Participation is part of what makes the good a good in the first place. That's why non-participants or free-riders, whether disaffected or distracted or just apathetic, are actively bad for the overall health of the public good. Like party-goers who won't join in the game, they bring the rest of us down: they reduce the goods in play; they don't just leave them neutral.

The slogan appears on every issue of *This Magazine*, Canada's best political periodical; for a subscription, call (416) 979-9429 or e-mail thismag@web.net.

"Individuals, Groups, and Rights to Public Goods," *University of Toronto Law Journal* 38 (1988).

To sum up: Distinctively public goods must be plural, discursive, moderately rational, and participatory. They must be oriented to the success of the social project, a success whose measurement lies, however unclearly for now, in the happiness of its participants. The public goods are not fixed or unchanging, but rather the result of ongoing debates, sometimes vexatious, between citizens who perforce share a stake in their society.

What, now, is the role of reflection? There are three difficulties we face immediately in answering that question, all derived from important criticisms of the social-democratic conception of the public good I have been defending. One: are we sufficiently stable as subjects to engage in public discourse, or is it rather the case that our much-scored and fluid status as concatenations of interest and power makes citizenship an impossible role to take up? Two: where should we go to engage in public reflection, given that the public sphere sometimes seems to be little more than a kind of "phantom" space, and the contemporary political landscape a ruin of isolated communities and jagged self-interest, governed only by the cash nexus and the mass media? And three: even assuming it's possible for us, and we can find places to do it, what exactly are we trying to achieve when we engage in public discourse?

Bruce Robbins, ed., *The Phantom Public Sphere* (1993); also Jürgen Habermas, *The Structural Transformation of the Public Sphere* (1989).

These are deep challenges, but not unanswerable ones. It's true that our contemporary selves are fragile social and narrative constructions. It's true that there is no obvious marketplace of ideas to walk to, the way Socrates could prowl the agora of ancient Athens. It's true that we don't always know what we are up to, in some final transcendent sense, when we engage in halting attempts at public utterance. It's true, in short, that we are never completely transparent to ourselves, either as individuals or as a society. Indeed, it may feel at times that the public good is opaque and unknowable, and we ourselves no more than brute clots of interest and conflict that neither reason nor God could make clear.

But I want to say: full transparency is the wrong criterion of success in public discourse anyway. We do not need to be entirely clear to ourselves in order to get on with the business of citizenship. Indeed, there is a better metaphor for social relations, though it is also a more challenging one. It is a metaphor that has exercised the imaginations of thinkers as diverse as Joseph Addison, Norbert Elias, Sigmund Freud, and Jacques Lacan. It is the image of consciousness as a kind of mirror: not Plato's mirror, reflecting some realm of true reality, but, rather, something like what psychoanalysts call the mirror-stage of self, which achieves consciousness only through being reflected by an Other—an Other who may well be perceived now and then as a threat to me and my private interests.

Democratic society thus resembles an infinite hall of mirrors, forever bouncing and refracting its light like that scene from *Last Year at Marienbad*. We shine only in the presence of others, and they help define us as who we are: reflection is the first activity, and first duty, of citizens. The public sphere always houses a kind of generalized Other for each of us. It is the place where we confront that which is enduringly alien and try to come to terms with it, and with ourselves as we do so.

And in this complex of reflections, the intricate cross-references and input-output protocols that define us as citizens, the public good emerges as that which makes private interest and personal comfort insufficient standards of justification. It is not enough that I and my family are financially secure if the gap between us and the majority yawns ever wider. It is not enough that I am educated and literate if the majority lack the basic skills of citizenship, reading and writing. It is not enough that I am happy if the majority is not. The public good is something both greater than, and reflective of, myself—something with which, as an ideal forever approached but never fully achieved, I identify as I identify with the image of myself in many mirrors.

The danger lately, of course, is that this complex hall of mirrors has become a sort of mad funhouse, with distorting surfaces and devious curves that create spectacle but not, as good mirrors should, speculation. Nowadays the play of images is so pervasive, indeed, that we seem to have reached a condition, as the philosopher Guy Debord expressed it in *The Society of the Spectacle*, in which "the image has become the final

Guy Debord, *The Society of the Spectacle* (1983): "The images detached from every aspect of life fuse in a common stream in which the unity of this life can no longer be re-established. . . . The spectacle is not a collection of images, but a social relation among people, mediated by images."

form of commodity reification." That is, we inhabit a culture in which images are produced and consumed so relentlessly that substance drains from both the public sphere and private life at once, leaving us, at an extreme, in the position of consuming not products and services, but the act of consumption itself: going shopping, using technology, or ingesting media product as ends in themselves, precluding any real or discursive forms of social interaction. In this pathological condition, we become distracted with the play of light rather than what light should illuminate. We lose track of the wisdom interpersonal relations teach us concerning the never-ending task of citizenship. For, like the series of doorways that extends into the infinite mirrored distance, our obligations to our fellow citizens are unending.

Fredric Jameson, *Postmodernism* (1991): "We must therefore also posit another type of consumption: consumption of the very process of consumption itself, above and beyond its content and the immediate commercial products. It is necessary to speak of a kind of technological bonus of pleasure afforded by the new machinery."

But to what purpose? What is the point of this or any kind of reflection on the public good? Well, the point of any society is *justice*. And the first thing to realize about justice is that, like happiness or wisdom, it is both demanding and elusive. It is not a state to get to and then call it a day, the political equivalent of Miller Time. There is no final goal here, no position we could reach where all our obligations had been realized so that we could, finally, relax. In fact, this desire to pass beyond obligation by meeting obligation is really an evasion of responsibility—the same sort of evasion you can hear in those who claim that paying taxes and voting absolves them of any further, more participatory, duties to society.

Now, you may want to say: *But there are only so many hours in a day. There is only so much one person can do. You're suggesting that nothing we do is ever enough.* Indeed I am. It is an obligation that I put on myself as well as on you, and that I fail to meet as much as anyone. Because when it comes to the public goods, there is no enough; there is always more to do. That is the nature of being a citizen. The late Canadian critic Bill Readings once compared citizenship with Freud's notion of adulthood. There is no template for complete adulthood. Likewise, and for the same reasons, there is no template for complete citizenship.

Bill Readings, *The University in Ruins* (1996).

77

No citizen *models* the public good in the way ancient republicans demanded, because there is no higher-order reality to be modelled. There is only the lower-order world of our multiple and provisional reflections, down here where we live with each other, with people who are somewhat—enough—like us to argue with now and then. We do not reflect an ideal city, we reflect only ourselves.

If we recall the very adult roots of the word, "public," that got us started on these reflections, these intricate turnings-towards and bouncings-back, then we see the point. When do we finish becoming just? When do we finish being good citizens? When do we finish realizing the public good?

Well, ask yourself: when do we finish growing up?

To the editor: "Today's 'philosophers' tend to sit in their taxpayer-subsidized ivory towers and deduce their conclusions from abstractions detached from reality ... rather than logically induce their principles from reality (as Ayn Rand did); Mr. Kingwell appears to be no exception."

Screen

....

Television and Film

For just over two years I wrote a regular television column for the monthly *Saturday Night*, and in the process did two things: (a) put my reputation as a serious thinker into question in some corners of the academic world; and (b) enjoyed myself thoroughly. Almost everybody despises the act of TV criticism, including many regular TV critics themselves, and yet I remain puzzled about why this is so. Television is the most powerful entertainment medium going; it seems strange not to give it the same careful attention we give film or music.

At the same time that I was writing about TV, I also found myself doing more of it, usually in the form of talk shows or panel discussions. Based on my admittedly limited experience, the big lessons about television are, first, that not everything on it is bad; and, second, that not everything bad is without its interest. This section includes a few of my TV columns—the ones I liked best—along with a couple of other pieces that focus more on films to pursue some larger cultural point. It starts with an attempt, possibly ill-judged, to convince some of my academic peers that television has more to offer them, and they it, than either side usually likes to believe.

The Intellectual Possibilities

of Television

It depends who you talk to, whether my appearance with the shock rocker Marilyn Manson was a high or low point of talk television.

If you ask my students or the young people who accost me on the street every now and then, it was the coolest thing a philosophy professor has ever done, may ever do. If you ask my departmental colleagues or the senior graduate students of my university, who live in a permanent state of disgruntlement, it was a shameless act of consorting with the cultural enemy.

One, wearing a Marilyn Manson T-shirt, actually chased me down the street for several blocks; but he proved friendly.

For those who don't watch MTV or pore through back issues of *Spin*, Marilyn Manson is the stage name of a Minnesota-born musician and songwriter who dresses in Nazi-style leather overcoats, paints his face deathly white, and has been known to disrobe or mutilate himself while performing his lugubrious hits. The members of his band all sport shock-monikers that combine a cultural icon of beauty with one of mass murder: Madonna Wayne Gacy, Twiggy Ramirez. Mr. Manson himself is a weirdly disjointed character with the posture of a slug and the meagre vocal talents of a bullfrog. His latest record, *Antichrist Superstar*, shipped platinum.

The poet was Lynn Crosbie, who whispered cynical comments in my ear as the show went on; she was the only panellist who praised Manson.

I was part of a panel recently gathered to discuss Mr. Manson's music and message, to talk to him and challenge his ideas, on the Canadian MTV-analogue, MuchMusic. Besides me, there was a poet, a music critic, a street worker, and a young man who called himself "a recovering Goth." We were in one of those open-plan music-television studios, the ones where art is life and vice versa, surrounded on all sides by dozens of dead-pale non-recovering Goths sitting on the floor or perched on the monitors and amp stacks. A hundred more fans milled on the sidewalk outside, powdered noses pressed against the glass.

Criticizing the musical stylings of Marilyn Manson in this setting may constitute a new post-modern test of moral courage, but I rose to it. "You do only one good song," I told Mr. Manson, "and it was written by someone else." (The band recorded a passable, if creepy, cover version of the Eurythmics' hit "Sweet Dreams.") Mr. Manson's brace of bodyguards, clad in top-to-toe black leather, folded their arms in a menacing manner. He stared at me. The crowd of vampiric teenagers growled and booed. I felt about a million years old.

What was I doing there? Over the past eighteen months, mainly as the result of publishing a book of mainstream cultural criticism on the topic of millennial anxiety, I have found myself in many situations of the same kind, asked to offer critical commentary on this or that event of the day, to contextualize this trend or that fad. I have reacted and opined, panelled and guested, expounded and expatiated. I have interpreted the cultural meaning of Princess Diana and "Xena, Warrior Princess," and spent a whole hour with just *Harper's* editor Lewis Lapham as my fellow guest, untangling the knots of hero-worship in North American culture. The go-round with Mr. Manson was an extreme but not an isolated engagement with contemporary culture. And you know what? I loved every minute of it.

I'm a little too pleased with myself here. Sorry.

You're probably thinking that says something bad, and maybe obvious, about my character, either as a person or as a thinker. The sociologist Pierre Bourdieu recently caused a sensation in French intellectual circles by penning a denunciatory ninety-five-page pamphlet, *Sur la télévision*, in which he decries the genesis of a peculiar modern character he calls, in what might itself have been a flashy television phrase, *le fast-thinker.*

Les fast-thinkers are those people who show up on the screen time after time to explain the world to us in thirty seconds or less, the experts of expertise. They are not genuine intellectuals, Bourdieu argues, only TV simulacra of same. Worse, they deaden public discourse by providing an illusion of exchange where there is only superficiality and self-aggrandizement. "Can one think in a hurry?" Bourdieu demands. "By giving the mike to thinkers who are supposed to think at an accelerated

83

rate, doesn't television condemn itself to having nothing but fast thinkers?" The polemic has already sold more than 100,000 copies, despite Bourdieu's refusal to do any television or print interviews.

Sur la télévision was virtually guaranteed to be a popular success, because it is an example of that enduring but disreputable genre, the no-cost palliative. Everyone loves to hate television, intellectuals more so than most, and so any censure of the medium is bound to warm the cockles of many a common-room heart—particularly since *les fast-thinkers* are contrasted unfavourably with "real" scholars and intellectuals, the ones who write the books that nobody reads. But there is bad faith at the centre of that reaction, and worse, a misunderstanding of the intellectual possibilities of television.

The bad faith first. My experience is that the standard academic reaction to television exposure runs along these lines: "Television is crap. [Pause] Why didn't they ask *me* to do that show?" Many academics, at least in the humanities, flatter themselves that they understand culture better than the talking heads they see on TV, just as they hold the same opinion about their abilities as potential governors. Of course they would not deign to sully their hands, get mired in compromise, and so on. Plato gave intellectuals this all-purpose piece of defensive armour 2,500 years ago, and it remains popular.

> The reaction is not about age: in a 1998 edition of the *New York Times Magazine*, young academics were quoted as saying that true status now lay in being "post-Paglia"—that is, disdaining all popular appeal.

But let's ask the deeper question. Is talk television as drastically impoverished, compared with "real" intellectual discourse, as Bourdieu and his supporters believe? Is it responsible for the democracy-undermining superficiality of opinion over argument?

In my experience, not at all. To begin negatively, let's acknowledge that television is hardly the only place discourse gets truncated. *Les fast-thinkers* are nowhere on more graphic display than during graduate seminars or the point-scoring exchanges that follow departmental colloquia, where the rhetorical skills of the quick draw and the snappy comeback thrive. Few people bother to check the reference when Doctor X has just coaxed a laugh from the audience at the expense of Visiting Professor Y. And in an age when the bulk of intellectual exchange happens at conferences in which twenty minutes is the maximum presentation time, television can hardly be allocated sole liability for endangering the subtle development of ideas.

But there's more than this rather cheap, what-about-you reply. I think one can communicate ideas—provocative, searching ideas—via the medium of television. Indeed, I believe I have done this, and done it with many of the same techniques I use in first-year lecture courses and upper-level seminars to draw students into foreign subject matter. Television thrives on energy, and it requires that you think *before* the camera comes on, but it doesn't necessarily demand fast thinking of Bourdieu's pejorative kind. And contrary to popular prejudice, not all viewers of talk television are stupid. They may be uneducated or badly read by academic standards, but some of them are actually watching because they are interested in learning something. (Strange but true.) Academic posturing will put them off; concrete examples and lively debate will fire their interest.

I was struck, for example, by the amount of thoughtful comment, positive and negative, I received after defending the feminist credentials of Xena. My TV discussion of heroism opened out into a searching critique of cultural production and the influence of the cult of celebrity that kept me in e-mail and phone calls for several weeks. I'm still hearing from people with fresh insights about the evolution of Diana as icon, and millenarian zeal has moved more than one person to share elaborate theories of the end of time, sometimes in thick hand-written tomes. What is clear to me from all this is that many undoctored, non-specialist people have a deep interest in how their culture works—and a desire to participate in a conversation about it.

Can you draw intricate distinctions on television? No. Can you say everything there is to be said, even everything you have to say, about a given topic? No. Can you back your way into the subject the way you might write the opening pages of a journal article? Also no. These are irritants to people trained in academic discourse, but they are not, in themselves, barriers to thought. On the contrary, I think it is the very

Not to mention straight abuse. A correspondent writes: "Diana was a real human being, making mistakes which many of us have done (though perhaps not Mr. Kingwell)."

sharpness of television discourse that dismays many intellectuals. It forces them to be direct. There is no time to gratify your ego by holding the floor, no opportunity to set the terms of the debate in your own favour, no licence for exclusive and proprietary language.

There are both rewards and risks associated with this kind of engagement, of course. You may find that mildly envious remarks about your ubiquity begin to take on a nasty rather than amused tenor. (The sentence "I see you every time I turn on the TV" can support many tonal variations.) Colleagues have sneered at me openly in the departmental mailroom after a TV appearance, and I have been accused of "pontificating" in one national newspaper and two local magazines—though I reassure myself that the word was applicable neither literally nor figuratively. I was educated by Jesuits: I may prevaricate, but I never pontificate.

I should probably mention that this article was written when I was teaching on contract, had been passed over for two permanent jobs in my department, and looked to be on my way out of the academic world.

Of course talk television is not a substitute for extended intellectual engagement with a topic. It cannot overtake the sustained attention of reading a book. But nobody I know has ever suggested that it can, or should. The fifty-minute lecture is no substitute for reading either, and, as most of us know, it is a preposterously inefficient means of conveying information or stimulating ideas. Yet we persist in considering it an essential part of our mission as professors. I would like to propose, modestly, that taking part in the daily conversation of what remains the most powerful communication medium in the modern world might be another such part.

A correspondent writes: "As an English Ph.D. and a person who has watched television almost every day since February 5, 1953, I found your article most engaging. I regret now that I refused an offer from Geraldo to discuss Walt Whitman on his talk show."

Don't expect to do this without challenging some assumptions and habits of thought familiar to the academic mind. Don't think it will leave you unchanged. But don't, out of some misjudged notion of intellectual purity, consider it beneath your scholarly dignity. As with most things in the marketplace of ideas, the more good capital there is, the harder a time bad capital will have.

The Uneasy Chair

"**You can outrage** people today simply by mentioning social class," the critic Paul Fussell wrote in his 1983 book *Class: A Guide Through the American Status System*, "very much the way, sipping tea among the aspidistras a century ago, you could silence a party by adverting too openly to sex." This may be especially true south of the border, in the land of egalitarian denial. Despite the most restrictive social ladder in the developed world, class is still, according to the sociologist Paul Blumberg, "America's forbidden thought."

> This is true in part because of the enduring correlation of class with race.

For the most part this wilful ignorance is evident on television, which seems bent on delivering, week after week, a series of postcards from the land of the good life as conceived by Ralph Lauren or *Gourmet* magazine. The utopian fantasyland of "Friends," for instance, TV's hottest comedy show, has six gormless twentysomethings battle un- and underemployment even as they sport designer wardrobes and cavort in airy Manhattan lofts. It's just the latest in a long line of plutocratic nonsense available in prime time. You might learn that twenty percent of the American population controls eighty percent of the nation's wealth if you read Lewis Lapham's brilliantly grumpy editorials in *Harper's*, but very little on television would lead you to believe it.

> These editorials get grumpier by the month: it's a fine spectacle to watch cultural decline reported with both deepening gloom and ascending articulacy.

It wasn't always thus. During the long years of the early Seventies, amidst images of jungle airlifts and gas-station queues and the Symbionese Liberation Army, Norman Lear's "All in the Family," the quintessential 1970s sitcom, proved television could tackle bigger social issues than whether Jan should apologize to Marsha or how Fred should tell Wilma a fellow Water Buffalo was coming over for dinner. "All in the Family" is now the subject of serious academic study—possibly a dubious distinction (so are Madonna, college football celebration dances, and

87

the rappers 2 Live Crew)—but, more important, dwells in viewer memory as a must-see show that put American class conflict right in our living rooms.

Archie Bunker, meticulously depicted by Carroll O'Connor, was a snapshot of America's underside, the cigar-chomping, beer-drinking, slur-slinging bigot in white socks, gabardine trousers, and vest undershirt. But there was also the running conflict between Archie, enthroned proprietorially in his armchair to deliver racist *bons mots* and philistine aesthetic judgments, and son-in-law Mike Stivyk (Rob Reiner, in his pre-*Spinal Tap* days). The Archie vs. Mike skirmishes obviously reflected post-1968 generational and cultural conflicts—that's what made the show so influential—but they also had clear class implications: philistine against intellectual, working man tackling university-educated youngster. A personal favourite: Archie reading the name of the artist Jackson Pollock on a gallery program so that it sounded like an ethnic insult to Mike.

I remember actually getting worked up with righteous indignation as I watched "All in the Family" as a teenager. Hard to imagine that happening today.

Archie rarely won the battles, because Mike always argued the emerging politically correct views, but "All in the Family" nevertheless acted as a sly defence of the blue-collar Bunker values. Never before or since has a television comedy given us a character so captivating, infuriating, emblematic, and ultimately, tragic. Archie Bunker was the post-war America consensus slowly dying, on screen, week after week. Whether "All in the Family" was really as good as we now choose to remember it is ultimately less important than the conceptual space it occupies: the socially conscious TV comedy that was actually funny, the hard-hitting yet thigh-slapping prime-time hit. Is there, we wonder, anything to take its place now?

The best candidate may surprise you. For it's not the Rust Belt chuckle-heads of "The Drew Carey Show," the faux-gritty efforts about plucky working-class moms ("Roseanne," "Grace Under Fire"), or even the burgeoning crop of struggling-black-family comedies—Sherman Hemsley in "Goode Behavior," Malcolm-Jamal Warner in "Malcolm & Eddie"—that provide the sharp hints of a society of growing disparity between haves and have-nots. These shows, in common with soft Seventies efforts

Both shows were cancelled after one season.

like "Chico and the Man," "Sanford and Son," and "Good Times," aren't really driven by class conflict. For them, working-class life is merely a surface premise, a convenient set-up for standard sit-com riffs on family conflict, secret love, or relationships. No, the socially conscious winner is instead an off-beat effort about a Harvard-educated psychiatrist whose tastes run to amontillado, Armani jackets, Le Corbusier furniture, designer coffee, and Bobby Short records.

NBC's "Frasier" is one of the most successful spin-offs in recent history, itself an unlikely tale. Frasier Crane (Kelsey Grammer) began life in the mid-Eighties as an oddball sidekick in the "Cheers" menagerie, a starchy, the-joke's-on-him minor character who haunted the Boston bar in order to (a) avoid the pressures of his lucrative psychiatric practice and ghoulish, type-A wife, Lilith; and (b) live vicariously, like the bar's other habitués, through the aging, hair-obsessed baseball hunk Sam Malone (Ted Danson). The Cheers bar was, famously, the place where everybody knows your name—the place where people are all the same. Frasier, an elitist through and through, knew that was laughably untrue. He was really just slumming, revelling in the egalitarian backchat and day-long drinking sessions of that implausible tavern, even as he cherished his Brooks Brothers suits and Beacon Hill brownstone.

Fair enough. But when "Cheers" folded and Frasier resurfaced, shorn of both Lilith and his psychiatric practice, it couldn't have looked odder. Now a radio phone-in therapist (!) in rainy Seattle, he was reunited with Niles (David Hyde Pierce), an exquisitely fastidious brother we hadn't heard about before, along with their working-stiff father, Marty (John Mahoney), a former cop. Personally, I wanted to know where the barstool saddies Norm and Cliff were going to go, but maybe that story—wandering the streets, eventual incarceration, possible clumsy suicide bids—isn't the stuff of TV comedy.

"Frasier" is now one of the most critically successful shows of the Nineties. It has won three successive Emmys for prime-time comedy, plus a fistful of international awards, including three straight awards from Canada's Banff International Television Festival. The critical attention has come mainly for the show's writing, now under the supervision of the novelist Joe Keenan, the author of two small masterpieces of social comedy, *Blue Heaven* and *Putting on the Ritz*. Keenan's campy wit and gentle but piercing satire have lifted "Frasier" above the usual prime-time run.

Critics often like shows nobody else does, though, and "Frasier" is not an overwhelming numbers hit like "Friends" or "Seinfeld." That's a shame, and the show's small but dedicated audience knows why. "Frasier" is deft and witty; it has no winking, posturing stand-up comic at its centre and no structural innovations to carry its comedy. If it's short on hipness and edge, it is long on an increasingly rare television commodity: charm.

All of which might suggest that it has no teeth. Yet that judgment would be too hasty. "Frasier" has more to say about class in 1990s America than many a sociology thesis.

In a sense, "Frasier" functions as "All in the Family" in role reversal. The show's central ironic conceit is that Frasier hands out advice for a living but doesn't know how to live his own life, a classic do-as-I-say-not-as-I-do intellectual. The product of Ivy League schooling and professional credentialism, the socially graceful clubman, oenophile, and gourmet—a winner, in short; one of the most having of the haves—expert Dr. Crane is also a bit of an idiot. Frasier Crane might be Mike Stivyk after grad school, a medical residency, and two decades of private fees: stuffy and snobbish, sophisticated in taste but not judgment, a supercilious fool.

By extension, Marty is Archie Bunker redux: no longer the working-class bigot, now the working-class sage, a twinkling wise man in flannel shirts and white socks who offers up parenting tips and romantic guidance in place of neanderthal social commentary. The upper-middle-class professional is here ever on trial in the court of the heart-of-gold working class, and now Marty, not bookish Mike, is the arbiter of the world's ways. (Ads for the show depict Frasier and Niles, also a polished and successful

It may not be obvious from the slightly cryptic way I have put it here, but Keenan is gay and his books are gay social comedies. Until "Will and Grace" premiered in 1998, "Frasier" was the campiest show on television.

psychiatrist, on a big leather couch with Marty sitting nearby, Freudian-style, notebook in hand.) But even while Frasier is shown to be a fool, his character—and his values—drive the show and, like Bunkerism two decades ago, receive its implicit support. Producer Peter Casey, accepting the show's latest Emmy, explained its success this way: "It sends a message to the pompous, long-winded and incessantly fussy of America . . . there is a place for you." To that list of adjectives, add "rich."

At the centre of this new class battle lies, significantly, the same talismanic object: the Bunkeresque armchair. The basic situation of "Frasier" was created when Marty, in rehab after a shooting wound (yes, he's a workaday hero too, cheerfully taking a bullet for the people of Seattle), moves into Frasier's gorgeous open-plan apartment. Neither is happy about it, especially when Marty insists on bringing his Jack Russell terrier, Eddie, and the ratty, puke green, duct-taped La-Z-Boy he's owned since the Eisenhower administration. The charged battle over the armchair went on for several episodes in the first season, with Frasier predictably attempting to purchase a new top-of-the-line leather replacement. He gives in only when Marty explains that he is, in a sense, the armchair; the armchair him.

"The Red Green Show" has made duct tape the all-purpose sign of male bonding and homespun virtue.

So there it sits, amidst Frasier's museum-quality knick-knacks and designer originals, with Marty permanently installed, beer can in hand, watching sports on TV. Meanwhile Eddie—who, along with the collie called Murray on NBC's "Mad About You," might force a new Emmy for Best Dog in a Satirical Role—sheds hair on Frasier's beautiful suede sofa. And every now and then, lovable Marty explodes in a paroxysm of solid working-man's disgust with the excesses of his two sniffing sons. In a memorable episode he dresses Frasier and Niles down when they begin to make fun of his favourite restaurant, a suitably down-home steak house where they shear off Niles's tie with a pair of giant scissors. ("A Hugo Boss tie," Niles points out moodily.) The boys, suitably chastened by this moralistic outburst, cast down their eyes as the studio audience cheers. In another, Frasier's increasingly desperate attempts to buy his son an "educational" Christmas gift are rendered null by Marty's grandfatherly good sense: he's secretly bought the kid what he really wants, the goofy robot toy that's all the rage.

"Frasier" doesn't usually preach this way, and you might even miss its social awareness under all that whimsy. It is, nevertheless, a thoroughly modern fable about the simultaneous privileges and misgivings of those in the top echelons of the winner-take-all economy. The series' defining moment: Frasier, alone in a grubby diner on Christmas Eve and unaccountably without cash, has his blue-plate turkey dinner bought for him by a street person who mistakes the affluent doctor for someone even worse off than himself. Taught a lesson in the true meaning of Christmas, Frasier heads out to climb guiltily into his BMW—only to discover that he left his keys on the counter and must return to get them.

We laugh because, for that moment, the joke's on him. But the bigger joke is that despite all his homespun wisdom, it is Marty and this wholesome bum, not the posturing sons, who are the real losers here. "Frasier" allows us to make fun of people like Frasier and Niles, and feel better doing it: they are silly upper-class fops, supremely fatuous. But the show never forgets that they're also the ones, at the end of the day, who drive off in the big German cars.

Class consciousness, Nineties-style.

The writing on "Frasier" has gone downhill in recent years, but it's still possible to watch for fashion tips.

Sad About You

When it was published last year, *The Rules,* a manual of advice for women striving to land eligible men as if they were rock bass, became an instant best-seller—proving, if nothing else, that when it comes to courtship nothing has changed since this sort of manipulative coyness was popular in the Betty-and-Veronica Fifties. "Always be the one to end the date," *The Rules* advise; "never accept a Saturday date after Tuesday." Most of all, do not share *The Rules* with any man, therapist, or other agent likely to be hostile to them. Like all ideology, *The Rules* folds itself into a closed system, immune from all rational challenge.

The book did provide sharp-tongued critics with plenty of fodder. Christopher Buckley's "Counter-Rules," published in *The New Yorker,* advised men on how to avoid Rules-minded women ("call out the wrong name at the height of sexual ecstasy; use sparingly") and identified something called Rules Date Deficit Disorder, which (Buckley said) "afflicts women who rigorously follow 'The Rules' and as a result never get asked out on dates, get married, or have children." And, as three of my single friends wondered, what happens after you land the man of your dreams anyway? Are there post-matrimonial Rules too, to keep the romance and mystery alive? "Always wear your makeup to bed"? "Don't ever let him see you pee"?

Soon a serious counter-manual for men, *The Code,* appeared on book-shelves, advising men on effective counter-measures. The whole thing began to resemble a CIA-vs.-KGB covert-action stalemate: the Gender Cold War. Sick, yes, but the ugly truth seems to be that, though *The Rules* and *The Code* were last year's phenoms, they are every year's staples. Their presumptions are deeply rooted in conventional notions of romance: the perennial and apparently universal interest in the narrative of seduction

Wendy Shalit's *A Return to Modesty* **and Danielle Crittenden's** *What Our Mothers Didn't Tell Us* **(both 1999) extend the genre—backwards.**

93

and conquest. In other words, straight boy meets straight girl, loses her, and gets her back—if girl is clever and boy makes enough money. Then they live happily ever after. Sure they do.

When it comes to meeting this all but hard-wired desire for romantic tension, television shows have a problem. Cinematic romance certainly lives by *The Rules,* for here mystery and desire are played out without regard for aftermath: we don't really care what happens to Meg and Billy, or Meg and Tom, or Fred and Ginger for that matter, *after* they finally hook up. The interest is all in the chase, and if the chase is a dance set to Gershwin, Berlin, or Kern, so much the better. But television's serial nature, the relentless week-after-week schedule, drains romance narrative of its tension, constantly deferring the cathartic moment of resolution that marriage (or sex) provides.

This truth is most obvious in attempts to spin out a romance between two attractive TV characters over more than one season. Kingsley Amis once said that the two conditions for romantic love were (a) thwarted sexual attraction and (b) ignorance of the other person's character. No sane person can stay in that state forever, and neither can somebody watching them. So there are only so many variations we can stomach on the theme of the unconsummated love Angela harbours for Tony ("Who's the Boss"), Maddy for what's-his-name ("Moonlighting"), Ross for Rachel ("Friends"), or Lois for Superman ("Lois and Clark"). The characters either fall into bed together, and the audience checks out. Or they fail to, and the audience bolts anyway. "Lois and Clark" may be the paradigm case of this failure, since it's only by a degree of suspended disbelief bordering on imbecility that the ubiquitous Net-babe Teri Hatcher, who plays Lois Lane, can fail to notice that Dean Cain, the ex-Princeton football god, is in fact both Superman *and* Clark Kent. Lois and Clark finally hooked up this season and ratings have plummeted, proving that on television it's always the morning after rather than the night before.

As a result, TV comedy is forced into two desperate alternatives, neither

For those whose cultural memories might be failing, I mean Meg Ryan and Billy Crystal in *When Harry Met Sally* (1989) and Meg Ryan and Tom Hanks in *Sleepless in Seattle* (1993); I take it Fred and Ginger need no introduction.

This is once again from *Lucky Jim* (1954).

of which really succeeds in bringing romance to the small screen. The two options don't simply prove that television cannot be genuinely romantic because of limitations in the medium; they show, too, that when TV attempts romantic comedy, it can, even more than The Rules themselves, have distorting effects on our expectations of love.

The first is the urban-single comedy, a form that runs in an unbroken line from "The Mary Tyler Moore Show" and "Rhoda" to such current efforts as "Caroline in the City" and "The Single Guy." As a TV sub-genre, this one is not without its appeal and it should be the one that delivers the small-screen version of Hollywood romance. But the relentlessness of watching singles cheerily maintain a belief in true love week after week, caught on a merry-go-round of all too lifelike futility, is oppressive. This is *The Rules* in grim reductio: underneath all the campaign optimism, dating is actually hell; that's the point of trying to get married, after all. Sure, we happily watched Mary Richards confront her array of unsuitable suitors, the various nerds and weirdos, but that's because she was the first single career woman we'd seen on TV, and we thought (didn't we?) that she was probably better off alone anyway. Nowadays the appeal of endless singlehood is exploded—it just sucks.

Smarter shows like "Seinfeld" know this. It openly mocks the *Rules/Code* world-view, with Jerry routinely dumping one leggy desirable after another for the most inconsequential reasons. "Seinfeld" also points the way to TV's other desperate path, the urban-marriage comedy—singlehood's flipside. Paul Reiser's "Mad About You," the current champ of this sub-genre, actually became a running gag in "Seinfeld" when the horrible George Costanza was engaged to his doomed girlfriend, Susan. (In what is arguably "Seinfeld"'s blackest moment, she died from licking the cut-rate envelopes he bought for their wedding invitations.) While George was chafing under the new obligations of impending marriage, still fantasizing about trying to date Marisa Tomei, Susan would come over all couple-y, holding his hand in public and calling him into their shared bedroom to watch taped episodes of "Mad About You."

What made this funny was the romantic openness of the latter show's

The last show was cancelled after one season, while "Caroline" staggers on still. Could it be there is no audience for a show about a *male* urban single?

Background joke: "Mad About You" was nominally a "Seinfeld" spin-off; Paul Reiser's character was the previous tenant of the apartment occupied on "Seinfeld" by Kramer.

95

main couple, in sharp contrast to George's pathological duplicity and adolescent fear of commitment. "Mad About You," as the title implies, is meant to be courtship transmuted effortlessly into eternal matrimonial romance—one of the unlikelier pieces of emotional alchemy we know. The show centres on the endless married-life disputes between husband Paul and wife Jamie, played by former child star and blonde girl-next-door Helen Hunt. It's little more than a series of tiffs—over the couch, the food shopping, the TV remote, imagined jealousies, their quartet of exquisitely awful parents—with Paul cast as inarticulate (but charming) booby and Jamie as neurotic (but cute) shrew. The dubious background assumption here, and the same assumption apparently shared by delusional *Rules* buyers the continent over, is that marriage will be fun because of, not despite, all the little differences of opinion, taste, schedule, and desire that mark close co-habitation with another human being. The domestic conflict is all josh, never altering the fact that nothing bad ever really happens to these two: they're unfailingly cuddly, secure—and nauseating.

The constant bickering has led some viewers to recast the show as "Mad *At* You." It is the only show apart from "Ally McBeal" that I cannot watch with my wife, Gail.

Likewise in another stab at the same target, this season's surprise success and "Mad About You"'s Tuesday night NBC follow-up, "Something So Right." Starring Jere Burns and Mel Harris, the patrician beauty who played Hope Steadman on "thirtysomething," this show is about the mid-life marriage of two gorgeous, funny people with children from various previous marriages. Touted as a risky comedy of Nineties-style marriage, with all those differently sired kids throwing around barbed insults and cool cultural references, the show is really just more romantic fancy. Like the Buchmans in "Mad About You," the family live in a spacious New York apartment, enjoy a successful two-career income, and manage to invest domestic conflict with all the wit and playfulness of a Noël Coward play.

Also like "Mad About You," "Something So Right" is sharply written and its two stars have charm to burn. Watching it, though, you begin to imagine the Mel Harris character is, in fact, Hope Steadman ten years after the fact. On "thirtysomething" she and hubby Michael (Ken Olin, now working mostly as a director) were the obnoxiously perfect yuppie couple, with angelic children, a big house, and an enviable sex life. It couldn't possibly last. So now here's Hope a decade on, as lovely as ever but with a couple of nasty divorces behind her, that beatific kid now a teenager deep in some furious adolescent hell. And she is still gamely trying to make marriage into a romantic adventure. *That's* what's funny, really: not the situations or the one-liners, but the fact that she clings so desperately to this illusion of domestic bliss despite all the evidence, *even in her own character*, to the contrary.

I should probably admit that I found Hope Steadman on "thirtysomething" profoundly attractive.

Romantic comedy on television may dress itself up as Freud's reality principle in action, but it's really just a romp in fantasyland. Unable to sustain courtship in the cinematic way, television opts instead to romanticize both dating and marriage beyond all reason. No longer the genial Hollywood comedy, where we indulge in two hours of uncertainty with the confidence that the principals will get together, the TV version of romance masquerades perniciously as reality: selling not the fantasy of love but the fantasy of love amidst the pizza boxes or the dirty dishes.

I see it now. The final irony is that the basic situation of "Something So Right"—minus, of course, the lofty Manhattan condo, persistent good looks, snappy dialogue, and great sex—is probably *exactly* what happens in the end to people who follow *The Rules* and *The Code* too slavishly. They dance their little waltz of romantic measure and countermeasure, foster the mystery, and stoke the desire. If they're very lucky indeed, the process has some of the joys of film romance, not simply the cold tactical precision of a commando raid. But in any case they then get married, slide quickly into disillusion, get a bitter divorce, and have to start all over again.

I found, writing regularly about television, that I constantly came back to "The Simpsons" for deeper comment on almost any issue addressed by other shows. Go figure.

It's enough to make you watch "The Simpsons" for a dose of optimism about gender and relationships.

Homicidal Tendencies

I think it was the bike-gang air of the cops on "Hill Street Blues" that first drew me in to police dramas in the early Eighties. Compared to standard-issue Toronto constables—invariably six-four, beefy, brush-cut, and wearing immaculately pressed uniforms, the policeman as *Übermensch*—those New York City cops were all grunge and grit. Dark turtlenecks poked out of their blue uniform shirts, hair hung down over their collars, non-regulation weapons dangled from their thick rawhide belts, only half hidden by jackets of Hell's Angels black leather. When Sergeant Phil Esterhaus sent them onto the slushy grey streets with his patented "Hey, be careful out there," you thought, Jesus, look out: here come the badass *cops*.

The city was never actually identified as New York, but I could not shake these images when I first encountered New York City policemen, who were short, unshaven, and long-haired—more para-legal than legitimate.

"Hill Street" 's chaotic squad room, presided over by imperturbable Frank Furillo, was the command centre of a war zone, and the show twanged immediately with an audience world-weary and sophisticated enough to appreciate its nihilism, masterly tragicomic tone, and claustrophobic camera work. "Hill Street Blues" was perfect post-Vietnam television, probing, cynical, unsettling, and funny—a weekly dose of Robert Altman's *The Last Detail* in police, rather than Navy, blue. It was, at the time, the best cop show television had produced, and it vaulted its creator, Steven Bochco, into industry superstardom.

Bochco returns to the genre this fall with "Public Morals," and he'd better have something awfully good in store to vie for an audience ten years more sophisticated and already well served by three superb police dramas: "Law & Order," "NYPD Blue," and "Homicide: Life on the Streets." They are sometimes denigrated as excessively glamorous next to the more realistic Brit-grit of "Prime Suspect," "Spender," or "Cracker," but that's to miss their point. These shows are building on the dark legacy of "Hill Street

He didn't: the show bombed even more quickly than Bochco's bizarre TV-opera experiment, "Cop Rock."

98

Blues," plumbing the moral and psychological depths of police work. They make us realize why police drama is such an enduring genre: because it deals seriously with the mortal questions of death, justice, and evil.

The basic provenance of the police drama is clear enough. The detective story—a form invented, per consensus, by gloomy Baltimore resident Edgar Allan Poe in the 1840s—begat, as one of its branches, the so-called police procedural. Here the murderer is sought not by an aristocratic dandy or matronly auntie, but by real police using the slogging, detail-driven techniques of actual detective work. The grisly reality of violent crime, especially murder, is compellingly complemented by the methodical, minutiae-heavy investigation of the police: hunter and hunted, matching wits and luck, looking for (or hiding) clues—all of it given point by the ultimate mystery behind the mystery, the stark finality of death itself.

Poe (1809-49) was born in Boston but died wretched and penniless in Baltimore. His stories "The Murders in the Rue Morgue" and "The Purloined Letter," written in the 1840s, predate Conan Doyle's Sherlock Holmes.

The best police shows are rooted in this simple, deep confrontation between law and disorder, crime and punishment. The proximity to violence also underwrites the sometimes startling brutality of the dramas themselves. When the smouldering Jimmy Smits, as Detective Bobby Simone on "NYPD Blue," shoves some miscreant up against a concrete wall, his suit jacket bunching up beneath his armpits, or plants his feet and bitches out a weak-willed superior, you sense the anger and weariness that must come with looking at pools of blood on the sidewalk every day. On "Law & Order," which adds fact-based courtroom drama to police work, the conflict-ridden dialogue sometimes takes on a poetic, Mamet-esque quality in pursuit of the hard, ugly details of near-harassing interrogation and often cynical plea bargaining.

It was Smits's departure, not that of the overhyped redhead David Caruso, that sent "NYPD" downhill.

The implied question here: does dealing with death make you nasty, or do only nasty people slide into a job as hopeless and soul-destroying as trying to solve murders in a major American city, circa the 1990s? These shows walk a tightrope between maintaining the moral superiority of the legal system and overcoming its imperfections in order to put the bastards behind bars. This is "Hill Street Blues" revisited, in other words, but with the focus now squarely on dark character, not appearance. In fact, the police genre's evolution in the last decade or two has been decidedly *inward,* from the workaday detailing of "Hill Street" and "Police Story," through the flash-and-dash of "Miami Vice," which advanced camera work and backing music but not dramatic scope, to this almost painful degree of psychological scrutiny.

"Homicide" is the best of the three, and arguably the best show of any kind currently on television. Based on a 1992 Edgar Award–winning book by the *Baltimore Sun* crime reporter David Simon, the series was created by the film director Barry Levinson, the man who put Baltimore on the cultural map with *Diner* and *Tin Men,* and developed for television by the author Paul Attanasio. Apart from making a weekly mockery of Baltimore's claim to be "Charm City"—unlike other major North American cities, its murder rate continues to rise—"Homicide" is the true social realism of our age, the evolution of the Dickensian form. When *The New Yorker* reported recently that actors and crew sometimes find themselves spilling over into real crime scenes, or welcomed into a drug deal, it made a twisted kind of sense. Simon, now a story editor with the show, noted that the show's appeal spans the last big divide in American society, that between criminal and law-abiding citizen. "They're just as willing to host us in a crack house as in a fancy house up in Roland Park," he said.

The use of hand-held cameras and stop action gives "Homicide" a disjointed, jittery air appropriate to the violent action but never fading into the sea-sick excesses of "NYPD Blue," while occasional moody sequences backed by music, or shifts from colour to black and white, lend even more *film noir* ambiance than in the ill-lit sequences of "Law & Order." One "Homicide" opening sequence two seasons ago, in which a boy was killed by crossfire from a shopping mall shootout, was a dialogue-free stop-action essay on senseless violence so powerful and frightening it communicated more, in two minutes, than ten hours of Quentin Tarantino ever could.

"Homicide" also shows, to an even greater degree than the others, the intense demands on psychic equilibrium in those who make it their work

It may also have produced the best hour of television drama ever broadcast, the now-famous existential episode of a man physically trapped—and, in effect, pre-killed—by a subway train.

That would have been 1995, and a powerful reminder of television's potential as a dramatic medium.

100

to solve violent crime. The cast is an ensemble of superb character actors portraying an array of troubled, driven people: the former standup comic Richard Belzer's sarcastic John Munch, a man with three divorces behind him, for instance, or the Canadian Clark Johnson, whose character Meldrick Lewis, with one, is a mass of ill-feeling layered over with superficial good nature. The film veteran and Toronto resident Yaphet Kotto, the only member of the "Homicide" cast whose fame pre-dated the show—among other things, he got eaten in the original *Alien*—plays the homicide squad's commander, Lieutenant Al Giardello. A black man with skin so dark it gleams like polished mahogany, Kotto punctuates his rumbled commands with Italian curses and waves his hands around, fingers pressed together, to sing the praises of linguine alfredo. He is no reasoned Furillo clone, but a hulking presence at the show's centre, emerging from an award-cluttered office like an avenging angel to break up spats and hand out dirty assignments.

But the focal point of "Homicide," the show's most emblematic character, is brooding Frank Pembleton, a tortured Catholic intellectual played with startling intensity by Andre Braugher. Last season Pembleton suffered a stroke, giving Braugher the opportunity to extend the range of his acting, but the development actually made Pembleton a little less interesting. He remained a constantly angry man, but gone was the sharply expressed intellectual arrogance, the evident contempt for his fellow men, combined with a religious believer's inescapable awareness that murder is evil because *every* life is morally sacred. When Pembleton railed at a partner who suggested that the death of a loving father was somehow worse than that of a street-based drug dealer, or demolished a posturing suspect by reading the man's own Greek copy of Plato's *Republic* ("Let me show you what the Jesuits taught me"), he was like a flaming sword of justice slicing through human evil, St. Michael in braces and a slouch hat. Yet the conviction came only at the price of an enduring doubt, an emptiness at the moral centre, when Pembleton, or any of the other detectives, was forced to confront the futility of trying to combat Baltimore's human depravity.

When Braugher left the show, it lost its centre, just as Smits's departure crippled "NYPD." Only "Law & Order" has managed to maintain a high quality level across numerous changes in cast.

All of them are, in one way or another, fractured people, the walking psychological (and sometimes physical) wounded. Beneath the barbed dialogue and well-pressed suits the detectives, lawyers, and medical examiners of "Homicide" are actually mild sociopaths. They have lost spouses, parents, children, or siblings to death, argument, and distance; they can't relate to other people except in argument or threats; they can't leave their work in the office at the end of the day. The police genre's question of which came first, the condition or the career choice, is thus rendered somehow not just unanswered but unanswerable, enclosing these damaged individuals in an unbreakable feedback loop of cause and effect, good and evil.

And that is the hidden essence of police drama: here it's not just mortality at issue, who dies and who doesn't, but *evil.* The police drama, alone among serious television genres, relentlessly forces us to confront not just the limits of life in death, the realistic issues of life, but the specifically moral failures of human justice in dealing with human violence, mendacity, and weakness. The greaseboard in the "Homicide" squad room, on which solved cases are written in black, unsolved in red, is a harsh roster of hope and despair, a scorecard of the most basic human confrontation since Cain slew Abel. Realistic surface aside, cop shows may be in this sense the only truly biblical drama on television.

Indeed, by being so gritty and compelling, "Homicide" does what other, more obviously religious shows cannot. It paints the stark contours of faith and belief in a highly imperfect world. Compared with the infantile hooey of "Touched by an Angel," in which some perfidious unbeliever is each week confronted (and converted) by a gravel-voiced, motherly angel played by Della Reese, or the apocalyptic maunderings of "Millennium," where every second person seems to be a Bible-quoting serial killer, "Homicide" is religious drama for grown-ups: moral, angry, profane, funny, and raw.

Which is, I am sad to say, among the most popular shows currently on television.

Dopes on a Soap

First of all, I watch it. Yes, I watch it—faithfully, obsessively, even passionately. I remember the times Kimberly died, only to rise again, with her psychotic episodes and demonic possessions. I remember Alison in detox, sneaking quarts of vodka into her handbag and giving Billy fits. I remember Billy also possessed by a demon, though a different one from Kimberly's and maybe, weirdly, the spirit of Amanda. I remember, probably better than he does, all the women Michael has slept with and/or been married to. I remember the time Jane and Sydney tried to kill Richard in a botched *Blood Simple*–style, buried-alive caper. I remember weeping when Sydney was hit by Samantha's father's car just as she, Sydney, was about to marry Craig.

Well, no: I have never wept. But yes, I watch "Melrose Place," the Fox Network's hit show about a group of gorgeous Los Angeles sociopaths—have done (obviously) for years. I admit this freely and not, as in a celebrated "Seinfeld" episode, only after being subjected to a prolonged police interrogation, including brow-beating and a lie-detector test. This, I realize, is odd. Among those who talk about television as well as watch it, there is a felt imperative to deflect devotion to "Melrose Place" into either irony ("It's so bad it's good, and that's why I like it") or a feeble groping after substance ("It says a lot about the emptiness of life in glittering, twentysomething Los Angeles"). I watch "Melrose Place" *because I really like it.*

Sure, I like to offer shrieking reactions to the absurdity of the characters and the drama, often with a group of cackling, like-minded friends who deliver a witty running commentary on, say, Taylor's mad staring eyes, crazy hair, and ridiculous collagen lips. But that making fun is only part of the show's appeal—the part of consumption, as Michel Foucault

That word again: you might be forgiven for thinking I see sociopaths everywhere. I think it's more accurate to say that TV presents sociopaths everywhere. That's what it's for.

A favourite double-play:
Foucault and Butthead
in one sentence!

once said, that is trying to bring culture under control by demonstrating one's superiority (the Beavis-and-Butthead approach to television viewing). At another level, at once simpler and altogether more complex, "Melrose Place" is just excellent television.

It is, first and foremost, a prime-time soap, a running serial in the tradition of "Dallas," "Dynasty," and more recently, "Beverly Hills, 90210," which add glamour and superior technique to the bed-hopping and scams typical of their daytime counterparts. (Various lawyer and cop shows, notably "L.A. Law" and the current Canadian effort "Traders," borrow some of this sheen, but they are too focused on the professional milieu to count as pure prime-time soap. People in them work too hard.) Prime-time soaps are blackly funny shows in which beautiful people do ugly things to each other. We might call them sick-coms. And "Melrose Place" is the hit-and-run Porsche of the genre: fast, utilitarian, precisely machined, and out of control.

The show's ground zero is a Spanish-mission-style apartment complex in an L.A. neighbourhood known for its young professional population. It is owned by a feisty blonde advertising executive called Amanda Woodward, who is played with expressionless intensity by Heather Locklear: she looks the same declaring her undying love as when threatening to sue. For some reason, Locklear is still being billed in the credits as a "special guest star," even though she's been a fixture on the show for years and is its dramatic focus. Rumours that Locklear is leaving the show after this season strike fear into the hearts of fans: without her, "Melrose" must die.

The show was cancelled
after the 1998-99 season.

There are other sites of action, including Amanda's advertising agency, a couple of restaurants that the characters frequent with brain-dead regularity, and a hospital, Wilshire Memorial, where several of the characters fill in unstructured positions as staff physicians, leaving them plenty of time for adultery and elaborate revenge plots involving drugs stolen from the hospital dispensary. But the apartment complex is home base, a throbbing, claustrophobic concentration of anger, ambition, and libidinous energy. Fights in the courtyard and confrontations on the stairs are common; there is a pool into which people and furniture are regularly thrown; once, the entire building was wired to explode by mad Kimberly.

Of course the situation is absurd—I have just broken up with my wife after a flaming row over my infidelity with her best friend; where else am I going to move than the apartment right next to her?—but that's precisely the point. "Melrose Place," both show and location, is a crucible, a forced human chemistry experiment that burns off all extraneous norms of civility, compassion, and respect in order to force a residue of naked greed, sexual rapacity, and pure, unadulterated will to power—all in great clothes. It's the state of nature as dressed by Dolce & Gabbana.

In his novel *Microserfs*, Douglas Coupland's narrator explains that the group of young computer programmers he lives with like to take a break from hacking code in order to watch "Melrose" and observe some people going random and non-linear all of a sudden. But that is exactly wrong. The characters on "Melrose" and the plot-lines they inhabit are as predictable as the most basic algorithm. Push Amanda, with her tiny twitching skirts and leopard-spot sheets, and she will cut you off at the knees. Tempt Michael with sex and he becomes a mastermind of deceit to rival Cesare Borgia. Give Taylor an opportunity to show off her aggressively aerobicized body in mam-spilling dresses that would embarrass a Victoria's Secret model—and, well, she will.

So the first deep pleasure of "Melrose Place" is seeing the characters behave with all the economical elegance of lines in a logical proof. Their actions, relentlessly pushed forward by the serial story's unceasing energy, snap into place with a satisfying click: Michael gangs up with Taylor to dupe Peter out of the chief-of-staff job, Lexi flies off the handle at Coop because she's on drugs, Kyle takes a swing at Eric because he offered blandishments to get Amanda in bed. There is no resolution here, no cessation of the tension. There is only an interruption: for dedicated viewers, the name of executive producer Frank South, flashed on the screen after each episode, is synonymous with a feeling of obscure disappointment.

Obviously another favourite cultural reference point for me.

Cesare Borgia (1476–1507), the illegitimate son of Pope Alexander VI, suspected murderer of his own brother, was a brilliant Italian soldier and priest whose ruthlessness and single-minded pursuit of power called forth the admiration of Machiavelli in *The Prince* (1532).

The regularity of the action even makes it possible to extract normative generalizations from the "Melrose Place" world. For some time a list of twenty "Life Lessons from Melrose Place" has been circulating on the Internet, a distillation of the vision that informs the actions of these distant handsome crazies. "A good way to unwind after a hard day at the office," says Life Lesson No. 3, "is to build a fire, curl up with a good book, and rapidly drink seven large glasses of straight vodka." No. 4: "Every once in a while, just go ahead and slap somebody in the face, really hard." No. 14: "Call your ex-wife 'Baby.' " No. 15: "If you've got to fix your Harley, you might as well take off your shirt and do it by the pool." No. 19: "A good way to aggravate your sister is to tell her that Mom liked you best. Another good way is to sleep with her husband a bunch of times." No. 20: "Just because you're in the midst of ruining someone's career doesn't mean that you can't carpool to work with them."

Every year I distribute this list to my first-year philosophy students as a perverse introduction to an essential point of ethical theory: it's not enough to have a life plan, you need to have a *valid* life plan.

No, it doesn't! The great thing about this list is how accurately it reflects the principles that the characters actually use to guide their lives. In fact, they follow them much more consistently than most of us cleave to our life-guiding nostrums. The acts of theft and betrayal are still outrageous, but the characters never acknowledge that this is so, even when referring to the long checkered past of their group. "Trust me, it's a job you don't want," Peter said recently to Lexi, his newest troubled babe. "The last two ex-receptionists are dead, the third just came out of a coma, and all three were married to Michael." Peter again, in a rare philosophical mood: "I look around and think, what do I have for all my troubles? Nice condo. Stock portfolio. Broken marriages."

Over time, this failure to notice the startling immorality of the "Melrose" world becomes extremely funny. It's great TV because it generates in the viewer a peculiar form of giddy pleasure—call it the joy of confirmed outrage—where you know exactly what's going to happen but still can't quite believe it when it does. The second deep pleasure of "Melrose," then, is this escalating degree of shock.

We call these serials "soaps" for short, but in so doing we miss the other side of the equation, the operatic scale and appeal of them. The figures in the drama are larger than life, their roles and proclivities loudly proclaimed in signature arias of insult or seduction, and their clothes as finely differentiated and recognizable as the costumes in *commedia dell'arte.* (Dedicated fans can instantly spot the difference between a tie Michael would wear and one that Billy might favour, the sort of dress Samantha would buy versus one of Megan's. I'm not kidding.) There is no development of character here, really, only a heavy Clash of the Tokens.

Nor is the show instructive in any practical way: it simply provides us with the endlessly entertaining spectacle of people consistently and energetically acting out an ethical code that is wholly different from our own. In contrast to some earlier examples of the prime-time soap genre, which offered crude morality plays and deliciously nasty villains to hate (J. R. Ewing, Alexis Carrington), "Melrose Place" is morally unfocused. There are a few likeable characters, even some—the reformed bank robber Samantha, the reformed prostitute Megan—who come close to being good; but they're all perfidious now and then, and even the nastiest ones (philandering, scheming Michael, say, or Amanda) have their moments of warmth. As in more traditional opera, in other words, the appeal of "Melrose Place" is not moralistic but campy: it is obviously overdrawn and funny, yet without sliding into the self-consciousness of parody or the didactic self-congratulation of irony.

Still, there is a kind of perverse moral point to "Melrose Place." It shows that even someone who is calmly engaging in behaviour you or I would consider insane is still acting according to a plan. The "Melrose" inhabitants are unreflective but they are not undirected; that's why they never see fit to change, forever trapped in their cycles of betrayal, assault, theft, and deceit. In this way "Melrose Place" could be seen, negatively, as a kind of Socratic challenge to ethical reflection, a point of entry for the examined life.

On the other hand, can you *believe* Taylor was wearing that dress? At Sydney's funeral?

I'm not kidding, because I do this all the time, as do many of my friends. "Melrose" may be the only show better than "Frasier" for collecting good fashion pointers.

With Amanda it's more a matter of insane touchiness: every objection is a challenge to her sense of self, every divergence of opinion a threat to her power. She's like the chair of an academic sub-committee.

Buffy Slays Ally

"Ally McBeal" has been the talk of the town this past TV season—the winner of a couple of Golden Globes and proof, for some, that the cheerfully low-brow Fox Network is finally growing up. A "comedy-drama" about the ups and downs of a nonconformist Boston lawyer looking for love and respect, the show has been praised for its "sharp, off-kilter dialogue" and its "storylines hot off the cultural zeitgeist." Ally herself is often said to be the quintessential late-Nineties woman, played by the young Broadway veteran Calista Flockhart with "the perfect, appealing balance of self-confidence and uncertainty," as *The New York Times* put it. Some even consider her a new feminist icon, Naomi Wolf in a wardrobe of miniskirts and sexy Anne Klein suits.

This was before the notorious *Time* magazine cover that put Ally's picture alongside second- and third-wave feminist icons like Gloria Steinem and Naomi Wolf, and asked, "Is this where feminism has brought us?"

Doubt it. Doubt it very much. In fact, underneath the high-gloss sheen of her Cosmo-girl sophistication, beyond the slick gimmickry of the show's know-it-all comedy, Ally is perhaps the most regressive female presence on television since Edith Bunker, a walking time-bomb of sham equality and invited sexism. Viewers looking to "Ally McBeal" to offer sharp commentary on contemporary gender relations, or to illuminate the pitfalls of office politics, would be better off with re-runs of "That Girl" or "The Mary Tyler Moore Show." Failing that, they should tune out Fox and tune in a show about a teenage girl who's still in high school but happens to kill vampires for a living.

The trouble with "Ally McBeal" begins with its very premise. Ally has left an old-fashioned Boston firm after being sexually harassed by one of its senior associates, and joined a young firm founded by a law-school classmate. But wouldn't you know it, her former lover, a doughy guy named Billy with a fondness for loud suspenders and bad neckties, is also a member of the new firm—and is now married to somebody else, who is also (yes) a member of the firm. (In a piece of cultural savvy so delicious it's probably unintentional, Billy's wife, Georgia, is played by Courtney Thorne-Smith, she of the perfect chiselled features, blonde mane, and ice-blue eyes, best known for living with *another* goof named Billy on "Melrose Place," the show that leads in to "Ally" on Fox's Monday night schedule.)

The firm on "Ally" is all exposed brick and clouded glass, a postmodern environment in which both men and women, an assortment of oddballs and geeks in expensive clothes, share the same bathroom—numerous scenes of revelation and confrontation there—and dash from office to office, doors slamming, with all the energy of a French bedroom farce. But despite the hip setting, we somehow feel we have been here many times before. The law firm is one of television's favourite stomping grounds, because it affords a virtually limitless supply of conflict-driven stories, topical social issues, and (not least) an aura of impressive wealth and power. The fact that most law offices are actually very dull places where nothing much ever happens, their inhabitants slowly measuring out their days in billable hours divided into six-minute tenths, has not loosened the grip of lawyers on the popular imagination as a nexus of high drama, especially in the litigious U.S. "Ally"'s creator, writer-producer David E. Kelley, also responsible for "The Practice," a more straightforward legal drama on Sunday nights, is now mining the vein profitably.

But not necessarily to much effect. The characters here are one-note sketches, stick figures given tag lines and pet obsessions to mark them out from week to week. There is an intrusive, lascivious secretary, Elaine, forever offering unwanted advice both personal and professional; a moral cipher called Richard Fish, given to gnomic utterances ("Bygones!") and the happily unscrupulous pursuit of client dollars; and a nebbishy, socially dysfunctional senior partner, John Cage (played with mounting hammishness by Peter MacNicoll), who is undergoing something called smile therapy and utters lines like "This troubles me" and "I won't stand

Not that I have anything against lawyers, or law firms; some of my best friends are lawyers. They do happen to be more self-involved than most other people, but that may be a matter of self-selection.

to be disparaged" when he is, well, troubled or disparaged. The whole thing, from the love-triangle set-up to the ensemble cast of office screwballs, is about as unpredictable as a pre-flight safety demonstration. It's "Cheers" without the charm.

Even the much-praised special effects, used sparingly at first but now becoming obtrusive, are not particularly original. Like the Marshall McLuhan cameo in *Annie Hall* or the television allusions of "Dream On," they are simply broad visual representations of Ally's neurotic running monologue: when she is faced with sudden bad news, a volley of arrows thwack into her chest; rejected by a date, she goes tumbling into a dumpster from a garbage truck; turned on by a client, she slurps a long reptilian tongue towards his head. The monologue itself, meanwhile, smacks uncomfortably of the intrusive, worldly-wise voiceover of "The Wonder Years." *Shut up already!*

The show can be funny, and occasionally a delicious bit part or vignette enlivens it (a hilarious turn by Tracey Ullman as a whacked-out therapist who uses a sarcastic laugh track as part of her therapeutic technique saved two recent episodes), but its ideological assumptions are as hackneyed as its style—and far more dangerous. The romantic tension among Ally, Billy, and Georgia is locked in the familiar, and frankly tedious, situation of a married man who can't quite decide whether he still loves his former girlfriend. Lawsuits are revealed as exercises in female smiling ability or winsome laughter. Ally seeks dating advice from her female roommate, only to be told that, lacking large breasts, she should pout her lips more.

As a self-conscious misfit, Ally might be thought an expression of strong female identity, refusing the expectations of her world. "I like being messed up," she says in one episode. "It's who I am." A running gag has her hallucinating the presence of Dancing Baby, a computer-generated infant familiar to dedicated Websurfers, who dances to Blue Swede's early-Seventies version of the song "Hooked on a Feeling." The dancing baby communicates secret messages to the perpetually conflicted Ally, with her sweet grimace and knotted brow. The other characters, in

Which, when you think about it, is really saying something.

Favourite "Simpsons" moment: Homer yelling at Bart as he repeatedly wanders off into that smarmy I-didn't-know-it-then-but-I-know-it-now bullshit during a typically gobbled meal at the local Krusty Burger.

turn, accept this notion of Ally as impressively troubled, a strong-minded refusenik in the social world. "You're a wacko, Ally," Billy says to her in his exasperated, ex-boyfriend way.

But Ally's not a wacko, she's a kook. Very different thing. Barbra Streisand, in those endless and infuriating Ryan O'Neal comedies, was a kook. Katharine Hepburn, in *Bringing Up Baby* and *Holiday*, was a more tolerable kook. Audrey Hepburn in *Charade*—beautiful, but also a kook. The kook is no feminist challenge, just a certain kind of man's wet dream. (An ad for "Ally" in the recent *Sports Illustrated* swimsuit issue played on her status as "the thinking man's sex symbol"—even while showing off her pretty face and perky body.) Kate Millett in *The Loony-Bin Trip*, Esther Greenwood in *The Bell Jar*—now there's a couple of wackos. And not women most men would want to date.

Ally's driving ambition is not to be a good lawyer but to land a man; her amorous and emotional conflicts are just power plays and struggles for advantage, stuff straight out of *The Rules*. Even her power-girl aerobic kick-boxing leads only to a catfight with Georgia, watched over by the aroused male lawyers. She's no Murphy Brown; she's not even Mary Richards. She's just the comic-strip character Cathy, only with thinner legs. All this smart, late-century feminism—the careerism, the penis jokes, the makeup crises—is mere candy-coating for deeply sexist, and banal, presuppositions about life in contemporary North America. The show's jokes and sly devices, the cool soundtrack, mask its essential conservatism, the way it purchases laughs at the expense of a predictable, and depressing, regression.

Unbelievably, Flockhart has got even thinner as the show has continued its successful run. Soon she will disappear completely into the collar of one of her swishy skirt-suits, and the suit will have to continue on alone.

For a true 1990s TV heroine, you have to look in a less obvious place. To, for example, "Buffy the Vampire Slayer," a show about a young woman really struggling with the limits of love and death, will and destiny.

Unlike "Ally," where the cartoon elements and smart humour are smokescreens for the rearguard nature of the drama, "Buffy" is closer in spirit, and in writing—in sheer cleverness—to the satirical possibilities of an animated series like "The Simpsons" or "South Park." It is no surprise that it is, like them, ostensibly directed towards (and in practice, enjoyed by) adolescents—even as it pulls in an adult audience of greater presumed sophistication.

The series is based on the 1992 film of the same name but has several key alterations. Buffy, now played by Sarah Michelle Gellar as a tough-talking vamp-killing machine, with a repertoire of roundhouse kicks and Jackie Chan kung-fu moves, is no longer the happy cheerleader of the cinema release but, instead, a chippy, angry teen who resents the fact that she has been chosen, from among all her peers, as the Slayer.

Living in generic Sunnydale, California, which just happens to be on top of a Hellmouth—the point of entry for vampires, demons, mummies, and other assorted monster-movie creeps—Buffy is now a social misfit. She spends most of her time with the school librarian, Giles, who is her Watcher—a sort of nerdy scholar-guardian, played with elaborate finesse by Anthony Stewart Head, best known as the guy from those serial Taster's Choice commercials. Nights find Buffy prowling the graveyard looking for vampires to waste when she should be doing her homework, backed up by a computer geek called Willow and a wise-cracking nerd called Xander. The three form a love triangle you actually care about: Willow loves Xander but Xander loves Buffy. And Buffy was in love with a good-hearted vampire called Angel, until she made the mistake of sleeping with him, at which point an ancient curse made him turn nasty again.

This might all sound a bit goofy, but Buffy is a surprisingly deep character, her personal and social conflicts rich in resonance for anyone who is, or ever has been, in high school. And Gellar's edgy performances are a pleasure to watch: unlike Calista Flockhart, she brings nuance and bite to the condition of being out of tune with things. The heart of the show lies in its kinetic action sequences, with their exaggerated sound effects and boffo death scenes, when Buffy turns into a self-assured professional who doesn't kick-box just for the exercise, coupled with the deadpan wit of

There is probably a Ph.D. dissertation in the topic of why the best television of the late 1990s is ostensibly directed at teens. McLuhan: "Adults are just obsolete children."

the characters, coolly accepting their bizarre situation. Explaining why they're stealing a rocket launcher from an army base, Willow says: "We don't have cable, so we have to make our own fun." The show is sharp and funny, layered with pop-cultural allusions and crackerjack banter: a screwball comedy without the pat romantic resolution.

Finding strong leading women on television is no easier now than it has ever been. Too often, when a female character does come front and centre, she is, like Ally, handcuffed by second-guessing and faux acuity, becoming a perverse, and pernicious, caricature of Modern Womanhood. Luckily we have, with Buffy, at least one tough, strong-willed, culturally savvy young woman—a woman of the Lisa Simpson school of feminism—who knows the world is full of monsters and, by God, is going to kill as many of them as she can.

I **borrowed** this characterization of genuine 1990s feminism from Michelle Rotstein.

Dr. Action Man

In 1963, the distinguished American historian Richard Hofstadter published *Anti-Intellectualism in American Life,* a book that has become a minor classic of social diagnosis. Fear of and contempt for intellectuals was, he said, "pervasive," from "the atmosphere of fervent malice and humourless imbecility stirred up by [Senator Joseph] McCarthy's barrage of accusations" to the presidential campaign of 1952, which "dramatized the contrast between intellect and philistinism" in Adlai Stevenson and Dwight Eisenhower.

Despite the presence now of an ex–Rhodes Scholar in the White House, there is no reason to imagine Hofstadter would have cause to think differently today. Lately, though, popular disdain for intellectuals has taken on subtler, more insidious forms. If you pay attention to television and the movies, you might have noticed a bumper crop of Ph.D.s recently making their way across the screen in the guise of leading men like Nicolas Cage, Kurt Russell, Alec Baldwin, Harrison Ford, and David Duchovny.

A reassuring sign that brains are sexy? New respect for the trials of graduate school? I don't think so. Because the significant thing about these products of graduate education is that they cannot be taken seriously by audiences—until they become killers.

Take Cage's character in the brainlessly loud thriller *The Rock.* Cage plays Stanley Goodspeed (Ph.D. biochemistry, Johns Hopkins) as an unnerving mixture of dopey-eyed goofiness and manic sarcasm. He is, in the words of an FBI superior, "a lab rat" who, because of his expertise in chemical weapons, is dragooned into a squad of counter-terrorist SEALs about to lay siege to Alcatraz. Of course.

Goodspeed's trial by fire becomes the central motif of the movie, especially once the SEALs are wiped out and he's left alone with a former SAS man and ex-con played by Sean Connery. Backed into a corner, he has to come up with the manly goods. So he shoots people in the head; he fights hand to hand; he gorily ends the lives of terrorists—all the while complaining to Sean that he was not cut out for this sort of thing. "I drive a Volvo!" he screams at one point, "a *beige* Volvo!"

A similar arc of "development" is traced in *Executive Decision*, a film whose main virtue is that the counter-terrorist played by Steven Seagal gets killed in the first ten minutes. Kurt Russell's character (Ph.D. in political science, university unspecified) is an expert in counter-terrorism. When some Islamic—what else?—crazies hijack a plane, he is called to an emergency strategy session. Having evidently followed the example of Henry Kissinger (Ph.D. history, Harvard) for appearances on "Nightline," he arrives wearing a tuxedo. Everyone calls him doctor.

It's clear that they don't really respect the dinner-jacketed doc, though. Not, that is, until he strips off his bow tie and picks up a gun. This follows the obligatory sequence, reproduced almost frame for frame in *The Rock*, of the hapless academic being shipped out, via helicopter, with a crew of gung-ho, armed-to-the-teeth military men. Russell looks sick during this implausible ride; Cage, overacting madly, injects a bizarre humour into his nervous imitation of the SEALs' pre-battle rituals.

There's more. In three different movies based on Tom Clancy's novels *The Hunt for Red October, Patriot Games,* and *Clear and Present Danger,* Baldwin and Ford each play the same character, Dr. Jack Ryan, as a mixture of bookish family man and lethal agent. Ford had prior experience, of course: he starred three times as Indiana Jones, the cinematic anthropology professor who favours fist, bullwhip, and revolver over specimen box and textbook. On TV's "The X Files," David Duchovny depicts Fox Mulder (D.Phil. psychology, Oxford) as a gun-toting FBI agent who bravely investigates "the paranormal." None of these guys turns into a pure killing machine like the Russell or Cage characters, but each must become violent to vouchsafe his status as hero.

This is a sign of clear cultural savvy; compare Stanley Fish, "The Unbearable Ugliness of Volvos" (1994), an indictment of self-righteous academic slobbery.

The tuxedo theme again; see "The Voice of the Pundit" (Section II). Once more, for the record, I have a Ph.D. *but no tuxedo.* I may entertain fantasies of this kind, but I'm clearly out of the running.

What's going on here? It is, I think, a weird form of cultural domestication: the transformation of nerds into the most regular of regular guys.

I am not, by the way, here equating "intellectual" with "academic"; on the contrary, sometimes.

Intellectuals traditionally pose a threat to the established order because they are skeptical, imaginative, and probing; by definition they don't accept received wisdom at face value. Hence their routine excoriation, during U.S. election campaigns, as the central corrupting influence in modern social life. Almost always localized to "the East Coast," if not to the Ivy League itself, they are blamed for everything from the decline of the family to the fact that computers dominate our lives.

At the same time, many of those identified with the intellectual class—the so-called cognitive elite—are now defecting from social responsibility with alacrity. They respond to anti-intellectualism with equally aggressive anti-philistinism. The result, as Hofstadter himself glimpsed, is a cultural impasse that has clear class implications: "a running battle between the eggheads and the fatheads."

This was the phrase employed by Richard Herrnstein and Charles Murray in their influential book The Bell Curve (1994); Christopher Lasch pursued the theme of elite defection in The Revolt of the Elites (1995).

In this stalemate of mutual hostility, then, what better way for mainstream America to bring the intellectuals on board than to initiate them into the purest form of its macho gun culture? The message is clear, if paradoxical: ordinary folks can relax and stop fearing the nerds. Sure that guy has a Ph.D.—but look how he emptied his .45 into that other guy's chest!

The Nihilistic Noir of a Reservoir Pup

In recent issues of the tonier American magazines—*Harper's*, *The Atlantic Monthly*, *The New Yorker*—there appeared a quarter-page ad that marked a significant cultural watershed. The ad was for the Library of America editions of Raymond Chandler's novels and screenplays, and it sported a large-type headline identifying Chandler as "America's Poet of Pulp Fiction." "Raymond Chandler took the pulp murder mystery," the text said, "and transformed American writing." Added the novelist Paul Auster, in a blurb: "Raymond Chandler invented a new way of talking about America, and America has never looked the same to us since."

These claims are straightforwardly true. Chandler did transform American writing, popular writing anyway, and he did invent a new way of talking about America, the clipped cynicism of his novels' dialogue and of film-noir screenplays. But in the context of the ad they have a somewhat forced quality. Hovering behind the ad was an odd presence: the young movie director Quentin Tarantino, now known to anybody who watches movies, whose film *Pulp Fiction* was among the most talked-about releases of 1994. "A work of such depth, wit and blazing originality that it places him in the front ranks of American filmmakers," one intemperate critic wrote at the time. The film's mainstream success, following the cult success of his first film, the bloody heist-gone-wrong tale *Reservoir Dogs* (1991), made Tarantino among the hottest of today's Hollywood properties. *Pulp Fiction* had, by the summer of 1995, grossed $107 million (U.S.) and garnered Tarantino an Oscar for best original screenplay. "Quentin Tarantino is, if not God, then proof at least that there is one," another gusher said; "he has almost single-handedly brought the cutting edge back to the forefront of contemporary American cinema."

Indeed, Tarantino's ascension into the popular consciousness seemed to herald the mid-decade dominance of hip, moody, and ultra-violent films like *True Romance, Seven, Heat, Casino,* and *The Usual Suspects,* as well as quirky versions of the same that added comedy to the stew of guns and heists: *El Mariachi, Desperado, Get Shorty, True Lies.* The trend was so obvious that one American film magazine gave it a memorable name: "Bleak Chic." It seemed to many that, for a variety of social and economic reasons—racial hostility, cheapness of life, even millennial anxiety—the movies were exhibiting an upsurge of cynical consciousness, a noir revival. Call it neo-noir.

The troubling thing is how empty, how *virtual*, this new genre of cinema really turns out to be.

I first saw *Reservoir Dogs* at a screening during the 1991 Toronto International Film Festival, a screening I merely happened upon while in temporary possession of one of those platinum or titanium passes that grant admission to any and all films. I was struck by the enthusiasm of the audience, most of which was young, male, and white. They were apparently Tarantino fans before the fact, having heard the news of this new talent on some kind of sub-cultural telegraph. As the final frames of the film hit the screen, the entire fractious gang of thieves imploding in a cathartic gunfire outburst, the fans shrieked with insane approval, as if Quentin had just hit a World Series–winning home run.

I still don't know how those people could have known about *Reservoir Dogs* before the rest of the world, except that film-festival crowds are an odd bunch.

For my part, I admired the film's artistry, especially the dialogue, which, as everyone by now surely knows, combined hard-talking gangsterism with an occasional comic eloquence that I found oddly—and disturbingly—reminiscent of Wodehousian quipping. The artful backchat between Mr. Pink (Steve Buscemi) and Mr. White (Harvey Keitel) on the nature of professionalism in theft is, in its nasty way, as satisfying as a Jeeves and Wooster exchange or, more appropriately, as the famous "are we talking or are we discussing" fugue in the film of David Mamet's superbly unpleasant tale *Glengarry Glen Ross* (1993).

But what was the adolescent reaction all about? What was the source of this intense acclaim from the young white males? It was one of those dislocated moments, when you wonder why you are keeping company with people. Sitting there, I found the festival audience even more frightening than the guys I sat behind at the opening of the original *Die Hard* (1988), who yelled out the make and model of every weapon used by the gang of Euro-trash terrorists led by Alan Rickman.

Like *Pulp Fiction, Reservoir Dogs* is an accomplished cinematic pastiche, piling movie allusions one atop the other in a bravura display of late-night flick savvy: there are references to *The Taking of Pelham One Two Three, Asphalt Jungle, The League of Gentlemen, The Thomas Crown Affair, Topkapi,* and a half-dozen other heist movies both grim and witty. It also shows the structural canniness, the sly reversals and convergences of plot, that Tarantino would use to even greater effect a few years later in *Pulp Fiction*. It was, at the time, one of the most violent films I had ever seen, and I can now no longer hear the Stealer's Wheel song "Stuck in the Middle with You," which I remember from Saturday morning "American Bandstand" broadcasts in the 1970s, without visualizing the lovingly filmed torture scene in which Mr. Blond cuts off a police victim's ear and speaks into it: "What's that? I can't hear you." *Reservoir Dogs* made me feel manipulated and condescended to, even while it asked me to join in the nasty fun.

There is perhaps nothing new in that. Filmmakers, especially ones given to violence as a form of artistry, have often taken audience to places they didn't really want to go. The real question is, why have we lately proved so amenable to that invitation?

You have to admire, if nothing else, the moxy of Tarantino. He muscled his way into the film business without benefit of connections or money, and he has the true fan's knowledge-base and passion for film. His former fellow clerks at the now-defunct Video Archives in Manhattan Beach, California, tell tales of him launching into full-scale lectures on the women-in-prison film sub-genre (*not* identical with the violent-women film sub-genre) and insulting know-nothing customers in

The heist movie is a great genre, encompassing, as well as these nasty thrillers, such comedies as *Oceans Eleven* (1960), *The Italian Job* (1969), and *The Brinks Job* (1978).

Which is troubling, because, let's face it, that's a pretty funny moment in the film.

language that later helped him, together with fellow former clerk Roger Avary, take away the 1995 Academy Award for Best Original Screenplay. *Don't tell me you don't have the tape, you fucking bitch! I'll fucking shoot your ass dead!* Which might even begin to suggest a new violent-video-clerk film sub-genre: in *True Romance*, Christian Slater plays a vid flunky, presumably based on Quentin himself, who starts waving guns around when he hooks up with Patricia Arquette's waif-like prostitute; and the nastiest (and funniest) character in the 1994 slacker hit *Clerks* is, yes, a video clerk. I worked in a video store myself when I was a teenager, but it seems to have left me with no serious sociopathic urges.

Michael Medved, *Hollywood vs. America: Popular Culture and the War on Traditional Values* (1992).

Despite the slightly hysterical claims of anti-Hollywood Jeremiahs like Michael Medved, it is not the level of violence that is new in the latest crop of movies. The films of Sam Peckinpah, now much admired by critics, are as graphically violent as anything by Tarantino. In fact, Peckinpah's masterpiece, *The Wild Bunch*, which was re-released in 1995 in the director's original 1969 version, is an obvious touchstone of the younger director's vision. William Holden—a middling actor whose best role was as the doomed Joe Gillis in one of the best Hollywood noir films ever made, *Sunset Boulevard* (1950; screenplay by, among others, William Faulkner)—plays the reluctant leader of a cutthroat gang of thieves caught between American law and the Mexican army. It's a brutal, stylish film with—speaking anachronistically—some trademark Tarantino-esque moments. Holden, shot in the back by a woman, watches blood spurt out of his shoulder and then wheels on the woman, growls "Bitch" and shoots her dead.

Peckinpah's best-known film after *The Wild Bunch*, the thoroughly disgusting *Bring Me the Head of Alfredo Garcia* (1974), has Warren Oates playing a hit man who must show his vengeful boss the severed head of a troublesome rival. Oates performs the decapitation and the rest of the movie depicts his tortuous journey across Mexican badlands in a beat-up American car, the head in a burlap bag on the passenger seat. When he starts talking to the head, the film veers off into the kind of appalling comedy we have come to expect from our latest movies, making it, in the words of a CBC radio producer I know, "The best Quentin Tarantino movie ever made."

This line is from my buddy Greg Sinclair.

Violence aside, there are crucial differences between the garish, brightly lit violent thrillers of today, with their "Miami Vice" aesthetic and cool retro soundtracks, and the moody, ill-lit movies of the 1940s—differences that extend beyond the change in dominant aesthetic. The Chandler ad marks the tensions, for, while clearly playing on the popularity of these films, especially Tarantino's, to sell Chandler's books, its ultimate import is to lay bare the emptiness of the new noir efforts. Consider: the phrase "pulp fiction" is chosen not so much as a reference to the genre of cheaply produced drugstore magazines that, during the 1930s and '40s, served up murder mysteries, science fiction, and true romance in cheap, garishly coloured packages, but rather as a facile allusion to Tarantino's film. Chandler was genuinely rooted in that genre, even as his novelist's art and eye for the moral soft spot raised the material of tawdry violence and crime to new literary heights.

Tarantino alludes directly—and rather clumsily—to pulp fiction, but the allusion, like all of his art, lies entirely on the surface. He borrows the heightened colours and harsh light of pulp-fiction covers to create a cinematographic mood, and then apparently plays with some of the violent conventions of the genre in a way that is wholly Nineties in its bleakness. And yet there is no art to the process, beyond the unarguable talent for narrative construction: a loosely connected assemblage of characters weave their stories together, opening scenes are closing scenes, and so on. Clever, but hardly inspired. There is no elevation here, no transformation of material.

I think I'm being excessively pedantic (and moralistic) here; but Chandler was a *much* greater pop-culture artist than Tarantino will ever be.

Likewise with Auster's comment about Chandler's language, which (I take it) is meant as a fairly direct comparison to Tarantino's much-discussed talent for dialogue. The suggestion is that Chandler did on the page something of what Tarantino is doing on the screen. Though perhaps obvious, the comparison is not very flattering to Tarantino. Chandler's screenplay dialogue is exquisite, the combination of deadpan dread and unconsciously poetic diction making for, indeed, a new way of looking at America. "How was I to know that murder can sometimes smell like honeysuckle," the character Walter Neff (Fred MacMurray) muses in voiceover during the opening scenes of Chandler's subtly wicked screenplay for *Double Indemnity* (1944), based on a James M. Cain novel and co-written with the director Billy Wilder. "I had a feeling that everything would go wrong," he says later—when we know that it has gone wrong, that the plot to murder his lover's husband for the insurance money has led him into a mortal trap. "I couldn't hear my own footsteps—it was the walk of a dead man."

Compare the stock routines of *Reservoir Dogs* or *Pulp Fiction*, now writ large on posters or repeated by fans with the same assiduity once devoted to Monty Python sketches. "You know what they call a Big Mac in France? Royale with Cheese," says the heroin addict and hit man Vinny (John Travolta). "What?" asks his partner (Samuel L. Jackson). "Royale with Cheese." The best lines in *Pulp Fiction*, so good they're used twice, are actually stolen, namely, the threatening biblical verse, Ezekiel 25:17, that Jackson's character magnificently quotes every time he is about to kill somebody.

"I shall perform frightful acts of vengeance and inflict furious punishments on them; and when I exact vengeance on them they will learn that I am God." The citation became a sub-cultural icon, appearing on T-shirts and baseball caps.

To be sure, it's probably *nolo contendere* when it comes to a comparison between Chandler and Tarantino as artists. But that is precisely what makes claims that Tarantino has spearheaded a renaissance of film noir so troubling. For it is not simply a matter of current cinematic art being less accomplished: in many ways, that judgment is false. The moodiness of *Seven*, for example, or the intricacy of the screenplay of *The Usual Suspects* certainly approaches, if it doesn't quite match, the high points from the standard film-noir canon of *The Big Sleep, Laura, The Maltese Falcon, The Blue Dahlia, The Postman Always Rings Twice*, or *Murder, My Sweet*. This is, anyway, a tough field to swim with. These films, all of them made between 1941 and '46, featured the talents of, among others, John Huston, Howard Hawks, William Faulkner, Humphrey Bogart, Alan Ladd, and of course Chandler himself. Who, speaking of plot complexity, once confessed that even he couldn't figure out who had committed one of the murders in the film version of *The Big Sleep*.

Stiff competition, yes; but really the downfall of neo-noir is not aesthetic but moral. Whereas original film noir was *cynical,* neo-noir is *nihilistic.* It has sacrificed the moral core, the high binding standards, of all genuine cynicism—think of Machiavelli and the intensely dutiful tone of *The Prince,* the sense that there are things that *must be done*—for the emptiness, the surface cool, of free-floating irony. Nihilism is not cynicism, for cynicism retains a sense of justice and the bitterness of long experience. Cynicism says: sometimes bad people are punished, sometimes they aren't, and the world is a cold, nasty place. That realization makes Philip Marlowe or Sam Spade world-weary, even fatalistic, but by no means does it render them moral neuters. Nihilism, by contrast, has no message and no point. Its response to the sense that bad things happen to good people, or good things to bad ones, is captured in the title of director Jefery Levy's 1994 cult hit about a young man on a crime spree who becomes a cultural hero: *S.F.W.*—So Fucking What?

The difficulty in seeing this has been largely owing to the efforts of some critics to suggest that depicting nihilism of this kind is tantamount to criticizing it. Tarantino and Levy are made to join the ranks of Oliver Stone, whose 1993 film *Natural Born Killers* was, indeed, a straight-ahead didactic lament for a culture that renders murder, in the words of Mallory (Juliette Lewis), "so cool." Stone's preachy approach to the issue made the film less enjoyable, and less disturbing, than it should have been. There was none of the irony about celebrity-driven, TV-saturated North American culture that made Buck Henry's screenplay for *To Die For* (1995), the film that proved Nicole Kidman could act, so deliciously funny. According to the apologetic critics, Tarantino is like Stone crossed with Henry: murderous but funny with it; moral but with a light touch.

Yet we find no sense of this critical distance in the recently popular neo-noir films. What, after all, is going on when an entire audience laughs uproariously during the now-infamous scene in *Pulp Fiction*

On the contrary, it is their adherence to the code that makes watching them so intensely absorbing: we are made to see that intricate evil cannot be exposed in any other fashion.

Buck Henry also wrote the screenplay for Mike Nichols's *Catch-22* (1970) and worked on the 1970s TV series "Get Smart."

where a bump in the road causes John Travolta's gun to go off and annihilate his hapless colleague in the back seat? Who—what—are we laughing at then? Is the scene funny because it's so outrageous? Are we laughing, too, at our embarrassed enjoyment of the shock? Maybe yes, on both counts. But what is the attitude of the filmmaker who offers us such a scene? Is it social commentary, as some critics have claimed: the scene shows us just how brutalized we have become by cinematic violence. Tarantino (the claim goes) is not brutalizing us; he's actually upbraiding us for our state of brutalization.

But there is no glimmer of this critical attitude in the presentation, no hint of authorial distance. In fact, the scene is what it appears to be, just another instance of cinematic brutalization, not a critique of it. The director is doing nothing, offering nothing. Worse, he is expressing contempt for his audience in the process. He says, in effect, "I can make you laugh at anything. Even this. And it doesn't mean anything except that you paid eight bucks for the privilege. Oh, and by the way, *fuck you.*"

That attitude is obvious in the person of Tarantino who, whatever else you might want to say about him, clearly has little respect for his audiences. The matter is less clear with the other examples of Bleak Chic, in particular those independently influenced by genuine noir conventions, but it returns to sharp focus in the reaction to the films themselves. If, as Mallory says, murder is so cool, it's likewise true that the only cool thing is being cool—which is to say, not caring, and not caring that you don't care. This is more than simply a further application of the dimorphic value judgment embodied by Bart Simpson or Beavis and Butthead, all elements of the moral and aesthetic universe reduced to the binary choice between "cool" and "sucks." What we find cool about *Reservoir Dogs* and *Pulp Fiction* is what we should probably find most disturbing: the glibness, the unruffled surface of irony, the form of seen-it-all knowingness that passes for insight. This is not cynicism; it is only *virtual* cynicism. The hard truth is that Quentin Tarantino isn't deep enough even to be cynical. Morally, he's still a teenager—with all the annoying poses of sophistication and cultural pessimism combined

I **stole** this characterization of contemporary bivalent morality from my colleague Arthur Sheps, who uses it to mock me every time I utter the word "cool."

with a puerile fondness for guns, blood, swearing, low comedy, and racial slurs. He's Bart gone bad.

By early 1996, a predictable counter-movement had set in among the very same writers who had lauded Tarantino so vociferously when *Pulp Fiction* was first released. The CBC radio film critic Don Irvine, writing in *The Globe and Mail* in February, charted the worm's turn in a mea culpa article ("Quentin Tarantino, Your Bus Has Left") that was thick with millenarian imagery. We critics thought Tarantino was the Messiah, Irvine sighed; he was really just the Antichrist. "While we've all had our faces to the dirt in worship, Tarantino was on the talk-show circuit showing off the triple sixes on his forehead," Irvine wrote. "We have just been cruising along on our own illusions while this dopey ex-video employee makes us all look like idiots." He added that Tarantino would survive mostly as a useful short-hand adjective for "petty, mean-spirited, adolescent, misanthropic, filled with contempt for an audience."

Well, yes; and some of us weren't getting our faces dirty, either. Irvine's second thoughts rang pretty hollow, considering how hot he and dozens of others had been for the brash upstart. They simply missed the emptiness of Bleak Chic the first time around—largely, one imagines, because the films were so technically accomplished, and this confused their judgment in a way analogous to, but far more subtle than, the way the distractions of special effects and explosions can conceal the emptiness of so much contemporary cinematic science fiction. There is no noir revival, they now rush to say; it was just our desires gone astray, tantalized by guns and blood and some snappy dialogue.

Is film noir then, as some critics have argued, a form so specific to its time and place—immediate post-war America, the dark wet streets of the Forties reconstruction—that it is no longer possible for filmmakers to exploit its attractions? That judgment is too hasty, not because there is so much of the neo-noir out there as because the moral lessons and atmosphere of noir seem still very much a relevant avenue of artistic

This tendency continues in the pervasive use of the word "nigger" in Tarantino's screenplay for *Jackie Brown* (1997), otherwise a very good movie.

expression in these cultural endtimes. There are a few films of recent years that, in their different ways, take the genre of film noir and update it for our own era, without surrendering to the nihilistic emptiness for which there is, unfortunately but evidently, a much larger audience. These films, of necessity quieter and less celebrated than their bleak neo-noir opposite numbers, retain the moral centre of noir and resist a descent into didacticism or facile allusion. They do so in one of two ways: the stylized noir homage, either updated or transferred to a new setting; or, more interesting, the development of a Nineties-specific but genuine noir aesthetic.

Steven Soderbergh's 1998 effort, *Out of Sight*, continues the noir tradition in a superior way.

Examples of the first kind are not mere remakes, as, say, the passable 1970s British productions of *Farewell, My Lovely* and *The Big Sleep*, featuring a granite-faced Robert Mitchum as Philip Marlowe. I'm thinking instead of Ridley Scott's *Blade Runner* (1982), in which Harrison Ford plays a Los Angeles police detective called out of retirement to hunt down a group of escaped "replicants," or intelligent androids, who are wanted for murder. The film sacrifices a good deal of the philosophical interest in the story on which it is based, Phillip K. Dick's *Do Androids Dream of Electric Sheep?*, but it creates new interest with a depiction, novel for its time, of a near-future L.A. of rain, multiculturalism, and human/machine racism. Purists object that voiceover is a copout in any screenplay, but it has always been a staple of film noir, and Scott uses it to good effect in *Blade Runner*. A more straightforward version of this transfer strategy is 1995's *Devil in a Blue Dress*, more or less a period piece but with one crucial shift in focus. Based on Walter Mosley's best-selling novel, the film's detective-protagonist is Easy Rawlins, an unemployed black machine worker (Denzel Washington).

Two recent films don't opt for transplanted noir but instead a vibrant new version of the old form, genuine Nineties noir. They are *Red Rock West* (1994) and *The Last Seduction* (1995), both directed by the talented young American John Dahl. *Red Rock West*, which bears a passing resemblance to Joel and Ethan Coen's excellent noir-homage *Blood Simple* (1984), depicts an aimless loner (Nicolas Cage) who is haplessly caught up in the machinations of various money-hungry, unscrupulous, and occasionally violent small-town hoods. Cage's sleepy-eyed performance masks a deep intelligence in his character, and in the script, and when he eventually triumphs over the people trying to use him, it is only at the cost of our realizing he is the marginally least of available evils. Justice—of a kind—is served. In *The Last Seduction,* on the other hand, there is no justice at all. Linda Fiorentino, in a gorgeous performance, plays a femme most fatale on the run with a sackful of money. Smart enough to bend the world, especially lustful men, to her calculated desire, she gets away with it. The clear-eyed malice of the script, which moves with mounting grimness from one deception to another, is so evident that it starts to take on an inherent pleasure. It's horrible, but somehow funny—and not in the merely shocking manner of *Pulp Fiction*'s blown-away head. When I saw *The Last Seduction,* a man down front started chuckling about halfway through; soon he was snickering, then laughing full-bore as the full extent of Fiorentino's wickedness unfolded.

That reaction is not sick; it is rather the genuine pleasure of recognizing stupidity and nastiness in unequal contest, the glee of *Schadenfreude*—a form of catharsis not mentioned in Aristotle's *Poetics,* maybe, but a powerful aesthetic force nevertheless. The film calls out genuine irony, insightful distance between audience and action, not the mere appearance of it—not simply the sly wink that passes for irony. Like Lawrence Kasdan's *Body Heat* (1981), *The Last Seduction* is really an updated version of *Double Indemnity,* with a big lug cornered into taking the fall for murder, seduced by sex and his own weakness of character. But like Kasdan's film, it pushes the conventions of noir in new directions, acquiring an energy all its own, distinctively contemporary in tone but without the pandering, brutalizing surface of the bleak neo-noir. How were we to know that murder can sometimes smell like honeysuckle? Or Chanel No. 5?

In the end, Fiorentino's character gets away with murder—inventively and intricately, but scot-free. Why, then, is the film so much more

As my friend Mark Thompson likes to say, "The Germans have a word for it." *Schadenfreude* means "joy at the misfortune of others"—an experience not limited to those who speak the language of Goethe.

ethically satisfying than the paroxysm of gunfire that closes *Reservoir Dogs,* or the rounded-off concerto of *Pulp Fiction*'s forward-backward chronology? Because injustice observed can, in the right hands, be justice underlined. Because cynicism done with a straight face is itself a moment of moral insight: the realization that bad things happen to good people, and good ones to bad. And that this matters. It is indeed the starting point of ethical reflection.

Without the straight face, though, the bottom falls out. In the hands of so many of today's young filmmakers, cynicism and irony have declined into nihilism, showy gunplay, mere cleverness. We are left with nothing but chic (and cheek): artfulness, not art. We have gone along for the ride, but it's now time to get off, for this decline insults our brains—and our hearts.

As I argued, maybe a little less plausibly, about "Melrose Place."

Speed

Going Fast, Talking Slow,
Playing

We live in a culture obsessed with speed, constantly gripped by the desire to go faster, and that fact has in turn become one of my personal obsessions over the past few years. What with one thing and another, I have found my own life moving at a quicker pace as we hustle towards the liminal cultural event known in some quarters as the millennium. Time for reflection, and spaces in which that time is welcomed, seems harder and harder to come by.

That is one reason I join here some thoughts on speed with some reflections on sports and technology. This conjoining is not perverse. Indeed, I think no separation of them is possible any longer. Sometimes a sport like baseball can give us a place, maybe the only place, where we escape the tyranny of the clock and pass time in outs and innings instead. Just as often, we see that the insistent drive for transcendence is alike part of sport and speed—that they cannot be untangled, any more than a world record in sprinting can distinguish the champion runner from the stopwatch that timed his running.

The Storyteller's Game

The first radio sportscast—like, say, the first military use of the air-plane—is an event much scored by myth-making acids. The way it's usu-ally told, Harold Arlin, a plodding daytime foreman at KDKA in Pittsburgh, just *decided* one day to haul a carbon microphone and power generator over to Forbes Field, where the Pirates were hosting their cross-state rivals, the Phillies. Arlin, who was twenty-six years old, paid his way into the park, took up a seat directly behind home plate, and simply started talking play-by-play. It was August 5, 1921, and the first sports broadcast was invented, sprouting whole from the forehead of Harold Arlin. Who heard him? What did he sound like? We'll never know for sure. The record says the Pirates won, eight runs to five.

This is the only one of my articles ever to be reprinted in *Reader's Digest*, a coup for which I received no payment; I still suspect David Warren of *The Idler* of using the cheque to settle a printer's bill.

In the next ten years and beyond, radio proved itself surprisingly well suited to the visual medium of sports. This is surely in part because the natural idiom of the fan is gab, and gab was just what the first sportscast-ers did best. Like all fans, they indulged themselves with aggressive dis-putes of plays, questioning of coaches' judgment, displays of historical knowledge. Talk, talk, talk—what would sports be without the commu-nal discussion, the bull session, the great conversation of devotion? The first sportscasters satisfied the back-brain dream of all fans, that once, for a while, *everyone else will shut up and let them talk.* Here was the impera-tive of the story-line, the drive to narrate, the longing to be the camp-fire focus. Who among us, after all, does not imagine that he could tell the game-story better than anyone else?

Indeed, some of the first radio men talked about what they had not even seen, for early radio sports relied heavily on studio "re-creations," imaginative talk-throughs of telegraph reports on game action. These announcers—among whom one could find, in those days, young Ronald

132

"Dutch" Reagan—thought nothing of inventing actions and plays, sometimes adding a string of nonexistent foul balls to their patter when the telegraph signal had been severed. Even at the park itself, accuracy was not always a virtue in announcers. NBC Radio's Bill Stern, for one, was well known for his mis-calls during college football broadcasts in the 1930s. Stern, who sported not only artificial hair but also an artificial leg, was famous for losing sight of Yale halfbacks' numbers as they pounded down the field against Columbia. "If we have a man with the ball on his way to a touchdown," he once told a rookie spotter, "and we discover at the five-yard line that we have the wrong man, *we will have him lateral to the right man.*" I think this must account in some way for the popularity of the last-minute lateral in sandlot football.

Another time, when Stern had the bad grace to criticize a fellow radio man, Clem McCarthy, for calling the wrong winner during a Kentucky Derby broadcast, McCarthy shot back: "Well, you can't lateral a horse."

These and other tales are the primitive mythology of radio sports, which found its heroes in unlikely places. There was Mel Allen (actually Melvin Allen Israel), a bookish—and Jewish—Southerner whose mellifluous tones on CBS Radio were synonymous with the fate of the New York Yankees from 1939 to 1964. Allen had a sure-fire signature line— *How a-bout that?*—which he developed during a rip of four home runs by Joe DiMaggio in 1949, whom he dubbed both "the Yankee Clipper" and "Joltin' Joe." Allen's outsized tones and the centrality of Yankee fortunes made his arguably the most famous voice in America during the 1940s and '50s. (Aficionados call him, simply, The Voice.) He also, unlike Stern and others of the first generation, managed a successful transition from radio to television: in later years he telecast Yankees games, World Series, and was to be heard until just a few years ago doing the baseball magazine show called "This Week in Baseball."

The other great in early sports radio was Mississippi-born Walter Lanier "Red" Barber, who for years broadcast Dodger exploits out of Brooklyn's Ebbets Field. The contrast with Allen was, and is, much discussed, for together the two plot the opposite poles of radio propriety.

Reagan says he received the nickname because his parents thought he looked, as a boy, "like a little Dutchman." Whatever that means.

Joe DiMaggio, one of baseball's greatest, died in March 1999, aged eighty-four.

133

On the one hand, the hollering, rollicking Allen, a man dedicated to obliterating dead air with his barrages of partisan, over-excited patter; on the other, Barber's quieter, gentler, and more balanced narration, long on detail and short on intemperate outbursts. ("That Barber," a Brooklyn taxi driver is supposed to have said one day in the Forties, "he's too fair.")

Most of the early radio voices were local heroes, tied to the fortunes of a single team their entire careers. There was Byrum Saam in Philadelphia; the irrepressible Bob "Gunner" Price, a Pittsburgh institution given to diving out of hotel windows on a wager; Harry Caray in St. Louis, who originated the "Holy cow!" tag later adopted by Phil "Scooter" Rizzuto in his Yankee broadcasts; and Curt Gowdy, voice of the Boston Red Sox, later a television star. There was, finally, J.H. "Dizzy" Dean—though Dean is perhaps better remembered for his Hall of Fame performances with the 1930s-vintage St. Louis Cardinals, the storied Gas House Gang. Dean, like Barber and Allen, was a Southerner, but in his case from po-dunk Arkansas and possessing no education beyond the second grade. But Dean's drawling down-home shtick struck a note that sports broadcasting has always loved, and he too slid (or, in Dean vernacular, "slud") easily from radio to TV. Of course, it was precisely the rough-edged ungrammatical cornpone of Dean's 1950s TV broadcasts ("Somebody's complaining about my syntax? I didn't know they was taxing that too"), and the mild lower-class aura that then clung to professional baseball, that kept some network executives from getting enthusiastically behind baseball TV.

Like silent-screen stars attempting to keep pace with the talkies, not all the radio wizards could master the peculiar demands of the TV sportscast. For most, it was as simple as this: in radio, the announcer is everything, master of his fate. ("In radio," said the veteran Ernie Harwell, "nothing happens until I say so.") In television, the announcer is no more than another prop under a producer's iron control. Lindsey Nelson, one of the radio–TV success stories, put it this way: "I love radio—you're totally in charge. To me, broadcasting baseball all season that way is a delight. You just let yourself roam. And you're the entire show—you paint the

From *O Holy Cow! The Selected Verse of Phil Rizzuto* (1993): "What kind is it? / Ohhhhh! / Pepperoni! / Holy cow! / What happened? / Base hit! / A little disconcerting, / Smelling that pizza, / And trying / To do a ball game."

picture. If you get in trouble, you can get out of trouble just as easily—and because there's no picture, nobody knows it. You have much less freedom in TV. You're at the mercy of what the producer and director show. In language, you have to be more selective. And always, your destiny is in someone else's hands." Not surprisingly for the great talkers of baseball radio, the diamond game made the contrast especially acute. "I guess I notice it so sharply," Nelson concluded, "because there's no radio sport better than baseball to do stream-of-consciousness—the slow pace, the time to improvise. It's an English major's dream."

What is most remarkable about the early history of sports broadcasting, and hardest to recall now, is that radio continued to dominate long into the television age. The thin electric beam of banter was not shoved aside by the magic of pictures right away. Television was well into its adolescence, in the late 1950s and even early 1960s, before its malevolent masterminds began to sense just how much there was to be had from sports TV. Partly this was owing to technical limitations. A three-camera studio could give you an effective show like "Jack Benny" or "The Honeymooners," both really just transplanted radio shows with minimal sets and studio audiences, but the same three cameras, scattered ineffectually around a baseball park, were certainly no improvement on Red Barber's masterful narration. "Baseball was made to look slow and dull," said one veteran broadcaster recently, "because TV was not ready to do justice to baseball. It was like watching grass grow or paint dry."

There were other factors. According to the TV critic Ron Powers, whose history of early sports TV, *Supertube,* is the best source on the rise of network power in sports, the men in control of television's early destiny were more than a little contemptuous of the American sports audience. They were, almost without exception, golf and polo men, and the drawling, brawling aura of baseball and boxing and wrestling was not for them. It is perhaps no surprise that the first major sport beamed out on television was one born of Ivy League tradition: college football, which had yet to acquire its reputation for recruiting violations, drug money, and free Corvettes from the Booster Club. Like rugby in Britain, football

This is not obvious to most of the English majors who have passed through my classroom, but I keep encouraging them.

135

was a brutal game played by gentlemen, while baseball was a gentle game played by rednecks. In the Fifties and Sixties, college football was depicted as a titanic battle of crew-cut young giants with pure hearts and indomitable school spirit, letterman sweaters and penny loafers in their lockers. So ran the mythology anyway—and it was, after its fashion, as effective as the election-year propaganda of a Roger Ailes. Roone Arledge, the man who almost single-handedly invented sports TV, carved out his niche at ABC by constructing college football telecasts that were masterpieces of visual manipulation: long shots of ivy-strewn campuses, tan cheerleaders flinging their bodies in collegiate glee, fans carousing in paroxysms of good cheer and fight song, sophomore cornerbacks giving up their bodies joyfully for the ball.

These opening sequences continue to be the most compelling parts of some broadcasts, the Pearl Jam and Offspring soundtracks and tattooed protagonists lending them an edgy, MTV–or maybe WWF–quality.

Arledge's style of "total package" sports broadcast set the standard for TV sports through the 1960s, and ABC quickly crushed every other major sport to its money-making bosom. And make money they certainly did. Some sports, like hockey and soccer, resisted the demands of the tube; others, like football, seemed born for them. It was not long before the television producer was controlling the pace of the game, calling commercial time-outs and dictating kick-off times. In exchange, the suddenly popular professional National Football League was waging a war of escalation over the sale of television rights. New leagues in both football and basketball (the AFL, the WFL, the ABA) were created just to fan the fires of television money-making. Then new networks (ESPN, SportsChannel, USA), new technologies (cable, pay-per-view), were created just to broadcast the new sports that had been created for them. Baseball suffered through neglect and the nature of the game, which was not given to the kind of violent visual dissection that makes football fans so happy or the fast pace and intricate movements that amp roundball watchers. It is hard to recall today that baseball's demise was confidently predicted in the early 1970s, by sources as diverse in tone and integrity as *Time* magazine, *The Wall Street Journal*, and Howard Cosell.

Predictably, baseball survived the threat of pro football and other telegenic sports only by becoming more telegenic itself, adding more cameras to game coverage and taking the instant replay to new heights of absurdity. Though purists rightly balk at the new tele-consciousness of players and fans, the game probably could not have done otherwise. The cycle of TV rights and TV profits, a dollar-producing turbine set on high speed, was up and running. Major-league sports are now dead in the water without television contracts, and network competition means that profit margins are just about as wide as those lucrative ad contracts from NFL Sundays, the World Series, the NBA finals, college football bowl games, and the college basketball Final Four. To see where the unholy alliance of sports and TV has brought us, one has only to tune in, once a year, to the Super Bowl. Keep a vomit bowl at the ready.

The Super Bowl has become the window of choice for major companies with huge ad budgets. Given the often one-sided nature of the game, the ads are frequently the only point of genuine interest.

Against a background of such all-consuming TV dominance, radio now seems an unlikely medium for sports—the medium of the past, of the early days. We are taught that *serious* sports fans must have massive dish antennas, six-foot screens, and cable. Sports radio, with its meagre broadcast schedule and early-era technology, starts looking pretty feeble by comparison. Radio? Who needs radio? I've got forty-nine channels of twenty-four-hour-a-day action here. I've got NCAA softball at two in the afternoon! Australian rules football at five! Fat guys throwing darts from seven to nine! One game of baseball a day on radio? Don't make me laugh.

But the argument soon founders. To nobody's astonishment, the quality of this programming is inversely proportional to its quantity. Now that I see what cable actually offers, I can prove what I only suspected when, as an impoverished graduate student with a borrowed cable-free TV, I had just one thin channel beaming into my life: the more there is, the worse it gets. And yet, because the visual medium is so seductive, whatever the subject, sports fans may actually find themselves watching things they would have sneered at a few years ago. Monster trucks roaring over mounds of dirt! Has-been football players shooting skeets! Competitive croquet from Long Island! This lowering of personal standards, the murder of moderation, leads in turn to a second negative effect: fan burnout. Immersed in inclusive coverage, drowned in all that professionally created imagery, today's TV sports fan has lost the ability to tell good from bad. It's not couch potatoes we need to worry about, but rather couch potatoes who can't tell the difference between the NBA playoffs and the under-sixteen synchro-swimming trials from Port St. Lucie. Dimmed by plenty, overcome by an embarrassment of visual riches, the cable TV sports fan has lost the ability to *turn the TV off.*

There are now entire channels devoted to single sports, including motor racing and golf. It's one thing to watch the final round of the Masters; quite another to sit through consecutive hours of instructional videos and phone-in shows with unknown PGA Tour veterans.

And it is precisely here that radio comes (or comes back) into its own, where the magic of sound actually outstrips the flood of information pouring from its audio-visual rival. Here is the fertility of imagination, the enchantment of inner vision, the power of the invisible. Radio pulls its audience with true drama, the unseen game more exciting for being unseen. It works the tired muscles of the imagination.

This is not true of all sports, of course. Most sane people would still rather watch a basketball game than listen to one; a basketball radio broadcast consists mainly of updates on the score. Football and hockey remain borderline radio: I have happily driven through upstate New York, en route from Toronto to New Haven, listening to college football broadcasts, picking up local relay stations one after the other, or monitored the Stanley Cup playoffs . But even devoted fans will miss the sight of the complex play as it develops, or the geometrical excitement of a three-on-two break. Baseball, by contrast, is a sports-radio natural, a game where medium meets message with joyous results. Listen to the slow rhythm of balls and strikes from, say, Tom Cheek and Jerry Howarth of Toronto's CJCL. You hear them, and the neurons of imagination and mental representation, the circuitry of the mind's eye, fire through your brain like scatter-shot tracer bullets. Big explosions of spastic bio-electronics. The splashing fireworks of inner seeing. There are no instant replays here, no flashy stats graphics, only the moseying words of the old-pro announcers, the rising voices of long balls, and the arcana of old baseball vocabulary.

"Baseball is the last theatre of the mind," says Cheek, a veteran of thirty years behind the mike, "and so baseball and radio are a natural marriage." Cheek, whose doughy face he describes as "made for radio," grew up in Pensacola, Florida, where his daily stick-ball routine included elaborate play-by-play descriptions that drove the other kids crazy. His is the classic story of childhood dream come true, the dirty kid with only a wooden spoon to talk into, hired, decades later, into his dream job: 162 games of action, seen from the best seats in the house. Along the way, he broadcast everything from Yankee League college football to amateur wrestling matches and pro bowling. Now, in his perch in the Telemedia Network broadcast booth at Toronto's SkyDome, he is in fan heaven.

Cheek and partner Howarth amble through the summer lineup of Jays games with the effortless grace of Fred Astaire and Ginger Rogers, making the hard look easy. Trading their elaborate courtesies like a couple of Victorian clubmen, they are the heroes of my radio world. Like all life-long fans, their knowledge of baseball trivia is encyclopedic and bizarre. For someone like me who can barely remember a World Series a few years on, this is astounding. They remember double plays turned a decade ago, lineup changes from the 1970s, clubhouse quips from three seasons back.

I have often been struck by this difference, which I can only imagine is genetic. My friend Alison Gordon, admittedly a professional baseball writer for much of her life, has an astounding memory for baseball minutiae.

Impressed by Curt Gowdy's intimate Red Sox broadcasts while working in Burlington, Vermont, during the 1970s ("He always seemed like he was talking just to me"), Cheek developed a warm, even presence on the airwaves. Now fifty-three years old, he grew up on radio—on Mel Allen and Bob Price and the rest. Yet he's more Barber than Allen, and doesn't go in much for the shouting, slangy noise of the old-time heroes. "It's not my style to have signature lines," he says. "I never went through a period of thinking, 'Now, how am I going to call a home run?' I don't spend my time trying to come up with nicknames for the players. Whatever the moment dictates, I call."

The calls are good, with Cheek's vibrant twangy voice a power source he modulates at will. He sets the scenes and "paints word pictures," while the more stats-minded and in-depth Howarth complements the broad strokes with detail. And the talk! Inside and outside, sliding and curving, dropping and rising, bouncing and chopping—the words of baseball radio jump out at us like lively Haitian baseballs, peppered with technical language and down-home vocab, filled with diamond wit and ball-yard bravado. It is a joy to listen to these gabmeisters, to hear the lifting excitement of a ball hit hard, the ranging fielder, the stumble onto the warning track, the clearing of the wall. Baseball on radio is pure summer joy, three hours spent in outs and innings, in the company of those voices and ourselves.

"Baseball is more than a game," Cheek says eventually, as baseball people always do. "It's a lifestyle. It's a long season, it's every day, it's continuity, and it's simple arithmetic. It's also mobile. You can take Tom and Jerry to the lake, on the bus, to the office, out in the garden, anywhere. You might be doing a lot of things, but there's no reason you can't have your Blue Jays." Surely this is the real magic of baseball radio? I remember driving from Toronto to New Haven one September, the Jays closing in on the American League pennant, and the rental car's antenna picked up the fading Tom and Jerry as we skidded through the rainy streets of Batavia, New York. I parked the car, got some coffee, and sat there with the rain pounding on the roof, straining to hear the wavering beam of talk as it skipped across Lake Ontario—a huddled caveman listening to big stories from far away. I was completely happy.

When I lived in Britain and worked for a literary quarterly, we used to paste up the galleys while listening to BBC4 broadcasts of Test cricket, another great radio game. Those broadcasts lasted six hours at a stretch, and the veteran announcers, John Arlott and Fred Trueman, filled in the frequent gaps in the action with disquisitions on local politics, the profusion of hedgehogs in the Home Counties, fashion commentary, even recipes. Norman Webster, now editor of the Montreal *Gazette*, once told me that, when he was London correspondent for *The Globe and Mail*, he and his wife drove all the way from London to Cornwall listening to cricket on the radio. He was, as I would have been, riveted—so much so that he didn't notice she was bored to tears.

You can't do this kind of thing with television. TV sports are fascistic,

Notice this instance of the media-age tic of third-person self-reference. I think we should all start doing this. "I just have to do what's right for Joe Blow and his family ..."

It was the *Edinburgh Review*; watching cricket, when you've never played it, is hard enough–listening is surreal.

totalitarian—and not just in terms of the sheer dollar amounts they control. The medium itself is authoritarian. You must sit there, watching. You could just listen to the announcers' voices, but they're not giving much away, saying things like "Look at that one!" You have to watch a TV, that's what it's for. It works its will on you. Nothing is left to your imagination—how could it be? Missed a play? Here's an instant replay. Missed it again? Here it is again. Here it is three more times. Want to compare that play with one last week? Here it is. Here, look at it again. JUST SIT THERE. WE'LL LET YOU KNOW WHAT'S INTERESTING. DON'T MOVE!

TV destroys the imagination, and so it usurps the human element in sports. Consider for a moment the phenomenon of *slow-motion* instant replays. What are these but stylized, melodramatic versions of the play, the play laid over with a thick wash of manufactured drama? Slowing the motion provides the illusion of greater significance or accuracy—but it's instant, disposable mythology. It is the sports-TV equivalent of the sort of hyper-realist art to be found in Nazi recruiting posters or Soviet labour murals, visual propaganda that undermines the reality of the action or subject depicted. The play is no longer the thing; it is the replay. Have you ever watched fans at a sports park with a Jumbo-Tron? They look to the TV after every play. At what point, I wonder, do they realize that they needn't even go to the park? Then there's the special nonsense of pro football replays, with crucial decisions determined by a faceless group of officials hunched over a bank of televisions. Can we no longer even play this game without TV?

Television should, in theory, be the perfect medium for sports, the medium that makes staying home better than being at the game. But in practice TV flattens the games out, makes them stagey and forced. Not surprisingly, today's players, so media-minded, are starting to modify their play to TV's demands. They get special haircuts before big games. College sport, once the preserve of true amateurs, is no more or less than a junior league for the pros, with huge television contracts dictating not only play but also league structure. The Notre Dame football team, for example, has its own network deal to show all home games. Because

One of my philosophy colleagues, explaining her inability to appreciate baseball in Toronto's SkyDome, said, "My *eye* knows where to look, and it's not at the field."

they're a TV popularity lock, the Penn State football team now has a guaranteed invitation to a bowl game, whatever their regular-season record. And worst of all, TV all but owns major team sport these days, underwriting huge portions of annual budgets with the sale of broadcast rights—forty-seven percent in the case of baseball. One major reason the National Hockey League may not survive the Nineties is that its television revenues are so minuscule—just $5 million a year, compared with the more than $200 million raked in by pro basketball and football.

Radio imposes no such demands on the game. Nor can it dictate the responses of the fan. Like all great and genuine mythologizing, sports radio is oral, a matter of storytelling and narrative power. Its force comes from the suggestiveness of words and the allusiveness of the described but not seen. Its power depends on the reality of the game itself, a game played and judged by real people somewhere else. That's why baseball, that most mythological of North American sports, is the perfect game for the medium of radio, that locus of elemental magic. When we listen, the feelings of subtle joy and solidarity are the feelings of being gathered to hear tales of people braver and more talented than ourselves. The game is filled with pregnant moments—the 3-2 delivery, the sailing long hit, the catcher's throw to second—and lulls and depressions, which can explode into sudden, dramatic action. Baseball, the storyteller's dream game—the summer game—belongs on radio, the medium of the mouth and ears and mind.

Not to be Luddite about it, but some technical advances just put us farther in the hole. So I've got my new TV now, and the cable that gives me way more than one channel. But on summer evenings and weekend afternoons, it's the radio that's turned on.

TV revenue continues to be a problem for hockey; and dumb Fox Network innovations, particularly the blue-glow puck, went bust–thank Christ.

Actually I'd really rather be at the park, with Alison Gordon, having a beer and a hot dog.

X-Rated Sports

Okay, forget the in-house slang, the stupid snowboard fashion trends, the teen cultism, and the hero-worship of media darlings like skysurfer Patrick de Gayardon or in-line skater Arlo Eisenberg. The beauty of extreme sports is in the eye of the camera.

The luge-cam angle is the best. Hurtling down an urban runway—steep grades, winding streets, ninety-degree turns, and all—a human is laid full-length and feet-first on a modified aluminum-rail and urethane-wheel skateboard contraption so rickety, so close to the blurred asphalt, that . . . Jesus, it's scary just to look at it. Other camera angles show that the human is wearing all the protective gear of a backyard gardener plus, maybe, a bike helmet, meanwhile reaching speeds (as they like to say) *in excess* of seventy miles an hour. *Street luge*: now why didn't you think of that?

Because (a) you're sane and (b) you're not Bob Pereyra, inventor of the sport that now provides what can only be described as a grisly form of sporting entertainment on ESPN2, the alterna-game branch of the big U.S. sports-TV network. "Grisly" because there is something horrible buried in the heart of street luge, like all extreme sports: a desire to observe the body at risk, meat in peril, the soft hominid flesh suspended delicately from gossamer wings or rubber bands, mere inches from the gashing rocks and abrading concrete of more stable matter.

In excess of . . . More extreme than . . . Pushing the envelope of . . . The culture of extreme sport is inherently a transcendent one, one organized around the conditions of physical possibility, probing performance boundaries that are drawn only to be exceeded. It is hubristic, arrogant, Icarean. It is also entirely human in its restless desire for more stimulus. The old motto of the Olympics, expressing the relentless drive to greater

Or as they say in the
more elegant Latin,
"Citius, altius, fortius."

performance—"Faster, higher, stronger"—here receives its appropriate late-century modification: "Riskier, scarier, crazier." As the ads for the X-treme Summer Games say: "The Truth Is Way Out There."

What kind of truth? Well, the purity of risk, for one thing; the peculiar relationship of trust between human and equipment. The clash of knowledge and fear. (I know the bungee cord will hold me up. So why can't I let go?) And of course here, as elsewhere, too much knowledge can be a dangerous thing. Reflecting too deeply or too long on the risks involved is sometimes precisely what makes you prey to them. The real mind-body problem, when you engage in BASE jumping or downhill mountain-bike racing, is the opposite of Descartes's celebrated "I think, therefore I am." It is instead "I think, therefore I'm meat." As baseball coaches, the untutored Zen masters of the sports world, so often say: just don't think too much out there. Merge with the machine. Become one with your equipment. Or die.

In fact, the inner logic of extreme sports is cybernetic. In order to succeed, we must integrate more and more with the metal and plastic prostheses of the bike, the cord, the skateboard, the luge. Can on-board computers be far behind? And still the human element must be present to haul this new meat-metal machine back from the edge when it threatens to go over. Sometimes the old human self, risk-averse and sane, intervenes. The downhill mountain-biker Kim Sonier recently explained to an ESPN interviewer why she balked at a wicked jump on the course, a decision that cost her first place in the event. "I decided to be smart," she said, "and stop. It was better than dying."

It was better than dying. So there are limits. But these are now the limits of failure, the sharp lines of nerve and skill that mark winners off from losers. Some extreme sports even reverse the very idea of limit. In BASE jumping, for example (the acronym means Building, Antenna, Span, and Earth), extreme parachutists try to jump off human-made buildings, or natural cliffs, that are *near* the ground. *How low can you go?* Experience the GRE: no, not the Graduate Record Examination, pointy-head; the Ground Rush Effect. In a world of security and isolation—not to mention the deadening alpha-wave effects of television saturation—why not seek extreme risk and the helpless rush of liberating fear? Manufacture some fear; it's better than amyl nitrate. And like any intense physical experience, it's pretty addictive.

Also spectacular, for both old and new reasons. The Greeks called the clash of wills and testing of limits *agon*, struggle, and they found much wisdom in watching it: struggle was revelatory of character, of fate, of courage and intelligence grappling with contingency. Hence, by extension, our word "agony," as in—I can't help thinking here of that doomed ski jumper on "Wide World"—the *agony* of defeat. Once confined to the arena or tragic stage, agony is now tailor-made for TV. Josh Krulewitz, a spokesman for the 1996 X-Games (nine sports, twenty-seven events), said in an interview that the 1995 gathering of extreme athletes "won an Emmy for camera production" and called the games, accurately, "spectator friendly."

Of course, the horrible irony is that this very success threatens to remove X-sports from their original scene of youthful urban rebellion, the skateboards on railings, in-line skaters "skitching" rides on passing cars in New York, and plop them right back into the commercial arena they set out to resist, even mock. When Turner Broadcasting Systems launched a slick X-sports Web site called SPIV earlier this year, that form of commercial intrusion into the purity of extreme became unavoidably obvious. "SPIV offers must-know information about entertainment, fashion, sports and technology to an audience who would rather eat with their hands than be spoon fed," the slightly hysterical promo sheets said. "The users, 15- to 24-year-olds, reflect the editorial approach: topical and cutting-edge with a large dash of cynicism."

Probably the only real cynicism operating there is Ted Turner's desire to haul more gear-buying viewers into his sick-o broadcasting universe, but okay, we'll still bite on the idea. Extreme sports, bottom line, are sexy. Alaska Bungee Safaris, an outfit that takes bungee-maniacs to leap off the 238-foot bridge at Chitna, Alaska, knows it very well. "An extreme 'airgasm'!" their Web site ad screams. "And always remember, if you

Amyl nitrate again. I should probably tell you that the stuff used to circulate in my high-school locker room before class; I can't speak to whether it improved academic performance.

My friend John Loonam, a Brooklyn native, claims to have done this; so does the novelist Tessa McWatt. The tough-guy Winnipeg variation, bumper-shining, involves grabbing on and sliding along on the snow-covered street.

145

jump naked, you jump free!" Snapping your body off the end of that gravity-defying elastic band gives new meaning to the word "G-spot."

Even as the search for extremity, the drive towards transcendence, is pushing the limits of human/equipment performance and spectacle in X-games of various kinds, the nature of more traditional sports is imperceptibly changing too. This isn't just an issue for the equipment-heavy team sports like football or hockey. Even the old Greek games of the Olympic ideal—running fast, jumping high, throwing things a long way—are being vortexed into a virtually technological performance imperative. Old speed and height records, like old car or computer models, are constantly rendered obsolete. Equipment is slowly moving in from outside the body to colonize the athletic flesh. New techniques, slight innovations, and new fuels power the latest prototypes to ever-greater levels of performance, bending the speed needles by minute increments over the previous benchmarks. Here the athletic performance actually merges with technology, because only the super-sensitive Swiss measurements, the precision nano-technology of Bauer or Rolex, can accurately determine the outcome. Without the fine tools of electronic chronometry, in other words, every 100-metre final and every downhill ski event is a dead heat. *Boring.*

It has become almost truistic to say that the body is being transformed in these media-saturated techno-times: To argue (like the Canadian cyber-philosopher Arthur Kroker) that television signals are physically altering our bodies, rearranging our very cells. Or to opine (like the American nano-technician B. C. Crandall) that our bodies are just meme-nests anyway, unwitting hosts to an array of parasitic chunks of coded information that need flesh to survive in these four spatio-temporal dimensions. It's also obvious that the flesh is indeed weak—so weak that we shore up its fragments, Borg-like, with metal and plastic girders: prostheses, implants, fillings, pins, splints, and rods. Artificial limbs. Replacement joints. Even our ideals of physical beauty are now irreducibly infected by

Crandall, "The Nanotech Future," *CTHEORY* 19 (1997): "A 'meme' is a piece of patterned information carried and expressed by a human brain, just as a 'gene'–which rhymes with meme–is a piece

146

the technology of the laboratory and the surgeon's art: those breasts, those pecs, that trim waist. What a fine *specimen*. What a masterful *creation*.

But if that is obvious, the implications for the culture of sports perhaps are less so. The purity of the Olympic ideal is long dead. It is only speciously maintained in the rhetoric of Juan Antonio Samaranch and the other poobahs of the International Olympic Committee. This is less about the incursion of "sports" like beach volleyball (a transparently sensationalistic marriage of sex and game, the "Baywatch" of ball games) or ballroom dancing (please!) than it is about the accelerated evolution of athletic performance. The Olympics are no longer pure because the athletic body itself is no longer pure. It is now programmed by the non-flesh logic of the mechanical, and the external equipment of sport—the bicycle or shoe or swimsuit—now merges by degrees with our more basic equipment, the body itself. Steve Austin, the bionic man, is no longer the preserve of cheesy TV science fiction. In fact, if we wanted to mark the midnight of athletic purity, the final demise of the Greek ideal that still cynically condemns steroid use, it would be easy.

It is 1994. Bo Jackson, the great Auburn University prodigy, pro-level skilled at both baseball (Chicago White Sox) and football (Los Angeles Raiders), accepts a plastic-and-metal hip joint. An awkward tackle and a freak infection have destroyed his physical hip, taking him from successful two-sport poster boy to medical case study. But what Bo really knows is that this quasi-cyborg status doesn't bar him from returning to professional sports if he can make it. And for a time, he could. Bo was never the same, of course, and now he has accepted retirement from the sporting arena, but that—surely?—is really just a small problem of engineering. In the future, Bo's hip would have made him stronger, not weaker. Faster, not slower. And then, just watch out for that guy coming around the end of the blocking line or spiking into second base.

The body-machine; the machine-body. Watching television, it's sometimes hard to tell them apart. First lesson in the cyborg heats: power is

of patterned information carried and expressed by DNA. By taking in that last sentence, you become infected with the meme about memes."

Where have you gone, Lee Majors? A nation turns its lonely eyes to you.

Where have you gone, Bo Jackson? A nation turns ... Oh, never mind.

nothing without control. The American sprinter and long-jumper Carl Lewis demonstrates that truth in a series of recent ads for Pirelli Tires, including the now-infamous effort of him in red stiletto high heels, poised for the race-starting gunshot. In one of the TV spots, Lewis, running so fast he skips across water and so hard he leaps huge distances, is dressed in nothing but a campy black leotard. Perched finally on the strut of a Manhattan office tower, he turns over one of his bare feet and fondly strokes the distinctive rubber swirls of the Pirelli tire tread that are now there, part of him.

Of course the body as machine requires fuel. Rival sports-drink companies now compete for market shares with an all-out assault on the old ideas of bodily purity. Because we must now accept that it's no longer enough simply to eat food and drink water in order to build a successful sporting physique. The ambitious athlete has to enhance his or her performance with a trademarked performance beverage: Gatorade, All Sport, Powerade. These drinks contain vitamins and minerals. The body absorbs their fluids more quickly than water. They come in toxic-looking neon green or Slurpee orange. And if the ads can be believed, they taste great even as they take performance levels to unimaginable new heights.

Or a male hormone that happens not to be banned by Major League baseball, like the androstenedione used by 1998's record-shattering home-run slugger Mark McGwire. (Andro is banned by the NFL, NHL, and NBA.)

"Welcome to the 2020 Global Games," says a barely aged Jim McKay from his floating commentary hovercraft, introducing a host of new performance-enhanced Olympic-style events in one ad campaign: the highly uneven bars, the one-tonne power lift, the dolphin relay, the graduated hurdles. Athletes in full body suits, some with armour—those graduated hurdles not only get higher, they have spinning rods that have to be knocked aside—plough through these events in superhuman feats of athletic performance. But then, not superhuman at all. "The world of sports is ever-evolving," the voiceover tells us. We're all headed to greater levels of performance. And a jug of All Sport might be just the thing to push you over the current limit. Go ahead. Stretch the boundary. Drink some.

In a recent TV ad for Powerade, Donovan Bailey, the great Canadian sprinter and current world champion, lines up on a drag strip next to a top fuel racer, one of those rangy rear-engine machines with the big spoiler and fat slick tires. Sprinter? Meet sprinter. The drag-strip staging lights flash red, amber, green—and the two finely tuned speed machines peel away from the line. Donovan Bailey: World's Fastest Human. It used to be that sprinters were compared with swift animals, cheetahs or antelopes, shots of the fleet human intercut with Marlin Perkins-style "Wild Kingdom" footage of these even fleeter mammals. No longer. Now only a rival fast *machine* impresses us as a viable opponent. Will Bailey add an Olympic gold to his world title at the 1996 Summer Olympics? Well, forget being a cheetah. He's got to be a *dragster*, to flash past the light-trigger a couple of hundredths of a second before the hungry challenging field of overmuscled speed merchants. To do that he must, apparently, drink jugs of Powerade. And by the way, so can you. Drink it, that is, not win gold medals. "You may never set a world record," the ads tells us, "but you can enjoy the power of Powerade." Just don't try to beat any cars across the street after you do.

The answer to that is, of course, Yes, both for the 100 metres and for the 4 x 100 relay.

These fuels for the human body merge with more conventional machine fuels in yet another striking TV ad. It features two admirably grungy tennis players sweating out a gruelling match on a wide stretch of red desert. The court is massive, unprecedentedly large—a football field. The players dive for the ball, serve with robotic intensity. Then the disembodied holographic referee calls time in his voice-of-doom tones. One player goes to sit down, takes a cup, and pulls a draught of . . . Powerade? Gatorade? No: Pennzoil motor oil. An aperture whirrs open in the back of his head and he pours the lubricant in. And now back to the court for the final set. Robotic intensity is right. Look at that 300-mph serve! Android tennis: the new media spectacle. And the ad's tag line? "There are no limits." Not when it comes to what the Unabomber taught us to call, in his famous "Manifesto," the doctrine of technological inevitability.

These fuel pitches demonstrate two things. First, that the controversy surrounding steroids and other performance-enhancing drugs is really

149

pointless, a long-dead issue that limps along on the resentment of certain athletes for their rivals—Carl Lewis and fellow American sprinter Gwen Torrance are the most voluble whiners—and the face-saving dissembling of various athletic authorities. Athletes and governing bodies alike are vocally in favour of superior performance, and yet they go on maintaining this false demeanour of athletic puritanism.

The result is absurdities like Silken Laumann being stripped of her medal at the Pan-American Games because she took the wrong cold medicine (one version is banned, another not), and the uproar caused when a renegade Chinese running coach produced a crew of record-shattering distance runners by feeding them a diet of, he said, special herbal remedies, turtles' eggs, crushed bones, and seaweed. Most people still feel Ben Johnson was rightly stripped of his Olympic gold medal in Seoul in 1988 after he tested positive for anabolic steroids, but that moral disapproval is really about the unfair advantage of cheating, not the use of the drugs themselves. Is there any real difference between kinds of fuel, after all? Most extreme-sports kids favour beer and fast food, according to one on-line discussion group; their bodies can take it. What's wrong with performance-enhancing drugs? The whole drive of contemporary sports culture is performance enhancement. Many things are legal and a few aren't.

Meanwhile, innovations in equipment are unceasing: a new swimsuit has just been developed by Speedo, artfully designed with water-shedding qualities superior to those of human skin, that will shave a few hundredths of a second from a swimmer's time. The only issue with this new suit is, when can everybody get it? Sports is now an arms race, a kind of escalating fugue of measure and counter-measure, advantage gained and nullified: the one remaining constant in this, the original genetic fluke of native athletic ability. Genetic fluke also, of course, seems to be the thing that makes sports worth watching in the first place. If tennis stars really were robots, would we care? Probably not. But if they are quasi-robots instead, virtual androids hopped up on steroids with fairly matched bionic prostheses and super-efficient

In a forward-looking but evidently misguided move, Samaranch argued in 1997 that the IOC should lift its ban on any performance-enhancing substance that was not actively harmful. He was quickly shouted down.

Still not to be worn by anyone other than truly superior physical specimens; see "Running Low on Posing Pouches" (Section I).

food/fuels and graphite-titanium raquets, will we watch then? Yes, because that's what we do already.

Hence the second thing that the Powerade–Pennzoil ads teach us. We have an apparently insatiable appetite for the increases in performance that drive athletic contests, and that is part of why we watch the contests in the first place. But those increases must be tied, however tenuously, to bodies—however unusual. Basketball and football players get bigger and stronger by the year. Did you see Dennis Rodman morph from his noodly 1980s-vintage Detroit Pistons body, when he had black hair and no tattoos but won NBA defensive player of the year, into his multi-hued Superman physique, complete with body-art, circa 1996? Sprinters are now more muscular, and swifter. Donovan Bailey can bench-press 225 pounds and squat a Volkswagen-like 505 pounds. Distance runners have pared whole minutes off world records.

Technology plays its role here, too, of course. Better bodies come from better machines. Lighter shoes. Hyperbaric-chamber sessions. The weight room. Immersion tests and muscle isolation. Once again science and technology creep into the realm of physical contest, this time from the training end.

I can attest that the technological aspect of even a low-equipment sport like running is pretty hard to resist: you start to want those gel-filled heels, that flyweight polymer upper. In golf or skiing, with graphite and titanium in play, it must be at least half the fun.

Is there any upper limit to this seemingly parabolic arc of advancement, any point of contact between performance curve and physical asymptote? Not so far. And if the producers and consumers of athletic spectacle have anything to say about it, not ever.

Fast forward in your mind to the 2120 *Enhanced* Global Games. Your host is still Jim McKay, but now a prosthetically improved, artificially maintained version of him: his face a little bit saggier but otherwise unchanged, his internal organs largely replacement models, three of his limbs made of titanium-based alloys and Bakelite 3000, the new superlight, superstrong nanotechnology plastic. The new events? Naked beach volleyball (let's be upfront about this, for God's sake). Strip figure skating (ditto). The ten-storey high jump. The 500-metre sprint (world record 15.49 seconds). Nothing is banned, nothing censured. The only rule is captured by the new motto of the IOC: "Wetware Is Shareware." All new bionics, enhancing drugs, genetic-code manipulations, brain chips, and technological advances are considered public property, no patents are available on sports technology, and there is a strong ethical code, originally part of cyber-culture, that protecting information is deeply anti-social—not to mention bad sportsmanship.

Sure, some people still cheat, adding a new version of the Intel reaction-enhancer to a star sprinter, say, without informing the officials. But this kind of cheating is now much harder with the new program scanners available at every track and pool and ski run. And really, what's the point? Old records fall just about every day, and unless you find a genius scientist who can work just for you, real technological innovation is ubiquitous anyway. No athlete acts on his own; he's really just the point man for a corporation-sized group of technicians, trainers, micro-engineers, bio-geneticists, and psycho-philosophical counsellors.

The last group may be the most important, because here at the Enhanced Games the margin of victory—a pico-second or less—now lies mostly with the intangibles: attitude, desire, courage. With genetic differences more and more evened out at this, the high end of the gene pool, ancient techniques of mind control and focus-enhancement are now practised with an almost religious fervour. They are the difference between winning and losing. Who would have thought that philosophical reflection would become so important in sports? Who would have predicted that the mind—not its physical host, the brain—would prove so essential to athletic success?

In this future, a cult of sports puritans maintains a rear-guard position against the innovations and new media spectacles of sports, of course. They insist on a restrictive definition of sports and refuse all implants and prostheses. But lately their credibility is growing weak since their leader, the novelist and former wrestler John Irving, who extolled the virtues of pure sport in *The World According to Garp* and other works, recently accepted an artificial heart to ease him into his third century

This vision has its nightmarish aspects as well. The Ethan Hawke and Uma Thurman film *Gattaca* (1998) provides a vivid, stylish depiction of the soft tyranny of genetic determinism.

Well, probably only me. Philosophers now provide therapy, and therapists counsel athletes, but I rather doubt that I or any of my philosophy colleagues have a future on the staff of the Green Bay Packers.

of life. What these people don't seem to realize is that there is nothing to fear in cyber-sports. When meat meets machine, only the flicker of life distinguishes us from the new tennis-playing cyborg creation, Android Agassi. But that flicker makes all the difference in the world, the difference between caring about performance and merely being impressed by it.

Are there any limits in the clash of individuals on the field of athletic performance? Not as far as we can see. Is sports dead when the athletic body is no longer pure? Of course not. The pure athletic body really died with the Greeks, who ran and wrestled naked. That sort of thing might be *interesting* (in fact, the IOC is considering naked wrestling as a demonstration sport for 2124), but give us the Enhanced Games any day. For one thing, they're coming, like it or not; in fact, in a limited fashion are here already. And anyway, weren't records made to be broken, limits to be transcended? Isn't that how we demonstrate the deepest parts of humanness, whatever the precise contours of the machine-body we operate?

Extremity—not image, not even thirst—really is everything. And only the mystery of consciousness, the slow burn of the human soul, is finally equal to that challenge.

I'm **not** sure I really consider this a valid conclusion any more, though it is consistent with the logic of the position I have set out. I do wonder if there is an upper limit to the constant smashing of performance records in athletics.

Sportspace

This article was written as part of a series on the theme of "space"; I owe some points to discussions with my friend and colleague Mark Migotti.

There is space in games as there is in life, space defined and controlled, fought over and hard-won, created and nullified instantly, measured and celebrated by the passage of objects called balls, accomplishments called passes, triumphs called goals. Game-space is life space, metonymic and synecdochic, where nations battle (England v. West Indies) and cities tangle (Pittsburgh taking on New Orleans), where "the turf" is the entirety of horse-racing culture, "the pitch" is all that's cricket and "the gridiron" is a whole world of collective aggression. Game-space is also crucially *more than* life, an abstract critique of life advanced between the lines, within the boundary, inside the gridiron. Games are relationships, situations, that at their best reflect critically on the social possibilities of life.

Game-space is so much a part of us that we do not often take the time to separate it off from life, to contain it conceptually—contenting ourselves, instead, to contain it physically within the monumental architecture of spectacle, the domes, stadiums, coliseums, parks, and grounds of our social imagination. To enter these spaces is to participate in the game's critical possibilities, but also, paradoxically, to limit those possibilities. To succeed as more than diversion, to realize its possibilities, game-space must be both completely other than life and yet a crucial part of life. How can it be so? Well, begin with the inner spaces of game-space.

Game-space is, in professional team sports—the sports of social critique—either territorial or linear. It is, in other words, either rectangular or irregular, either measured and standard or idiosyncratic and conventional. Territorial games pit teams of equal number against each other in a battle of space control. Balls are advanced as tokens of ground won, strategic advantage gained. Goals await: the sheer advancement of the token beyond a certain line or plane (rugby tries, where the ball must be placed on the ground, football touchdowns where it must "break the plane" of the goal line); or the deposit of the token in a designated, defended space (the soccer or hockey goal, the basket). The ball is not merely a token, it is also a prize, deeply bound up with the conquest of space in the game. Notice the rituals of victory: Game ball. Spiking the ball. Writing a winning score on the ball and placing it in the trophy cabinet.

In territorial games the ball is also frequently the medium of movement. It can pass magically over the heads of toiling players bound to earth, advancing their territorial cause in great elegant leaps. One begins to understand the absolute dominance enjoyed by the Notre Dame football team, whose innovation of the forward pass in the early part of this century must have made their opponents taste instant despair. How could they—clay-footed mortals—compete with this death from above? Were they not now hapless infantrymen beset by aerial bombardment, out of their league, out of luck?

Territorial games, though circumscribed by defined space, work at the tactical level by the creation of space *within* the field. The field's limitations must be exploited, its spaces manipulated for advantage: the sideline pass pattern in football, the opening of "holes" in the defending line, the detection of "seams" in the "zone" defence—tiny unprotected spaces that open for a sub-second, only to close dramatically in an instant with the arrival of vengeful defenders. The quarterback, waiting for receivers to find the seams, has his own space worries. He surveys the forward field from a "pocket" of blocking teammates, keeping at bay for at best a few seconds the encroaching defenders. The pocket "collapses"—he is sacked. Or it holds, and his gaze picks out of the crowded game-space a receiver who is, or will be, "open" or sometimes even "wide open." The spiralling ball describes an arc, a curved line of power, from one open space, the pocket, to another, the open receiver in the seam. Success is measured in connecting open spaces, and the magic of football's forward pass is the magic of opening up small pockets of peace in a crowded battlefield of bodies.

As a lumbering intramural linebacker in high school, I always felt somehow god-forsaken when a long pass sailed over my head just as I was about to break through the offensive line and get to the quarterback.

155

Lance Morrow, "Deconstructionist at the Superbowl," *Time* (1999): "A professional football game is the mutation of inert muscle (noun) into pure historicized act (verb), framed in a matrix ('gridiron') of time and space. At a precise pencil-point of time, the quarterback's *cogito* presses urgently upon the possibility of the unthought.... Or something like that."

Football is the least fluid and most measured of the territorial games, the contest stopped after every move while new options are considered and reconsidered for the next. Moves are measured, motion is set, the game is laborious and sometimes tedious, but broken by explosions of movement and conflict. Yet even the more fluid territorial games like soccer and basketball turn on the creation of space: the pass to the open man, getting around a defender, placing the ball accurately and according to one's desires. Advantage is created, as in football, by drawing the defender into commitments that leave areas of the field unprotected, however momentarily, and thus open for exploitation. Skill in attacking consists in the ability to draw the defender and manipulate the resulting spaces; skill in defending is a matter of closing spaces quickly or preventing their creation altogether.

The field of territorial games is fixed, usually by statute; it is also usually rectangular and regular, measured by yard lines or offside boxes. All this is given: the field exists, immutable and consistent, before we step onto it as players. The field is the scene of the game, the circumscription of conflict. Moving off the field—going out of bounds, into touch, beyond the boundary—steals my status as a player, a participant in the game. The ball, beyond the boundary, is no longer a token of conflict. The question of whether the receiver's feet were in bounds when he caught the forward pass, now the subject of apparently interminable review by television monitor, is really the question of whether in that instant he is still a player, the ball still part of the game—or have they become mere furniture, indistinguishable from the rest of that surprisingly large milling crowd of spares, coaches, trainers, and hangers-on who throng the sidelines of every football game?

But these limitations, however powerful, are only the beginning of the game's spatial nature, for within the set boundaries the moves are not fixed. In the more fluid territorial games especially, players have enormous freedom of movement. They may have assigned positions, but with the exception of the oddball goalie (if there is one) these are tactical and do not represent limitations of the game itself. A defenceman may score in hockey, a forward may block his shot, and no coach will ruffle. A soccer sweeper may be the man who delivers the death-blow kick into the back of the opponent's net. Nevertheless, to prevent spatial chaos in territorial games there are frequently subtle and complicated "offside" rules—in hockey, rugby, soccer, and even static football. These rules limit the manipulation of the game-space in the interests of the game itself. Players cannot move in advance of the ball, or cross the blueline ahead of the puck, or enter the penalty area ahead of the last defender: the conflict of territorial games, in other words, must be head-on.

The rules, like the creation of the field itself, combine to make the game less like life and more like an idealized version of life, more like, indeed, a utopian critique of life. Unfair advantage cannot be taken within game-space. The teams are of equal number, if not of equal talent—but talent is the affair of God (and the general manager). The game is limited in time and space to produce the satisfaction of a result, never forgetting that a draw is a result too. Soccer, perhaps the most basic and certainly most universal of the territorial games, describes in its development a gradual drawing in of game-space, moving from its medieval English form of village-to-village conflict ranging over miles and days, marked by violence and cheating and irresolute cessation of hostilities, to its present limited form. Here, inside the defined green space, conflict is still basic but is now highly stylized, most obviously in the essential rule that no one but the goalkeeper may employ his hands, unless the ball goes, as they say, "into touch"—and thus out of the game.

What use is a game, after all, that is merely life by other means? The game can reflect on life only when its limits are clear, when it is clearly not-life in a definite respect. That game conflict spills over into life—in, say, the Honduras Soccer War or England's hooligan skirmishes—might be evidence of many things: a pathological inability to separate game from life, a continuation of deep hostility in a wider context, perhaps the profound effectiveness of the game's social critique. Contest reveals character, but so does response to conflict.

Offside rules are an attempt to impose order on conflict, the demands of fairness inscribed on the field itself, the drive for justice constraining the drive for victory. Somehow very poignant, and very human.

But conflict is the essence of some sporting contests, those confrontations that are not games and do not engage teams, but that are essential meetings of self with other, the struggle for recognition and dominance that characterizes the combative sports of fencing, boxing, wrestling, and others like them. Here space is not often of strategic interest, but defines the area in which one can run but cannot hide: the ring (another synecdoche there, as in the title of boxing's famous journal), the circle, the square. These combat spaces act, like the territories of game-space, to confine and stylize the conflict, to set artificial limits that pose questions of an essential nature—who is strongest, fastest, most cunning—within a controlled space. And just as two lawyers arguing does not always mean (though it sometimes can) that they disagree, two boxers fighting does not always indicate a hatred or even a dislike. Indeed, the brute nature of their conflict sometimes engenders a deep mutual respect: the recognition that after conflict—the struggle to the death—there is rest, and recognition.

Joyce Carol Oates, *On Boxing* (1986): "Boxers are there to establish an absolute experience, a public accounting of the outermost limits of their beings; they will know, as few of us can know of ourselves, what physical and psychic power they possess—of how much, or how little, they are capable."

In a few cases, the conflict of combat is itself about space, as, say, one thundering sumo wrestler attempts to push, throw, or knock another from the magic, sacred circle. More often it is about finding open spaces in personal defence, chinks in the armour of the boxer's dancing gloves—which "pick off" incoming punches to blunt their force—or the fencer's parrying épée. In wrestling, defended by John Irving's Garp as the most basic and essential of human sports, the object is even simpler: bring your opponent to the ground without aid of equipment or tool. This task, the planned destruction of the upright posture, that essential human achievement, is a return to the primitive both in method and in result. Once standing, I am felled; once independent, I am dominated. I lie on my back, looking up at my conqueror. No longer do I survey the world from atop my six-foot tower, master (as we say) of all that I survey. I am returned to the earth, with a thud, and against my will.

This toppling of the upright posture plays a role in boxing as well, though its achievement is not, in contrast to wrestling, the only way to win the contest. A knock-down brings a standing count, as the combatant is allowed to rise and collect himself; a knock-out is what happens when he cannot rise in the time (usually ten seconds) allowed him. Here it is not the opponent's body that pins me to the floor but the force of his blows, the violent punches to the head that will render me unconscious, or jelly-legged, or simply too dispirited to stand up for more. Destroying uprightness is also the essence of another violent confrontation, football tackling, that tiny instance of hand-to-hand combat within the larger spaces of territorial advancement. Bringing the man down is decisive, it stops play, which must begin again from this new site of man's fall. But here the conflict is not so controlled, so focused on the essential confrontation of ego and alter. There may be many tacklers, sometimes four or five, and they care not so much simply for bringing me to my knees— a man is down, in football, when his knee touches the ground—as for stopping my forward progress. But taking the evolutionary view, can we not say that these are the same?

That's in the college game; in the pros, his knee must be down and he must be, at the same time, touched by an opposing player. The classic tackle, which involves hauling someone violently to the ground, obviously satisfies both conditions.

Territorial and combative games are not the only arbiters of gamespace, nor the only or even best locus of social critique in the world of games. Territorial achievements and combat successes are, even when stylized and limited in space, to many minds still too much like life to offer much critical reflection. They may, in fact, simply reinforce dominant values of aggression and collective triumph, the values of warrior cultures and imperial nations. Linear games are fewer but their influence is sometimes wider, especially in defining national character at its best, what a people wants itself to be but often simply is not. In this sense the baseball diamond is a field of dreams in a way the gridiron will never be, and the cricket pitch says more about English civility and its attendant attitudes than the rough, militaristic game of rugby ever can.

Linear games are not territorial: there is no context for space, no obvious notion of ground won. The teams do not face each other as teams, but instead engage in a complex related series of individual efforts and confrontations. A player may find himself on the field of play with no

159

allies—or perhaps just one, his partner batsman or the next batter in the order. Success is measured in ritualized simulacra of progress: not attainment of goals, but movement along set lines in an elegant choreography of motions.

The ball, though now apparently less important because no longer a sign of territorial triumph, actually takes on a new necromantic power in linear games. It becomes a charged orb of menace and guile. It moves—"curves" and "slides" through space, "swings in" on a spin bowl—or it "takes a bad bounce," a bounce with evil intent. It passes beyond a fielder's reach, skips past an outstretched glove, or, in the most final of linear movements, leaves the field of play altogether: goes beyond the boundary, out of the park. In linear games, as opposed to territorial ones, to send the ball out of the game-space is to succeed wildly, not to fail or merely to stall play while it is brought back in. The ball remains a token of game progress but it takes on new technological roles: the ball as tool, not merely as marker. Roger Angell has reminded us that only the pitcher can, in the game of baseball, continue to regard the ball as an ally; it does things *for* him, but *to* everyone else. It is his tool, his weapon. The pitcher's success depends on an ability to control the ball's flight, to make it travel in lines that are not straight, in thaumaturgical arcs.

All else in baseball, meanwhile, is straight lines. The field is a diamond placed within two diverging foul lines, imagined in theory to extend to infinity. The diamond is fixed but the field is not, for the space opened up by the diverging foul lines may be contained in idiosyncratic ways. No two baseball fields have the same dimensions, and part of the game's charm lies in just this eschewal of rigidity. Fenway Park's Green Monster, for example, the massive fence in left field, compensates for urban encroachment on the field of play. Outfields vary in dimension from city to city, their changing lengths announced in large-scale markers on the fences themselves. No football field with such variance would remain a football field; and, by extension though less firmly by definition, no baseball field struck to rigidly controlled dimensions, outside the diamond

Measurement of the baseball field began in the latter half of the nineteenth century and was standardized by the 1880s, squeezing out other variations such as Cooperstown's game, known as townball, which involved five bases and two-way running.

anyway, would satisfy the spirit of baseball. Space is fluid here because the available space is infinite.

Likewise with the cricket pitch, whose precise boundaries are never drawn, not even (as now in baseball) measured. The game arises as though naturally, chthonically, from village green and country-house sward. The game is the sum of a set of relationships, not of rules and defined spaces. Linear games require, and embody, more culture than territorial games: their value-sets are more complex, less codifiable, more determined by social norms and conventions. It is only here that one can even attempt to argue, though perhaps with only limited success, for the presence of civility in sport.

A. Bartlett Giamatti suggests, in his book *Take Time for Paradise*, that baseball is a narrative of Romantic implications, an endlessly repeated and never-wavering quest to leave home and return home safely, against all odds, on a mythic patch of paradise. Here, in a little chunk of Eden, the enforced civility of the rules, and the more natural civility of the conventions of the game, make it effective as both critique and ideal. The game, though circumscribed by the city, is not the city: not the getting and spending for which cities evolve, nor the jostling and rudeness of city life; but instead an instant of peace, a moment of attention to larger-than-life events that take place, inevitably, in a "park." This plea for civility in baseball is, however quixotic in light of what now goes on there (Giamatti is dead; Pete Rose is alive, and coming back), a plea that simply makes no sense in the context of football. Michael Oakeshott's parallel claim, in *Rationalism in Politics*, that cricket is a practice whose integrity resides in its tradition, including centrally its tradition of manners (not its rules, that is, but its norms), meets a more favourable, though nowadays ever more threatened, reception. It is because linear games do not measure success simply with the attainment of territory that their social depth is more pronounced, and their possibilities of social critique that much more marked as they separate their game-space, little Edens, off from the rest of life.

There is nevertheless also here an issue of space creation. In baseball,

I still feel a thrill when I emerge from the concrete or brick tunnels, often dank, of a Major League baseball park and see the bright green space, the piece of paradise, enclosed by those projecting white lines.

balls are hit into the "hole" near the shortstop or to the "gap" between outfielders. The categorical imperative of baseball is, as Casey Stengel had it, to "Hit 'em where they ain't." To protect themselves from the onslaught of gap-seeking balls, fielders will "cover ground" to "track down" balls and so prevent hits. Occasionally they may be foiled by a "seeing-eye grounder," a ball that skips through an open space seemingly of its own volition, or by a "bloop" single that drops providentially into that troublesome square of open space between centre-fielder, second baseman, and shortstop.

Cricketers also seek gaps in the fielding, responding to shifts of the fielding players. In contrast to baseball, the language of cricket names positions, rather than players, when fielding is discussed. A shortstop is always a shortstop, no matter how close he is shading to second base, but the cricketer occupying the position known as silly mid-on may become the cricketer stationed at square leg merely by the whim of bowler or captain. The space of the cricket pitch is thus divided conceptually into a finite number of fielding positions, not all of them played at once, and with no firm boundaries between—but between is where the ball must go if a batsman is to score.

There are other issues of space creation. Both baseball batter and cricket batsman have safe spaces and dangerous ones. Vulnerability and security follow closely on one another, and one may be caught in the wrong place at the wrong time: run down between bases, or run out on the way back to the crease. ("There are no dragons in baseball," says Giamatti, "only shortstops, but they can emerge from nowhere to cut one down.") This may be owing to a teammate's ineptitude, bad judgment, or simply the exigencies of play. Success cannot be gained without risk—no runs are scored if I do not leave my crease or venture onto the basepath—but defeat can be swift. The ball returns with a vengeance, agent of my defeat: if it touches me, I am out; if it reaches the base or wicket before me, I am likewise dismissed. I cover space as a mortal while the ball flies over it, a winged harpy of destruction. Is it not something of a wonder that I get any runs or hits at all?

I never got many of either. As an extremely light-hitting

Reflecting on the difficulty of linear games is always to reflect on their spaces, on distances that must be crossed. In the room where I am writing this I have on the wall a reproduction of a baseball painting by John Dobbs. It is called *Stretching at First* and shows a baseball scene so familiar as to be iconic. The perspective, about ten feet directly down the first-base line in right field, shows a batter who, running full tilt, has placed his right foot on first base. The fielder, glove extended, is stretched to full extension while holding his left foot on the bag. The ball is not visible, though an umpire's head protrudes from the side of the frame. In this frozen instant lies the essence of baseball space, the paradigmatic linearity of the game. Think of the converging vectors: the pitcher's fastball delivery to the batter; the batter's sharp grounder to, say, third base; the quick throw over to first; the batter meanwhile covering the line from home to first at best speed. Batter and ball, who have parted so explosively a moment before at home, now meet again in the crucial convergence at first. Safe or out? The umpire's gaze is directed at the batter's foot touching the base, his ear concentrating for the sound of the fatal ball thumping into the fielder's extended glove. The ball remains, though visible neither to him nor to us, the scene's choreographer, its magic pill. Space separates and converges, and the game advances its slow ballet of lines.

What gives this confrontation its peculiar perfection? It is a commonplace that the distance between the bases in baseball (ninety feet) is arbitrary, based on no relevant authority except the dubious Doubleday. But the commonplace is misleading, for while the distance—the space to be covered—is indeed conventional, in that it has no grounding metaphysical rationale, it is not arbitrary. There is something, in other words, given the average speed of running athletic humans, the quickness of a thrown baseball, and the space created by the foul lines, that makes this contest one with meaning. Add five feet to the baseline, and batters would rarely beat out grounders for singles; subtract five, and they would perhaps do it all too often. Whatever the result, the game would no longer enjoy its delicate equilibrium of checks and balances—and so

shortstop for the Varsity Thunderbirds, and later an errant-armed outfielder for *Globe and Mail* summer-league teams, I stunk up softball parks all over Metropolitan Toronto.

would cease to be the game. Its space would be destroyed, and without its space baseball is not baseball.

It is thus possible that linear games are superior to territorial and combative ones precisely in their ability to give game-space more meaning in this fashion. Certainly it is true that watching linear games requires a degree of concentration and reflection unnecessary in the appreciation of the territorial. It also requires time, for the essence of both cricket and baseball is that the game is measured not by a clock, only by a set of tasks—getting the required number of men out. In Test cricket, that may take three or more days. And so anti-clockwise is the game of baseball that, as Giamatti reminds us, the players and the game proceed in that eccentric direction.

I'm **not** alone in thinking that, as commissioner, Giamatti might have saved Major League baseball from its recent troubles.

What this brings to our attention, and what the irregular contours of diamond and pitch finally emphasize, is that understanding game-space is not always a matter of conquering space, of gaining territory, or of defeating the other. Teamwork and aggression, the grammar of attacking and defending, do not tell us all we want to know about space. And to that extent anyway, space manipulated in that manner does not exhaust the meaning and the critical possibilities of the game. Ground is not always there to be won; opponents are not always to be brought down; life is not always to be conquered. The quest to reach home, or simply to create a small patch of regulated, civil endeavour—a piece of paradise, if you like, but perhaps just a peace of politeness on a greensward set amid the hurly-burly of life—is life's task too.

Fast Forward:

Our High-Speed Chase to Nowhere

Speed, according to the physics textbooks we all read in high school, is a function of distance over time: $V = d/t$. Space divided by time, the three dimensions of extension dissolved into the fourth, mysterious vector of duration. Miles per hour. Feet per second. Bodies rushing through time, into the future. But the indisputable fact that speed measures ground covered during periods of time fails to communicate why we yearn for acceleration, for the sudden enlarging of sensory volume that makes for the *feeling* of speed. This is a neurophysiological condition, familiar to most of us, that we might agree to call velocitization: the adrenal throb of neurons that accompanies large increases in velocity, the electrochemical, brain-fluid high we miss only when it's gone.

That's why coming down a freeway off-ramp makes us an overexcited traffic hazard, a portrait of unwilling deceleration still craving those now impossible seventy miles an hour. Or makes for the night of white-line fever following a daylong drive, the inside of our eyelids relentlessly patterned with oncoming dashes, one after the other, in an insomniac fugue of speed-jockey withdrawal. It is this sensation of speed that we desire, the impressionable meat inside our skulls lit up by that increase in sensory information. We want to be *velocitized*.

Speed is a drug, and not just in the old-time hepcat high of Dexedrine or bennies, those ingested, on-the-road amphetamines; or even in the newer, hi-tech crystal meth to be found, probably, in some corner of a schoolyard near you. The experience of speed itself releases into the

165

electrochemical soup of our heads a cascade of naturally occurring drugs, not the least of which are epinephrine and norepinephrine, the hormones that course through the brain in the bone-melting, stomach-clenching high of sexual attraction.

I have flown perhaps five or six hundred miles an hour while travelling in a commercial airliner. But the now-banal insight about this now-banal experience is that . . . there is no speed here. A slight pressing into my seat on takeoff, insulated from the engine's roar and cloaked in the unreality of carpeting and suit bags and laptops; a brief, fierce application of brakes and a reversal of engines on landing, especially if the airport is old and the runways are short. But otherwise, obviously, nothing. A sense of floating—music in my ears, a drink in my hand, peanut salt on my fingers, and not much in my head. A toboggan ride is faster, and more thrilling.

It would be different in a real plane. I grew up in an air-force family. My father, a navigator, pounded around the skies of the Maritimes in big four-prop patrol planes called Arguses, which, like their hundred-eyed namesake in Greek mythology, were ever-vigilant, searching for the conning towers of Soviet submarines or suspicious Grand Banks trawlers out of Baltic ports. The base where we lived wasn't home to any really fast planes, but they came through every now and then, hulking F-101s and insectoid F-5s slung with weaponry and wickedly slicked back from their forejutting needlepoints. Top speed: Mach 1.72. We looked at them with awe, the fast planes, observing their promise of barriers broken and limits overcome, the transcendental potential glowing on the matte-painted panels as visibly as the Day-Glo NO STEP and AIR INTAKE warnings. They said: speed transforms, speed kills, speed will make you free. I hung pictures of these jets around my room, glued together miniature simulacra of them, and dreamed of speed, of velocitization.

I start to read Milan Kundera's novel *Slowness* one snowy Sunday afternoon. I do it with the television on, a Bulls–Rockets game bouncing away in the background. "A picture-perfect fast break," Isiah Thomas

The suit bags and laptops are beginning to be the most salient feature of airline travel, those little battles for space in the overhead compartments our civilization's nearest return to a state of nature.

says to Bob Costas. Like many people, I often read while watching television. I'm not especially proud of this habit, but somehow I'm not appropriately ashamed of it either. Like most of us, I am also capable of simultaneously listening to music, carrying on a conversation, and eating—all while driving fifteen miles above the speed limit, scanning the horizon for signs of authority. Am I the proud owner of a parallel-processing new brain? Could I go even faster with smart drugs?

I have my laptop open to take notes, so I won't have to mark up Kundera's text. The laptop is a PowerBook 5300/100; it runs a 100-megahertz PowerPC 603e chip. This machine was considered pretty fast when I bought it eighteen months ago—not scary fast, just high-end quick. But now it feels slow, because I know there are so many faster machines out there, working at speeds closer to parallel. In fact, my 5300 has been placed in the "discontinued archive" by the Macintosh product developers, destined for quick-time oblivion in the big boneyard of machine death.

"Speed is the form of ecstasy the technical revolution has bestowed on man," writes Kundera on his book's second page. He is decrying the false "ecstatic" speed of the man in a machine—the artificial annihilation of time—as compared to the bodily speed of the runner. The man behind the wheel feels nothing but a mindless, futureless impatience, a desire to go faster that exists only in the present, obliterating all other modalities of temporality in a literal *ek-stasis*. The running man, by contrast, feels the many past, present, and future costs of speed, the burn in his lungs, the fatigue in his legs. Unlike the driver, the runner must resist the constant urge to quit, to slow down and rest. He must play mind games with himself, set intermediate goals, and then set new ones, knowing that eventually he will reach a point where the pain slips away, a fragile, short-lived euphoria of pure *human* speed.

I look up from Kundera's novel. Whatever the state of their lungs or feet, the Rockets and Bulls are in the dying moments of the fourth quarter and time is now being measured in tenths of a second, a precise charting that has the irritating effect of slowing it to a stutter. On an in-bounds play the ten young giants dash quickly around the court,

It also weighs a ton. Coupland, *Microserfs* (again): "I PowerBooked some code on ThinkC and so was able to remain productive. Batteries–the weight! They suck up gravity. They fellate the planet."

squeaking and grunting, even as no time at all passes on the game clock. The player with the ball, suspended in this artificial absence of duration, can't find an opening—he can't make time start again—and another time-out is finally called. The last three minutes of the game take twenty-five minutes to play.

This was the point I was trying to make in "X-Rated Sports."

"There is a secret bond between slowness and memory, between speed and forgetting," Kundera says, introducing a figure who captures something essential about the politics of speed. In a world forever overseen by television cameras, a world of instant forgetting, we witness the triumph of a particular character, *the dancer*. The dancer is that person who, through some expansive moral gesture witnessed by a TV crew, succeeds in putting his rival in an untenable position. The genius of the dancer is knowing when to make bold, skipping manoeuvres that seize the political high ground. What is crucial is that the dancer creates an image that instantly defines his opponent; a recent example of the dancer's art is Noel Godin's assault on Bill Gates with twenty-five cream pies, an image that within hours appeared on millions of television screens around the world, where it will be repeated endlessly. By choosing precisely the right moment to attack, Godin permanently inserted the image of Gates with pie on his face into our culture's image reservoir.

This was inserted by the editor; I'm not sure it's really a good example.

The dancer bears some resemblance to another character who was decisively labelled by a Parisian intellectual not long ago. In an essay called *Sur la télévision*, the sociologist Pierre Bourdieu lambasted the media-age creature he called *le fast-thinker*: the person who grinds out what appears to be intellectual discourse under the glare of the klieg lights. *Le fast-thinker* is not an intellectual, only the simulation of one; he is adept at the snappy phrase, the blustery and authoritative opinion, and, of course, the unanswerable statistical put-down. In the hurly-burly of talk television, on programs as disparate as "Meet the Press" and "Jenny Jones," the most successful performer is not the person with the truth but the one with the sharpest tongue and the handiest numbers.

See "The Intellectual Possibilities of Television" (Section III). I would seem to be contradicting myself somewhat, as compared with the argument in that piece.

168

Meanwhile, we sit at home and click nervously from one image to another, gazing at the disembodied heads of our televisual oracles as they flash across the screen. The medium, here, is the message, and the rapid-fire jump cuts seem to define not only our politics but our experience as well.

Alexander the Great and Napoleon moved through their respective worlds of overweening ambition and conquest at precisely the same speed. Top velocity for them, or anyone, was the gallop of a horse.

Machines change everything. Between December 18, 1898, when Comte Gaston de Chasseloup-Laubat set the first land-speed record in an automobile, his 36-horsepower Jeantaud achieving a top speed of 39.24 miles per hour on an open road near Achères, France, and October 15, 1997, when Richard Noble's ThrustSSC jet car broke the sound barrier in a car travelling 763.035 miles per hour (Mach 1.01) in the Nevada desert, the arc of human speed has bent its curve more and more steeply. Millennia of steady-state velocity have passed, and now in this crazy century of upthrust records limits are set and shattered in days, hours, even minutes. Chasseloup-Laubat held his record for less than two months, his Belgian archrival Camille Jenatzy taking it from him in January 1899 by hitting 49.92 miles per hour. The Frenchman managed, with some elementary streamlining, to respond by getting his car up to a respectable 57.6 miles per hour. But Jenatzy was more obsessed. He designed a new streamlined electric car, the first expressly built to break records, and shot to 65.79 miles per hour that April.

> Great name!

The name of this new car? *La Jamais Contente.* "Never happy." Here we have modernity in a nutshell, the same joyful fascination with speed—the same celebration of the sleek beauty of the machine age and its ceaseless imperatives—to be found a decade later in Emilio Filippo Tommaso Marinetti's original Futurist manifesto, published in *Le Figaro* in 1909. "Hoorah!" Marinetti wrote of the speedy machines he loved so much, the race cars and biplanes and swift war machines. "No

> Great name!

more contact with the vile earth!" But Marinetti's happy paean to "dynamism," his love of machine speed, reached its apotheosis, its own terminal velocity, only when he declared himself a fascist another decade later, in 1919. The speed of modern life had found its perfect political complement. Faster things for faster living. *Get with the program! Right now!*

The movement of our century can be plotted on a parabolic curve, a violent calculus of progress and quickness and neuronal excitement that is never, finally, happy, because it still has not achieved the pure limit-speed of infinity over zero. The upgrade imperative of the parabola is buried deep in the logic of speed, where machines not only go faster with each generation but also move from generation to generation at a brisker pace. The speed of personal computers, dutifully conforming to Moore's Law, now doubles in eighteen months or less. Technology's genius is that it plots its upgrade ambition on this striving curve, carrying us ever and ever more sharply upward. When it comes to our machines, nobody has to plan obsolescence. There is no military-industrial conspiracy to keep the eternal light bulb out of your hands, as suggested in a famous riff in the middle of *Gravity's Rainbow*. Obsolescence just happens.

Why? Well, consider gravity's rainbow itself. It is the other parabola dominating our era's span, the ballistic curve first plotted in the sixteenth century, when mathematicians brought forth the scribbles that could help them deliver cannon payloads more accurately. The two curves of speed and ballistics, the true golden arches, have never been far from the heart of war, our miserable keynote.

Speed, said Sun Tzu, is the essence of war. "History progresses at the speed of its weapons systems," adds the French philosopher Paul Virilio. "War has always been a worksite of movement, a speed-factory." It took ancient Greek warriors more than a decade to reach, and then destroy, a targeted city; we can now do so, from anywhere, in a few minutes. A single nuclear submarine can quickly reduce dozens of distant cities to molten glass and twisted metal. In the 1940s, the speed of naval "strike power,"

The bulb was called Byron. Thomas Pynchon, *Gravity's Rainbow* (1973): "Statistically, every n-thousandth light bulb is gonna be perfect, all the delta-q's piling up just right, so we shouldn't be surprised that this one's still around, burning brightly. But the truth is even more stupendous. This bulb is *immortal!*"

still the dominant form of military might, was measured in knots: in nautical miles per hour. By the 1960s, when the astronauts of *Apollo 10* achieved a record speed of 24,791 miles per hour, it was measured in Machs: thousands of miles per hour. Now operational velocity inches ever closer to light speed itself. Speed's annihilation of time and place means, finally, speedy annihilation of places—and times.

The inner logic of technology is not technical but commercial, and within the logic of commerce location is an increasingly meaningless concept. We confront, now, a new topology, a world of instant and direct contact between every point on the globe. The world's business, the totalizing globalization project, takes place at the speed of light, the speed accommodated by fibre-optic cable. Today there are 228,958 miles of such cable on the ocean floor. By the end of the century that number will almost double. The dominant material of our speedy world is not metal but glass: the glass pulled in phone connections, the silicon of chips and processors, the glass of the screen on which I am typing these words. In this silicon world, money flows ever faster, urged on its way by bulk-trading programs and electronic interfaces that replace the too-slow communication of the human voice. A million transactions a minute now pulse through the New York Stock Exchange alone; in 1900, there were fewer than two thousand trades per minute. The old-style trader, talking into his headset—or, still more primitively, shouting from the trading floor—is being replaced by a man watching the screen of his computer as representations of wealth and poverty, bar graphs and Cartesian plots, fluctuate up and down, wiping out South Korea's economy in hours or plunging Indonesia into international penury with the press of a key.

Everyone says: go faster. Everyone says: upgrade. Everyone says: be more efficient. We all hang on the curve, afraid to fall off. But the curve itself is not just a parabola; it is a paradox. It can never reach its ultimate

To the editor:

"Mark Kingwell believes that 'the movement of our century can be plotted on a parabolic curve.' The metaphor is not altogether apt. Personally, I would like to believe that it is a *hyperbola*, because this makes no sense whatsoever— much like our cultural desire to be constantly elsewhere."

goal, can only ever approach it more nearly by minute increments, because the end point of this insistent arch does not really exist. We know that Achilles must catch the tortoise in Zeno's famous riddle, but when we try to think about it logically he seems always thwarted, this famously fleet warrior, getting closer to the lumbering tortoise but never reaching him, no matter how quickly he runs.

In 1995, the science-fiction writer Bruce Sterling, whose body resides most of the time in Austin, Texas, posted a message on the Web inviting people to write what he called "The Handbook of Dead Media," an exercise in "media forensics," or (varying the metaphor) "a naturalist's field guide for the communications paleontologist." The idea was to track the history of the once-vibrant but now forgotten, the junk store of silenced communications along the road of obsolescence: the phenakistoscope, the teleharmonium, the stereopticon, the Telefon Hirmondo, the Antikythera Device, and a thousand more gadgets and extensions of human experience that once lived and do so no more.

See
www.islandnet.com/~ianc/
dm/dm.html

The point of the Dead Media Project, beyond its surface techno-anthropology, is to counter the hype of Net gurus, their tendency to champion nonexistent "vapourware" in terms otherwise reserved for the Second Coming and to load all technological change into the operating system we might call Progress 2.0. This "Whig version of technological history," as Sterling calls it, not only generates unspeakable hype but also spins off into aggressive, upgrade-or-die evolutionary imperatives—as if we're going somewhere in particular, as if technology really is teleology. Aging techies and watered-down McLuhanites can make a lot of money packaging and selling that brand of fear to the rest of us, but this is a phantom economy.

"We live in the Golden Age of Dead Media," Sterling writes on his Web site. "Our entire culture has been sucked into the black hole of computation, an utterly frenetic process of virtual planned obsolescence. But you know—that process needn't be unexamined or frenetic. We can examine that process whenever we like, and the frantic pace is entirely our own fault. What's our big hurry anyway?"

The Dead Media Project has a deeper lesson than historical awareness, though. It doesn't simply unsettle the fallacies embedded in techno-rhetoric; it doesn't just hint that the speed of technological "progress" has far more to do with money, power, markets, and politics than with simple technical efficiency. It also, more important, undermines the essentialism of speed, the dangerous and false idea that media them-selves have an internal desire to go faster. Media don't crave speed. We do.

Extreme speeds are not available to most of us. They are the preserve of the elite, who get to rise above the slow yet frenetic plodding of the urban lifescape. Sitting in traffic these days, watching the dollars count them-selves off in the red numerals of the taxi's meter as helicopters take off from distant office buildings, I realize that speed is the ultimate luxury good. Our cities' momentous flow of corpuscular traffic, pumping and squeezing in the arteries (physical and virtual) of our movement, our progress, is more and more sclerotic, slowing with the sludge of its own success. More than 700,000 cars enter Manhattan every day, joining the estimated 176,000 that are already there, along with the delivery trucks that block narrow streets and nearly 12,000 yellow cabs. Traffic crawls along in midtown at seven miles per hour. Mad cabbies honk and speed through the gaps and help maintain the average pedestrian-injury rate at about 250 per day. The bicycle couriers are the ones on speed.

The traffic stops, again. The meter in the taxi doesn't. I think: I can run a mile in seven minutes, but I have only a 14.4 modem and operating system 7.5 in my laptop. Am I fast? At what point, I wonder, do I get out and walk?

"Reading," says Virilio, "implies time for reflection, a slowing-down that destroys the mass's dynamic efficiency." Like Kundera, we feel we

Bruce Sterling writes:

"It may be that technology moves faster now because it's the last place left to go; the forces of repression have squeezed all the energy out of art, music, literature, cinema, politics and sex. It's as if you take the Concorde at twice the speed of sound so you can totter off the plane in London and tell everybody to stop smoking dope, join the Promise Keepers and return Western society to its heyday before Charles Darwin. Welcome to the Krokerian spasm, amigo."

should resist speed by engaging in activities, like reading or gardening or ambling, that are perforce slower. We feel we should make ourselves slow down. Indeed, there is an underground of this resistance in the culture, a theme of sundial slowness set against the overarching digital quickness of life—a theme that grows more obvious, and somehow more oddly frenzied, as we near the socially constructed limit of the millennium.

But notice the paradox. Time for reflection, the indispensable precondition of reading or any other "slow" activity, is possible only with the prior benefit of speed. Leisure time is a luxury good, too, the flip side of being able to move fast when you want to. Those idyllic gardens, so conducive to rest and restoration, are mostly found in rooftop condos or in the leafy confines behind million-dollar brownstones. For most of us, precious moments at the golf course or at a tropical-island resort are purchased only at the cost of long, harried hours on the expressway or waiting for connecting flights in Dallas, Texas.

United Airlines' notoriously busy hub.

Anyone who believes that the current young generation thinks and works faster than people in some notional, low-tech past hasn't been paying attention. And those who accuse kids today of a generalized attention deficit disorder, a compulsion to whip their heads around like distracted cats at the profusion of jump-cut images in our world, are also missing something crucial. Certainly there are more images and information now, more advertisements in our lives—three thousand "marketing messages" a day, according to some estimates—and kids seem to grow up faster, to *be* faster, than ever before. But it has yet to be proved that our enormous investment in computer technology in recent years has resulted in increased productivity, or that the ability to "process" hundreds of images and millions of bits of information has anything to do with *thinking*—with constructing or analyzing an argument, with making good decisions—much less with knowledge in the strong sense. And the sum total effect of this explosion of velocity is not a feeling of speed but one of boredom; the frustrating truth about the World Wide Web is that it is slow. Worse, it's often slow to no purpose, the seconds and minutes ticking away only to reveal that there is after all nothing of interest on the downloaded page. We are here approaching the metaphysical limits of speed, where the fast becomes the slow, and vice versa. In such moments, the newspaper as delivery system is state of the art.

Media have rates of speed, but not essential ones. Action movies get faster, and more kinetic, all the time—a sharp acceleration of retinal-nerve stimulation from the wide-screen scenes of old epics like *Spartacus*. But some movies are now, titanically, longer than ever; and John Woo, perhaps the best action-film director alive, has a fondness for extended slow-motion sequences, protracted exercises in the instant mythologization of anti-speed, that rival, in sheer unreality, the massed, from-every-angle replays of a televised professional football game.

In the late Seventies I used to listen to punk-rock singles that made it a point of pride to last no longer than two minutes, while my brother listened to prog-rock double albums with symphonic backing tracks and hour-long running times. The contemporary novel spans the continuum of speed from Elmore Leonard to David Foster Wallace, from Kundera's *Slowness* (which can be read and pondered in a single evening) to Don DeLillo's *Underworld* (which, suffice it to say, cannot). Short books sometimes demand many readings, however, and it is often necessary to read long books quickly. Is there more philosophy in John Rawls's *A Theory of Justice* (weighing in at 607 pages and more than two pounds) than in Donald Hall's poem "The First Inning" (three pages and as weightless as the limned parabola of a high fly ball)?

I have a new channel on my television now. It arrived late last year along with the Food Network and the Golf Channel and the History Channel and the Family Channel. (The package is called, amazingly, MeTV.) The new channel is called Speedvision. It is all about motor racing: F-1 cars, NASCAR cars, top fuel cars, funny cars, midget cars, sprint cars, Indy cars, as well as boats and planes. The commercials are

Donald Hall, "The First Inning," in *The Museum of Clear Ideas* (1993): "Well, there are nine players / on a baseball team, so to speak, and / there are nine innings, with trivial / exceptions like extra-inning games / and games shortened by rain or darkness, / by riot, hurricane, earthquake, or / the Second Law of Thermodynamics."

dominated by spots for crash videos, those technological snuff films so popular lately, in which fast boats and cars and motorcycles explode off the track or spin into the air, one after the other, amid hails of flame and smoke and flying metal debris.

Here is the secret of Speedvision: It is incredibly boring. There is no real tension, no suspense, because its creators have ignored the ancient narrative techniques that we use to manipulate speed and create drama. The speed-reading infomercials, on another channel, which play on our fear of being "overcome" by all the information that needs to be "mastered," are scarier. The Golf Channel, with its whispered commentary and endless instructional videos, is more exciting.

The sensory overload of speed leads necessarily to saturation, to senselessness, which is what the Greeks really meant by *ekstasis*. Not a singular rapture now but rather a digital version of the Rapture: the chosen ones carried into technoheaven, the rest of us left behind. A human body can tolerate no more than about seven g's of acceleration, the sort of load shouldered by an F-16 pilot pushing his ride to the limit in a sharp turn or power climb, a curve. After that, consciousness comes apart. The pilot blacks out, and the plane, still carrying his body, his fragile wetware, crashes.

The fastest man in the world right now is a Canadian sprinter named Donovan Bailey. In 1996 Bailey ran 100 metres in 9.84 seconds to set a world record. How do we know this? Because we measured it with a clock that tracks time to the level of one-hundredth of a second, an Omega or a Finishlynx or a Seiko—a clock that can, in short, model Zeno's paradox in machine terms, in increments of time invisible to the naked human eye. Is Donovan Bailey the fastest man in the world without that machine? Is anybody? Is a world record compelling, even intelligible, absent the slow-motion clock that can measure the man's incremental progress? At the limits of speed, not even the simple running human is free of the inbuilt upgrade logic of our machines.

Of course, Bailey isn't really the fastest man ever: in 1988 Ben Johnson ran 100 metres in 9.79 seconds at the Olympic Games in Seoul. He was later disqualified after officials discovered that he was using performance-

But the imperatives of speed, like those of utility and efficiency more generally, are crazily self-defeating. Speed's upper limit is found not in the laws of physics but in those of production: when the volume of movement, the rush of molecules or bits or consumer durables, decelerates, slows, and then stops. When nuclear war is so fast and so efficient and placeless that it surrenders to the frozen logic of mutual assured destruction, then we see not futurism's promise but rather the seized-up engine of material progress. War now has to be slowed down, artificially, to make it interesting.

enhancing steroids. Johnson was perversely in tune with the spirit of the times; he was just trying to upgrade his hardware.

Faster and faster can only mean, in the end, stasis. The logical outcome of efficiency is uselessness: solving problems has no point but the ultimate elimination of problem-solving itself. What is the point of being able to read a page every three seconds? To read every book ever written? Then what? Meanwhile, the vehicles of our speed ruin the planet as fast as we move around it.

Speed, we might admit, is our preeminent trope of control and domination. But even as speed excites us, we are drugged into a narcolepsy of cheap contentment whose danger we don't even recognize. The Canadian political scientist and performance artist Arthur Kroker labels ours "a crash culture," one in which we are always speeding up to a standstill, a spasm of useless speed that masks the coercion of "contemporary society as it undergoes a simultaneous acceleration and terminal shutdown." Not Marinetti's pure modern speed worship any more but rather a curious post-modern double movement of velocity and lethargy.

For the citizens of a decadent techno-utopia, boredom, not failure, is the great enemy of human happiness. And fear of boredom is the heart of the gentle domination of our new speed-driven regime. Yet there is no simple equation here, and the calculus of boredom's vectors and variables is more complex than we know. It is possible, even easy, to be bored at five hundred miles an hour. It is also possible for an instant to expand to fill the available space of consciousness, to watch a household accident or botched layup decelerate into the brain-jamming significance of heroic narrative, a real-time slow-motion sequence à la John Woo. We experience both hasty leisure and deliberate speed, moments that never end and decades that pass in a blink. How fast you move is not the same as how fast you are going.

Where, then, are we going in our fast-forward drive towards the future? Whence this urge, this speedy imperative? Is "technology" to blame? We might derive some solace from distancing ourselves from the principle of our rapidity, from blaming our machines and repeating the mantra that the medium is the message—but this would be too easy. And it would be a lie. Our machines do not make us forget. Our quick vehicles do not cause our panic, our wretched drivenness. The motor of speed, the transcendental impulse, lies buried not in the engine or the microprocessor but within each one of us, in our mortality. Speed was born of death, of both the desire to inflict it with weapons and the desire to transcend it. We are forever dividing more and more space by less and less time, yet we cannot escape time except in the liminal ecstasy of death. We love speed, because it means we can leave our unhappy consciousness in the dust—can for an instant pull apart the Cartesian mind-body confection with these superb machines. That's what the overload of sensory volume and pulsing adrenaline achieves: a minute and thrilling breach in the mostly impregnable union of mind and matter. We don't just risk death in speed; we press the limits of our mortality.

To the editor: "The real impetus for seeking speed through technology, this strained metaphor asserts, is not fiscal but spiritual.... I just cannot be convinced that the stockbroker or race-car driver is engaged in a philosophical striving for transcendental separation."

The final irony of our speed mania is that death, when we finally get there, may not be a kind of escape velocity at all but instead something like what was imagined by the ancient Greeks, a dull impatient wishing to be elsewhere. Hitting the wall, crashing into the ground, we may dissolve not into sweet unconsciousness but rather into a bleak waiting room of forever thwarted speed, a shadowy endgame in which nothing ever happens. And even when it arrives after a long, painful illness or years of institutional dullness, death almost always comes too soon. It takes us from the hurly-burly of this quick life and seizes us, suddenly.

The Bastard in Shakespeare's *King John* says, "The spirit of the time shall teach me speed." But while the velocities go up, our mortality remains unchanged. No matter how quickly you move, death drives the fastest car on the highway. In the end, death always does the overtaking. Our desire to escape the vile earth necessarily ends with us buried in it.

To the editor: "Some speed, such as that of the word processor or super-market scanner, does seem good. But one thing's for sure: those who drop out of the race become as invisible to their involved compatriots as the wraiths or spirits of the past, and are just as likely to be run over."

Thinking

Icons, Boredom, Wonder

The ancient Greek philosophers believed that wisdom began with wonder, with the awestruck and somewhat childish question "Why is there something rather than nothing?" Childish—or perhaps childlike. Almost everything in everyday life would seem to cut against this question, rendering it moot or banal or silly; but the original insight will not fade, the primal desire to understand will not be quieted. Wonder therefore remains, at once the infancy and the highest expression of our humanness.

The pieces in this section, including three examples of a column I write for the Vancouver-based magazine *Adbusters*, take wonder as an abiding theme, and confront both the possibilities of wisdom and the many challenges to wonder's integrity. The related sub-theme is the nature of the philosophical enterprise itself: what is reflection, and what is it for? As with wonder more generally, philosophy is a kind of return to infancy—an unceasing attempt to begin. Even at the farthest reaches of sophistication or argument, we are all doing philosophy for beginners.

Ten Steps to Creating

a Modern Media Icon

1. "Icon" is from the Greek *eikon*, which means "image," which is everything: The name of a camera. The word for all those little point-and-click pictures on your computer screen. Greek and Roman Orthodox religious objects, little oil paintings of saints with elaborate gold panel coverings. Anybody who represents something to someone somewhere. The image that gives a debased Platonic suggestion of reality without ever being it.

So create an image—one the cameras, and therefore we, will love.

2. The image must be drastically beautiful or else compellingly ugly. It must, for women, show a smooth face of impenetrable maquillage and impeccably "tasteful" clothing (Chanel, Balenciaga, Rykiel; not Versace, not Moschino, definitely not Gauthier), a flat surface of emotional projection, the real-world equivalent of a keyboard emoticon. Icon smiling at the cheering crowds: :-). Icon frowning bravely at diseased child or crippled former soldier in hospital bed: :-(. Icon winking slyly at the crush of press photographers as she steps into the waiting limousine: ;-). There should be only one name, for preference a chummy or faux-intimate diminutive: Jackie, Di, Barbra. Sunglasses are mandatory whenever the ambient light rises above building-code-normal 250 foot-candles. These can be removed or peered over to offer an image of blinking vulnerability.

Or else the image should be, in men, so overwhelmingly tawdry and collapsed, preferably from some high-cheekbone peak of youthful beauty, that it acquires a can't-look-away magnetism, the sick pull of the human car wreck. The only exceptions: (1) Athletes—Tiger, Michael—whose downy smoothness and transcendental physical abilities offer a male counterpoint that is almost female in appeal; they are the contraltos of the icon chorus. And (2) actors, whose malleable faces are so empty of particular meaning as to be innocent of intelligence. Folds of leathery skin, evidence of drug use and chain-smoking, the runes of dissipation etched on the pitted skin of hard living—they all have them. Johnny Cash, Mick Jagger, Leonard Cohen, Kurt Cobain, Chet Baker, late Elvis: the musician in ruins, the iconic face as crumbling stone monument.

Basic black attire is effective but must be Armani, never Gap. This suggests wisdom and sexual power, deep and bitter knowledge of the world—but with dough. The face need never change, its very stasis a sign of rich inner troubles. Sunglasses are superfluous. They smack of effort.

3. There must be a narrative structure that bathes the icon in the pure light of the fairy tale or morality play. Beautiful princess beset by ugly siblings or nasty stepmother. Lovely rich girl mistakes the charisma of power for true character. Overweening ambition turns simple boy into gun-toting, pill-popping maniac. Feisty rebel takes on the establishment of (circle one) Hollywood/big business/government/rock music/professional sports. Prodigy singled out for great things at an early age by psycho father.

Indispensable words in the story: "trapped," "betray," "tragic," "love," "promise" (as both verb and noun), "happiness" (always without irony), "fame" (always with venom), and "money" (never spoken). The details of the story may change, but the overarching structure cannot: you can improvise and elaborate, but never deviate. Sometimes a new story (thrill-happy slut consorts with swarthy and disreputable jet-setter) will be temporarily substituted for an old one that no longer applies (virginal

A correspondent writes: "You seem to think there is something suspicious about being beautiful. I have lived a long (and unsuccessful) life, and it is becoming clearer and clearer to me that outer beauty actually reflects inner beauty much more often than people think."

bride is unloved by philandering husband). We can't be sure which story will win out until . . .

4. Death. Already, at step four? Yes, absolutely, for iconography is very much a post-mortem affair.

The death ends the life but does not quite complete it: that is the business of storytellers and their audience, the cameras and their lights. Death is just the beginning. It should be, if possible, violent, messy, and a bit mysterious. Unwise confrontations with fast-moving industrial machines—sports cars, airplanes, cargo trucks, high-speed trains, bullets. Accidents are good, having as they do an aura of adventitious innocence, followed closely in order of preference by murder, assassination, execution, and suicide. If suicide, it must be either a gun or an overdose of illicit drugs, usually in colourful and nasty combination: alcohol and barbiturates, crack and benzedrine, heroin and anything.

In all cases, the death is "shocking" and "tragic," though in neither instance literally.

The reference book *Cultural Icons* (1991), a hipster's *Who's Who*, places a tiny airplane symbol next to anyone dead of "fatal confrontation with car, lorry, plane or other piece of modern technology." A black heart indicates "necromantic love-icon"; a pointing finger signals "astringent, difficult, modernist, élitist"; and so on.

5. Now, an outbreak of hysterical mourning, baseless and all the more intense for being so. (Nobody feels so strongly about someone they actually know.) Extended retrospectives on television. Numerous panel discussions and attempts to "make sense," to "assess the life," to "provide context." Long broadcasts of the funeral or memorial service complete with lingering, loving shots of weeping crowds. Greedy close-ups of the well-known people in attendance, the bizarre fraternity of celebrity which dictates that those famous for being born in a certain family have everything in common with those famous for singing pop tunes or throwing a ball in a designated manner.

News agencies and networks must spend a great deal of money sending a lot of people somewhere distant to cover the death. They must then justify that expense with hours and hours of coverage. We must see

184

images of the iconic face, beautiful or ruined, over and over and over. "Ordinary" people must be shown, on the media, insisting that the media have nothing to do with their deep feelings of loss. They must say that they "felt they knew him (her)," that "she (he) was like a member of the family." This keeps them happy and ensures that no larger form of public participation—say, protesting a tax hike or program cut, resisting a corporate takeover—will ever cross their minds as possible, let alone desirable.

6. A small backlash must gather strength, a token gesture of cultural protest that, in pointing out the real faults and shortcomings of the dead icon, unwittingly reinforces the growing "larger-than-life" status of the image. This is the culture's way of injecting itself with a homeopathic inoculation, introducing a few strains of mild virus that actually beef up the dominant media antibodies. Those who have the temerity to suggest that dead icon was not all he (she) is thought to be will be publicly scorned, accused of cynicism, insulted at dinner parties, but secretly welcomed.

The final storyline of the icon-life will now begin to set, rejecting the foreign elements as dead-ends or narrative spurs, or else accepting them as evidence that the icon was "after all" human—a suggestion that, in its very making, implies the opposite. The media coverage will fall into line in telling this story because individual producers and anchors will be unable to imagine doing otherwise. Tag-lines and feature-story titles will help set the narrative epoxy for good, providing catchy mini-stories for us to hang our thoughts on. Quickie books with the same titles will begin to appear—things like *Icon X: Tragic Ambition* or *Icon Y: Little Girl in Trouble.*

The producers and anchors must then claim that they are not creating this tale, simply "'giving the people what they want." Most people will accept this because to do otherwise would hurt their brains.

Roland Barthes, "Operation Margarine," in *Mythologies* (1973): "Take the established value which you want to restore or develop, and first lavishly display its pettiness, the injustices which it produces, the vexations to which it gives rise, and plunge it into its natural imperfection; then, at the last moment, save it *in spite of,* or rather *by,* the heavy curse of its blemishes."

7. The image will now be so widely reproduced, so ubiquitously mediated on television, at the supermarket, in the bookstore, that it will seem a permanent feature of the mediascape, naturalized and indispensable. It will now begin its final divorce from the person depicted. Any actual achievements—touchdowns thrown, elections won, causes championed—fall away like the irrelevancies they are. The face (or rather, the Face) will loom outward from glossy paper, T-shirts, fridge magnets, posters, Hallowe'en masks, and coffee mugs.

Kitschification of the image is to be welcomed, not feared. It proves that the icon is here to stay. The basic unit of fame-measurement is of course, as the critic Cullen Murphy once argued, the *warhol*, a period of celebrity equal to fifteen minutes. Kitsch versions of the image augur well: we're talking at least a megawarhol icon or better (that's fifteen million minutes of fame, which is just over 10,400 days, or about 28.5 years—enough to get you to those standard silver-anniversary retrospectives). No kitsch, no staying power: a hundred kilowarhols or less, a minicon.

8. There follow academic studies, well-meaning but doomed counter-assessments, sightings, and cameo appearances of the icon on a "Star Trek" spin-off series or as an answer in "Jeopardy." People begin to claim they can commune with the spirit of the dead icon across vast distances of psychic space. Conspiracy theories refuse to be settled by overwhelming evidence of a boringly predictable chain of events involving a drunk driver, too much speed, and unused seatbelts. Or whatever.

A correspondent writes: "Have you never gone out on a date with someone that other people thought was perhaps unsuitable? And was Dodi Fayed unsuitable to you because he was Egyptian and not from Toronto? Or was he just too rich?"

9. Television retrospectives every decade, with a mid-decade special at twenty-five years. The final triumph of the image: entirely cut off now from its original body, it is free-floating and richly polysemous. Always more surface than depth, more depiction than reality, the icon now becomes pure zero-degree image, a depicted lifestyle without a life, a face

186

without a person, a spiritual moment without context or meaning. In other words, the pure pervasive triumph of cultural exposure, a sign lacking both sense and referent. In still other words, the everything (and nothing) we sought all along: communion without community.

10. Now, for a religious experience, just point. And click.

Warning: The Topic Today Is Boredom

1. *We don't talk or write about boredom nearly enough.* It's true. Considering how much of daily life is given over to it, boredom is an underthematized subject. What is boredom about? A lot of people are bored a lot of the time; everybody is bored sometimes. Unforced, boredom is a lack of imagination, an inability to conceive of something worth doing. Considering how valuable our time supposedly is, it's amazing how much of it we spend not doing much of anything except regretting that we're not doing much of anything.

Are we afraid to admit this? "Life, friends, is boring," wrote the poet John Berryman. "We must not say so." Why not? Boredom is the great unacknowledged elephant doing circus tricks in our living rooms, the cavorting pachyderm we cannot admit to.

Bertrand Russell, *The Conquest of Happiness* (1936): "The most intelligent young people in Western countries tend to have that kind of unhappiness that comes of finding no adequate employment for their best talents. Cynicism such as one frequently finds among the most highly educated . . . results from the combination of comfort with powerlessness."

2. *Boredom is a great source of unhappiness.* Or so thought the philosopher Bertrand Russell, who identified it, along with fatigue and envy, as one of the three chief causes of human discontent. Boredom is related to those other two founts of mundane sadness. There is a peculiar form of weary boredom we call ennui, which creeps over us with too much exposure to banal cultural products—TV ads, Hollywood blockbusters, branded athletic-company clothing. There is also the boredom of dull, restless wishing to be elsewhere, a form of directionless envy that believes someone—anyone—else is having more fun than we are.

3. *Boredom is a mood.* Which may sound obvious but isn't. Moods, as Martin Heidegger once said, tell us how we are in the world, how we are faring. They also distinguish us from the world, because they make it clear to consciousness that it is separate from that about which it is conscious. When I am bored, my relationship to the world is hostile or frustrated: the world is failing to provide the stimulation I crave. The world is letting me down. The problem (I think) is not with me, it is with the world.

4. *But the world is just the world.* It cannot be more or less interesting than we find it. Being bored is a function of desire and attention span, and these lie within us. Some people, like multi-tasking television producers and quick-time teenagers, are proud of being easily bored: they think this form of voluntary attention deficit disorder is a mark of cultural superiority. They want their human neurophysiology, evolved over centuries to allow long-term concentration and deep meditation, to be more like that of a cat, which notices anything that moves—for a few seconds.

5. *This is not entirely their fault.* The culture in which we live is not one that happily tolerates boredom. The culture fears boredom, hates it. It banishes boredom in a growing firestorm of aural and visual excitement. But because our human brains are flexible sponges of neuron-firing wetware, we can take more and more stimulation all the time—even if the price of that expansion of volume is the decline of substance, and desire. The imperative here is an ever-rising scale of stimulation, a special-effects arms race.

6. *The first paradox of boredom is that more gratification can only mean more frustration.* Our desires can never be laid finally to rest. The world defies our cravings. And the more desperately we try to avoid boredom, the more we create a world of empty stimulation that seems only to invite boredom: a "crash culture," according to Arthur Kroker, "contemporary society as it undergoes a simultaneous fatal acceleration and

Arthur Kroker and Michael Weinstein, *Data Trash* (1994).

189

terminal shutdown." In such a culture, we are constantly falling into a state of *spasm*, in which we are fascinated but numb, excited yet bored, always "speeding up to a standstill."

7. *The second paradox of boredom is that it can, under the right conditions, be stimulating.* The writer Gore Vidal admitted in his wonderfully bitchy political memoir, *Palimpsest*, that he's had a lifelong fascination with boring people, the sort who stand in one place at a party and deliver long disquisitions on obvious topics, the kind of people who are handed from guest to guest like hot potatoes. Vidal loved these characters because he was compelled by personalities who had so little evident interest in anything but themselves.

See "Graven Images" (Section II).

Of course we don't all feel that way. And if you really do find boring people interesting, don't they cease, in some sense, to be boring?

And why are so many parties, often supposed to be the antithesis of boredom, so very boring? Why do so many of us continue to attend them with hope, even enthusiasm? The French call social functions *divertissements*: diversions—or, in a more judgmental mood, distractions.

Diversions from where? Distractions from what?

8. *Some things that people do when they are bored:* Eat even though they are not hungry. Go to bad movies. Channel surf. Play video games. Fret about the things they could be doing but are not. Sleep more than they need to. Call friends and bug them. Shop.

To the editor: "Mr. Kingwell lists supposedly boring places–'anywhere in England on a Sunday afternoon.' Really? Is it

9. *Some very boring times and places:* Anywhere in England on a Sunday afternoon. Your birthday if you are alone. Any commercial airline flight more than two hours long. Despite what everyone says, the beach. In front of the television during the day. In lots of university lecture rooms, but not mine. On almost any bus, anywhere.

10. *Topics of discussion that have become boring, through no fault of their own:* The future of the Internet. The millennium. Globalization. The alleged death of Marxism.

11. *Topics of discussion that are inherently boring:* How much you drank last night. Professional sports games after the fact. Unless you are very twisted indeed, your dreams.

12. *Boredom is not another word for nothing left to do.* Alexander the Great, looking upon the defeated soldiers of a hapless opponent, supposedly wept that he had no more worlds to conquer. But the bored are not the task-less, like him. The bored are rather like the teenager who, standing before a well-stocked fridge, complains that there is never anything to eat.

The bored have things to do. Lots of them. There are bills to pay, weeds to pull, calls to return, books to read. But in the face of this multiplicity of possibilities, the bored are paralyzed. They just can't be bothered. That is why boredom is the lesser cousin of depression. It drains tasks of their joy and their point. When we are bored we are vulnerable: it's just when we can't be bothered that we lose hold of why we bother at all.

13. *But boredom can be therapeutic.* The best essay ever written about boredom is called "On Being Bored," by the psychoanalyst Adam Phillips. Boredom, says Phillips, is "that state of suspended anticipation in which things are started and nothing begins, the mood of diffuse restlessness which contains that most absurd and paradoxical wish, the wish for a desire." Boredom is a kind of receptivity, a waiting that does not— that cannot—experience itself as waiting. If I am waiting, I am waiting *for* something. But being bored is the absence of that intention. It protects us from the commitment (and the danger) entailed by an actual waiting-for, a concrete desire for an elusive object.

possible to be bored in a country that has more history in one yard of its ancient soil than the United States has in its endless sea of shopping malls and tract houses?"

Arthur Schopenhauer, *The World as Will and Idea* (1818): "This is direct proof that existence has no value. For what is boredom but the feeling of the emptiness of life? . . . Real boredom is by no means an evil to be lightly esteemed. In the end it depicts on the countenance a real despair."

Phillips, *On Kissing, Tickling, and Being Bored* (1993).

191

The paradox is that we are still, in our boredom, waiting: not for something but for anything. In boredom we oscillate between desire and its absence, meaninglessness. Hence the peculiar *paralysis* of boredom, the "dreary agitation" and "cramped restlessness," which register as unpleasant moods but are really clues to our troubling immersion in desire.

14. *Life really is boring; we must say so.* We must say so because it is true, and the truth of something, absent regard for someone's feelings or a worthy political cause, is a sufficient reason to say it.

This is clearly a philosopher's view of things, I realize.

But to say that life is boring is not to make the dour anhedonic suggestion that we should take no pleasure in life. On the contrary. The greatest pleasures in life emerge against a background awareness of its often boring character. It is precisely *because* life is boring that finding pleasure in it is so important to us. We should have no fear of boredom, either in admitting it to each other or in dealing with it ourselves. It is the fear of boredom, not boredom itself, that leads us astray.

15. *Learn to love your boredom.* Most of us have one or two things we do that we don't find boring. If possible, arrange to be paid for doing one of these. Call yourself a professional, and be happy. For the rest of life, find out what boredom has to teach you. It is a form of meditation, an opportunity to look deep within yourself. Stop heeding the voices clamouring to dispel your boredom. Do nothing. Listen to the sound of wanting a desire.

What does it say?

16. *This column was not itself boring.* If for some reason you think it was, return to the top of the previous page and begin again.

Repeat as necessary.

Wonder Around

This is the story of my first, and probably only, appearance in *Strategy* magazine. *Strategy* magazine is not, as you might think, a war-gaming monthly or thinly disguised mercenary-training organ. It doesn't run detailed features on the comparative virtues of Beretta and Colt sidearms, or long columns of classified ads offering discount counter-terrorism services and cut-rate extraction missions. *Strategy* is, instead, a trade paper for marketers and advertisers. It's published every two weeks out of Toronto, on tabloid-sized newsprint, and has a circulation of about 15,000. It's a common sight on the magazine racks of design and ad firms in Toronto, Vancouver, and Montreal.

I'm not recommending you subscribe, but we all need to pay more attention to these internal organs of the ad business, these glimpses inside the throbbing brain of our commercial world. From the name itself, with its rather-too-obvious hint of precision planning and crack, quasi-military manoeuvring—the cheerful fascism of the ad *campaign* and the marketing *tactic*—to the articles inside, which lately have been celebrating "oddballs" and "leaps of faith" in advertising, against a presumed background of buttoned-down corporate conformity but really just in the service of wider profit margins, *Strategy* is a clear sign of the times. As was, in its bizarre way, my appearance in its pages.

For some time now I have been fascinated by the idea of wonder. This wonder about wonder started in graduate school, when I studied with an inspiring philosopher, Maurice Natanson, who shared the ancient Greeks' conviction that all wisdom, indeed all knowledge of any kind, begins in wonder, *thaumazein*, at the fact of the world. To remain astonished at the mere presence of things, against all the deadening, habitual tendencies of the everyday world, was for him, as it had

Natanson, *Edmund Husserl* (1973): "Philosophy is not divorced from the mundane world, nor does philosophy swallow up common sense. . . . *Wonder*, phenomenologically interpreted, is the recognition that the restricted field of my own experience is continuous with the whole of reality."

193

been for Anaxagoras and Plato, the source of all genuine insight—and happiness.

There is a scene in Plato's dialogue *Theaetetus* that illustrates the point. Socrates is conversing with a brilliant young man called Theaetetus, who has been excelling at mathematics. Socrates—who, incidentally, has the hots for Theaetetus—asks the young man if he has any acquaintance with logical puzzles and paradoxes, the kind of thing Zeno of Elea was so fond of, where, say, streaking Achilles can never seem to catch the tortoise waddling away in front of him because he must first cover half the distance separating them; and after that, half *that* distance; and so on. My students love this stuff: it blows their minds.

Plato, *Theaetetus* 155d. The Yale philosopher Sarah Broadie liked to say, "If you haven't read the *Theaetetus,* you haven't lived."

"This sense of wonder is the mark of the philosopher," Socrates tells Theaetetus. "Philosophy indeed has no other origin." The point holds firm through the ages. The twentieth-century philosopher Gabriel Marcel said, "A philosopher remains a philosopher only so long as he retains the capacity for wonderment, despite everything that tends to dispel it." And the existentialist Martin Heidegger, in his pre-Nazi phase anyway, spoke of the wonder occasioned by objects seen, suddenly, as *present-at-hand*: no longer the tools or equipment of the *ready-to-hand* world, thickly layered over with use values, but pure slabs of obtruding Being, the object suddenly illuminated as itself and nothing else.

Gabriel Marcel, *The Existential Background of Human Dignity* (1963); Martin Heidegger, *Sein und Zeit* (1927).

Now what has all this got to do with *Strategy*? In March of this year I was invited to give a lecture at Toronto's Harbourfront Centre as part of an exhibition of craftwork called "Masterpiece or Memento." I decided to talk about the complex relationship between objects and cultural forces, the way commercialization and reproduction can seem to drain objects of their significance and power to astonish—but also the ways that wonder can be found again, even in the midst of all this mediation and distortion and ideological layering. The way an object, even a tawdry or mass-produced or much-undermined one, can suddenly reveal itself as beautiful, as astonishing—if we have the eyes to see it.

The main point of all this is to see that wonder does not inhere in objects themselves, is not an internal property of them like an emanating aura. It arises, instead, from a complex relationship between us and objects. That's why issues of authenticity and originality are ultimately less important than the richness, the texture, of one's personal confrontation with a certain thing. The wondrous object might be a Picasso, with all its heavy cultural sanction and monetary approval; but it can, equally, be a cheap salt shaker, crumpled napkin, or unlaced workboot. The crucial thing is that we recognize the power of objects, at rare but accessible moments, to rise above their cheap utility—and the manipulating energy of packagers and brand-masters—to assume a wondrous new status, a glow of beauty. Wonder is personal, then, but it is also cultural and political, and so our experience of objects is ultimately fragile: it can be conditioned in countless ways, sometimes impaired or even stolen from us.

A few days after the Harbourfront lecture, I was invited to speak at a design firm in Toronto called Russell Inc. Russell is a big, multi-national design group with offices all over the world, and they have recently done some very successful designs, including a line of fruit-flavoured soft drinks that come in attractive chunky bottles and sport vivid floral and fruit prints all over them. I never quite know what people in firms like this will make of my lectures, given that they are full of criticism of advertising and (as we say in the trade) the ideological superstructures of late capitalism. But I went, and gave them a pared-down version of the argument for wonder as an antidote to the deadening commodification and kitschification of so much of contemporary life: the way images and objects are endlessly reproduced, and then endlessly chewed over by the ironizing, cheapening wit of current cultural re-reproduction.

The editor of *Strategy* was there. He snagged a copy of my original lecture, which had been made available. A week later, there I was in *Strategy*, being quoted in the magazine's editorial column. The editor got my name and institutional affiliation wrong, as it happens; but then, this kind of trade paper is not really journalism, is it? According to the editorial, I had argued that, upon being transported by an object into a state of wonder, "people see the world of the everyday as suddenly strange and

I didn't know this at the time.

195

mysterious." I had indeed. He quoted me again: "Wonder is three-fold. It invites investigation of the world, but also reflection on the subject who experiences that world, and on his or her experience itself."

The original insight is of course Husserl's, not mine. Husserl, "Philosophy in the Crisis of European Mankind" (1935): "We are absolute beginners here, and have nothing in the way of logic designed to provide norms; we can do nothing but reflect."

So true—if I do (and did) say so myself. That three-fold structure is certainly the key to wonder, the way it raises us up from the conformity and somnambulance of the everyday, forming this peculiar triangle of concern: the object of wonder, the subject experiencing wonder, and the feeling of wonder itself.

Okay, fine. But that's when it got strange.

"Could there be a better description," the editorial asked rhetorically, "from the point of a marketing executive, of the ideal receptive state of a consumer when he or she is experiencing a new product or seeing an ad for the first time? Hardly." He mentioned the new Volkswagen Beetle— which takes the same mechanical elements possessed by the original, adds a slight body rejig, and repackages the car for about $10,000 more than it should cost—as a successful example of marketing wonder.

Oh, boy. *The ideal receptive state of a consumer?* I stared at the page for some time, wondering (!) if I had read it correctly. As usual with printed text, it just kept repeating itself over and over, saying the same appalling thing again and again, like a malfunctioning CD. Was it really possible for someone to misunderstand a message so completely, to misread it so (let's give him credit) creatively, as to get it *exactly* wrong? Apparently it was. Where the lecture had argued the danger of commercial appropriation of wonder, he had chosen to hear the reclamation of wonder as a celebration of that appropriation. Wonder, which I had argued was liberating, a resistant strategy in a world of ubiquitous marketing, was taken by this Strategist as a way to make "consumers" more "receptive."

This would merely be funny, if a little depressing, if it weren't for the larger issue it brings to our attention. One of the most effective ways ideology functions is by recasting all available comments, however critical, in the terms of the dominant mode of thinking. Thus, for example, the remarkable creativity of the delusional psychiatric patient, who sees every therapeutic intervention as part, say, of the Cold War espionage narrative in which he is mentally stranded. Ideologues like Dr. Strategy are like madpeople in this respect—they turn everything, however critical, into grist for the mill of their own delusional narrative, which in this case is all about a world in which the only realities are marketing and consuming. Theirs is the same perverse, self-defeating impulse that draws some of the most talented, creative people in our society—not to mention those with aspirations to rebel—into the comfortable folds of Hollywood lawyering, Disney product development, and Time-Warner marketing.

Have you seen the newest ads in Microsoft's "Where Do You Want to Go Today?" campaign—the campaign that has sucked up some of the best (and worst) pop music from the last thirty years into its sick, Borg-like machinery, from the Jackson Five to the Rolling Stones? This campaign has a new slogan, I noticed recently. It says: Wonder Around.

Do that. But don't do it the way Microsoft wants you to. Don't do it as the ideal receptive state of a consumer experiencing a product for the first time. Do it for the joy of a world that is still, despite all efforts to take our inner selves and sell them back to us at a mark-up, full of truly wonderful sights.

Ronald Hepburn, *Wonder and Other Essays* (1984): "We can give no reason for the world's being rather than not being. We can meaningfully ask why it exists, but we have no resources for answering the question. Wonder is generated from this sense of absolute contingency; its object the sheer existence of a world."

The Future of Jurassic Technology:

Housing Culture at the End of Time

This article is a much-compressed version of a keynote address I gave at the annual meeting of the Canadian Museum Association in 1997.

My story begins with an unlikely account of the American neurophysicist Geoffrey Sonnabend. Afflicted by insomnia one night in 1936, Sonnabend conceived a radical new theory of memory, a revelation brought on by having heard, earlier that evening, a recitation of German Romantic *lieder* by the Romanian-American singer Madelena Delani. In one of those great near-misses of intellectual history, the two did not actually meet that night in the South American resort town of Iguazu Falls. Sonnabend was there to recuperate from a mental and physical breakdown, brought on in part by the collapse of his investigation into the memory pathways of carp. Delani, also in recovery, was herself a mnemonic anomaly, being a sufferer of Korsakov's Syndrome, which involves, among other things, the erasure of virtually all short- and intermediate-term memory—with the exception, in her case, of the memory of music itself. This peculiar condition gave her voice, according to critics, a uniquely plaintive quality, as if "steeped in a sense of loss." It profoundly affected Sonnabend, in any case, and in the sleepless reverie following the haunting recital he conceived, as a whole, the model of intersecting plane and cone figures that would become the centrepiece of his theory of "obliscence": the idea that memory is an illusion, since the natural outcome of any experience is forgetting, not remembering.

As Sonnabend put it in the Introduction to his book *Obliscence: Theories of Forgetting and the Problem of Matter*, "We, amnesiacs all, condemned to live in an eternally fleeting present, have created the most elaborate of human constructions, memory, to buffer ourselves against the intolerable knowledge of the irreversible passage of time and the irretrievability of its moments and events." In Sonnabend's resulting model, the Cone of Obliscence is forever being penetrated—bisected— by Planes of Experience, which hit the cone at varying but precise angles. Once through the cone, however, an experience is gone forever and any "memory" of its occurrence little more than illusion.

Now, you have to realize that none of this is true. Geoffrey Sonnabend and Madelena Delani never lived, and there is no actual theory of obliscence. There was no evening recital, no resulting attack of insight-laden insomnia.

No, this strange account is part of an elaborate critique of the idea of museums, an odd collection of stories, inventions, near-truths, and half-truths, the suggestive, the mysterious, and the bizarre, that is intended to put the idea of housing culture into question. In addition to the tale of Delani, Sonnabend, and the theory of obliscence, there are tales of bats able to penetrate solid objects, elaborate microminiature sculptures, executed in a single human hair and mounted inside the eye of a needle, and humans who grow horns—all part of recent exhibitions at that most unlikely institution of natural history, the Museum of Jurassic Technology in Los Angeles, California.

The museum is the brainchild of an eccentric filmmaker and performance artist, David Hildebrand Wilson. The story of Wilson's extended piece of performance art, this unceasing meditation on the institutional status and meaning of museums, is found in Lawrence Wechsler's superb 1995 book *Mr. Wilson's Cabinet of Wonder.* Wechsler's book, which began life as an article in *Harper's* magazine, details his various encounters with Wilson's oddball museum, and with the seamless irony of Wilson himself, who never seems to let on, in interviews or simply while taking money at the museum's entrance or explaining a particular exhibit's salient features, that the museum might be nothing more than a highly elaborate and dedicated post-modern joke. The most compelling aspect of Wechsler's encounter with Wilson and the MJT is his mounting research efforts to verify the truth, or whatever there was of it, in the museum's various exhibits. Were there really people with horns? Is there a theory of memory as forgetting? Can the image of Jesus Christ be carved into the head of a toothpick?

The result is a curious text, at once bemused and profound. By pursuing Wilson's lead, Wechsler comes to a realization about the nature of museums themselves: not simply routine insights about the history of authority and categorization, the social constructions of expertise and cultural memory—the sort of thing that might be found in any deconstruction of the institutional bases of museums—but also a richer awareness of the fundamental human impulses behind the housing of culture, history, and nature in buildings meant to instruct and delight. Leafing back through the historical record, Wechsler uncovers the notion of the *Wunderkammer*, the cabinet of wonders, which provides one of the important forerunners, and indeed, in some cases, the founding collection of artifacts, of the late modern, which is to say nineteenth-century, public museum. It is the sort of thing you might still glimpse in a quirky private collection, or in a museum whose idiosyncratic character is part of its point, as in, say, the weird shrunken-heads-and-potty anthropology of the Pitt-Rivers Museum in Oxford.

But the modern museum's dominant tropes—the aspirations of middle-class self-improvement, for example, or the idea of the museum as a palace of authenticity—give way, in this investigation's own kind of *wunderkammerlich* manner, to more attractive ideas of childlike curiosity and joy in discovery, but also arguably less attractive ideas of religious moralism and ethnic prejudice. The deep human impulses of cultural cataloguing seem always to contain within themselves both curiosity and prejudice, open-mindedness and censoriousness.

So, for example, the classical *Wunderkammer* typically grouped historical artifacts together with select works of art, religious curios like hair from Noah's beard or a sliver of the Cross, natural genetic sports and oddities, exotica of various kinds, and more didactic *objets*: memento mori, for example—a human skull, say—or dioramas illustrating

James Fenton, "The Pitt-Rivers Museum, Oxford" (1987): "Go / As a historian of ideas or a sex-offender, / For the primitive art, / As a dusty semiologist, equipped to unravel / The seven components of that witch's curse / Or the syntax of the mutilated teeth. Go / In groups to giggle at curious finds. / But do not step into the kingdom of your promises / To yourself, like a child entering the forbidden / Woods of his lonely playtime."

the seven deadly sins or depicting, in suggestive still-life, collisions of human aspiration and natural limit. They were meant to be didactic illustrations as well as simple groupings of objects considered fascinating in themselves.

One of the most celebrated of these conglomerations was the Musaeum Tradescantianum, operated in the early 1600s by the John Tradescants, Elder and Younger, and later devolved after a bitter legal battle to Elias Ashmole of Oxford, eventually to become the basis of the Ashmolean Museum of that city's university. Before the split of museums into art, historical, natural historical, and technological—before, indeed, the spirit of scientific inquiry narrowed the scope of museums from the inherently curious to the respectably provable, relegating curios to the circus sideshow or theme park—*Wunderkammern* were crucial repositories of knowledge, wisdom, historical sense, and of course, wonder. They were demonstrations of what was known as natural philosophy, the study that combined observation and preservation with theory, speculation, and moral judgment. Their rise in popularity through the early modern period is an important brick in the edifice of an emergent New World of discovery, classification, toleration, and democratization: the liberal world in which we still live.

But as so often, the creation of the "serious" has, here, the effect of relegating some fascinating but oddball material to the margins of cultural attention.

It is appropriate, at this cultural juncture, to consider the future of museums as cultural institutions through this odd lens of the past, to read the critique of Mr. Wilson and the MJT as more than a simple joke on the pretensions of intellectual and cultural authority. What I want to suggest is less about the day-to-day problems and challenges of running museums in this culture—even the admittedly pressing issues of political bias, government pressure, marketing imperatives—and more about the basic human and philosophical issues that arise whenever we attempt to place our culture within four walls. Those issues are always live ones, I think, but they become more pressing when we confront the kind of cultural reckoning represented by the calendar's imminent turn to a new century and, in the present case, a new millennium. I do not mean to suggest that that turning, arbitrary and contingent as it is in so many ways, determines our consciousness; only that it provides an opportunity for reflection, one that it would be folly to ignore. As I argued in *Dreams of Millennium* (unlike Sonnabend's, my book actually exists), millennial anxiety can take many forms, not all of them classically religious or, strictly speaking, millenarian. Apocalyptic expectation is all around us, if we only attend to the original meaning of the Greek word: to reveal, to lay bare.

So there are three points I want to make, points that will be, of necessity, more suggestive than definitive. All of them arise from the rewarding reflection on the idea of museums found in Wechsler's book, in Wilson's ironically informed museum, and in the idea of the *Wunderkammern* themselves. They are, first, that wonder is indeed at the root of museums, and indeed of human reflection on the world—of, we might say, philosophy in the widest sense of that word. Even if museums of today seem to have proceeded long distances from the curio cabinets of three centuries ago, there is a common thread between them and an experience of wonder at the world's novelties and intricacies that does not cease as long as we have eyes to see and imaginations to be fired.

Second, that the attempt to house culture becomes more and more problematic, if not self-defeating, as a culture accelerates towards temporal reckonings like the millennium's turn. Why? Because part of what makes us anxious at times like these is what the French cultural theorist Paul Virilio called the fascism of speed: the accelerating and apparently unstoppable generation of cultural product. There are more data and images now, more books and newspapers and films, than ever before. How can we cope with it all? We can't. My suggestion is that, contrary to the museological imperative that our high-modern consciousness has inherited from the previous century—an imperative that institutional bias feeds—we should give up trying.

See "Fast Forward"

(Section IV).

And therefore third, that, as the fictional Geoffrey Sonnabend insisted, and as the sly intentions and startling juxtapositions of the

Museum of Jurassic Technology suggest, when it comes to human experience there is as much to be learned from forgetting as there is from remembering. Sometimes, wonder is best served by the artful act of letting go, the refusal to codify, define, or pin down. The Talking Heads advised us to stop making sense in the 1980s but that message is more relevant than ever, as our culture mutates and expands beyond the kind of expectations and conceptual tools we now possess. And museums of the future may have to serve that fact, of our experience exceeding our received wisdom, as well as any other, more traditional purposes.

The process of directed forgetting has its dangers, to be sure. There is already much that we have forgotten in the years that brought us here from the days of the *Wunderkammer*, of course, and we cannot be confident that all of it was worth forgetting. Some gems surely went into the rubbish heap along with the dross. That need not worry us. Nor should it trouble us unduly that some things worth forgetting have probably been remembered, may indeed find a place within the institutional authority structures of the modern museum. Who has not had the experience of standing before a display case, diorama, or picture frame and thinking, What in God's name is *that* doing here?

It may seem strange for a philosopher to advocate making less sense. What I mean is that currently dominant forms of sense-making may prove inadequate to our cultural desires and aspirations as we move forward.

The future of Jurassic technology is clear enough to state in general terms. In these Last Days, the very idea of cultural authority no longer has the hold on us that it once did, when the modern age reached its full flowering in encyclopedic projects and universities that, as their name implies, attempted to encompass the universe within their ivy-covered walls. Instead we are confronting a multiplicity of cultural authority nodes, some of them very local and limited, others occasionally wider and apparently firm, but none of them absolute in the manner that our earlier aspirations promised us. Housing culture must mean in future responding to that multiplicity, surrendering the encyclopedic impulse, honouring the particular, the unusual, the strange. Legitimacy of the rigid kind will give way to smaller and more private culture houses, or to ones dedicated to particular, even sub-cultural, purposes.

In saying this, I am not trying to make some kind of cheap post-modern point or relativist call for exploding all myths of legitimacy and progress, drastically unsettling the norm of truth. The norm of truth may be local, or contingent, or open to constant correction; but it exists, and it must exist if we are to do anything as commonplace, and as remarkable, as sitting in a room somewhere reading these words printed in black ink upon a white page. Nor am I trying to suggest that a more and more diverse culture means, in doom-saying fashion, a disintegrated culture. There can be a kind of unity in the multiplicity, a form of order in the chaos.

No, I am simply trying to say that the point of culture is, the point has always been, to find and cherish those feelings of wonder that are, at once, the infancy and the highest expression of our humanness. As the fiction of Geoffrey Sonnabend reminds us, the idea of the perfectly captured memory is an illusion. But so, in a sense, is the imagined future of our hopes and dreams. The only thing that really exists is the present, the moment of the forever now. And in that eternal present, let us say to ourselves—and to the people we hope to communicate with, through our institutions and our other works, our writing and speaking—here, my fellow mortal, is something to marvel at!

That is why I am not, despite repeated accusations, a relativist; to be coherent, relativism must rely as much as hard-line objectivity on an exaggerated standard of what counts as truth.

The Fiction of Philosophy

When I was in graduate school at Yale, the philosopher Jonathan Lear used to run a wildly popular seminar on Wittgenstein's *Philosophical Investigations*, which he habitually began by quoting from A. A. Milne's *Winnie-the-Pooh*. "Piglet and Pooh have decided to make 'Aha!' mean 'We'll tell you where Roo is if you leave the woods,'" he'd say as too many people pressed into the stuffy, third-floor classroom in Connecticut Hall. "In this seminar we are going to try to make 'Aha!' mean something."

It was a canny and charming move, the flourish of a gifted teacher. Pairing Milne's simpleminded bear, that paragon of semantic and philosophical insight, and the hard-headed intensity of crazy Ludwig in his deckchair, arduously trying to write one meaningful sentence after a day of thought, only to tear it up the next morning and start again, fired our imaginations. It reminded us, as few things in graduate school do, why we were there. Like Pooh on a picnic, Wittgenstein's *Investigations* make philosophy a wild, careering adventure into the obvious. They restore the capacity for wonder that is the hallmark of a tradition of thinking begun by what Edmund Husserl once called "a few Greek eccentrics."

Of course they also sustain a detailed, intricate, and fractious scholarly industry that is of little interest to anyone outside of academic philosophy. The members of this philosophico-industrial complex have, on the whole, nothing but disdain for attempts by artists, writers, or filmmakers to "popularize" the ideas of someone like Wittgenstein. Derek Jarman's 1992 film about the Austrian philosopher, *Wittgenstein*, or Bruce Duffy's novel *The World As I Found It*, which dramatizes the philosopher's connections with Bertrand Russell and G. E. Moore, can drive them wild. One of my colleagues once pronounced the Jarman film "scandalous" during a dinner party and then, apparently unable to digest

Lear, *Open Minded* (1998): "Wittgenstein was a master in making us aware how philosophical perplexity can arise by asking questions in isolation from the normal contexts in which such questions get asked: it is then that 'language goes on holiday'."

the enormity of the offence, fell into a long period of wordless disap-

proval. (Whereof one cannot speak, one must simply mutter angrily.)

The same fate has come upon other attempts at rendering philosophical ideas palatable to what was once known as the general reader. The novel *Sophie's World*, by the Norwegian writer and teacher Jostein Gaarder, has become a surprise international best-seller since its publication in 1991. Translated into a dozen languages, available on audio cassette, even set to be produced as a musical, it has been a fixture on European best-seller lists for years, with German sales alone topping 1.7 million. Meanwhile, the German philosopher Walter Schulz's judgment that the book is "idiotic" is among the more civil assessments delivered by professional thinkers.

Sophie's World retails the history of Western philosophy through the thin device of a series of secret messages sent to a schoolgirl, Sophie Amundsen, just before her fifteenth birthday. The first one, found one day in her mailbox, asks these simple yet deep questions: "Who are you?" "Where does the world come from?" It is followed by long discourses on everything from pre-Socratic natural philosophy to contemporary ana-lytic philosophy, with stops along the way for Descartes, Spinoza, Hume, Kant, Hegel, and Kierkegaard, among others, all provided by a mysteri-ous stranger called Alberto Knox.

It turns out, about halfway through the book, that this narrative of Sophie and Alberto is a fiction being written by Major Albert Knag, a Norwegian army officer on United Nations post in Lebanon, for his daughter, Hilde, back home in Lillesand, on Norway's south coast. Sophie and Alberto are characters created by Albert for Hilde's amusement and edification, and other figures from nursery rhyme and literature, includ-ing Winnie-the-Pooh, soon make appearances in the book. The remain-der of it plays with the possibilities of this tale-within-the-tale, with the meta-fictional characters straining under, and at one point trying to escape, the direction of the first-order fictional characters.

This post-modern playfulness is not the book's appeal, however. The potted history of philosophy, sometimes communicated by Alberto within dramatic re-creations of famous scenes—the Athenian *agora* prowled by Socrates, a Parisian café where Sartre drank bitter existential coffee—is what seems to have captured the minds (and money) of millions of people, most of them young readers or those with no previous exposure to philosophy. And as the Princeton literature professor Theodore Ziolkowski pointed out in a recent essay in *American Scholar* ("Philosophy into Fiction"), the only thing exceptional about *Sophie's World* is the extent of its commercial success.

Fictional popularizations of philosophy are a booming industry, especially in Europe, a juggernaut trend of accessible primers on everything from Cartesian dualism to Hegelian dialectic. In Britain and North America, a series of comic-book "beginners'" introductions to the classic disputes and personages of philosophy (and academic discourse more generally), have appeared on bookstore shelves. *Philosophy for Beginners*, for example, is a whirlwind 184-page tour of Western thought, full of sardonic asides ("Boethius stands out like a Stoic at a chimpanzee's tea party") and smartass illustrations (Nietzsche in a Superman costume, Aristotle contemplating catharsis when he is barfed on during a play).

My personal favourite.

Winnie-the-Pooh, meanwhile, remains a favourite, with Benjamin Hoff's popular *The Tao of Pooh* and *The Te of Piglet*, with their air of toy-time spirituality and a Preciousness Beyond Belief, lately followed by a book by Oxford-trained John Tyerman Williams, *Pooh and the Philosophers*, which purports to "demonstrate beyond all reasonable doubt that the whole of Western philosophy—including, of course, Plato himself—is best considered as a long preparation for Winnie-the-Pooh."

C. S. Lewis called Boethius, author of *The Consolation of Philosophy*, itself a best-seller of astonishing, albeit posthumous, magnitude, "the divine popularizer," but few academic philosophers would be willing to accord the same honour to Gaarder or his ilk. I think much of the eloquent sneering may be traced, on this continent, to the popularity of Robert Pirsig's *Zen and the Art of Motorcycle Maintenance*, which functions, culturally speaking, as the progenitor of *Sophie's World*.

Pirsig's quasi-fictional account of a cross-country motorcycle trip, with its mentally disturbed first-personal narrator, his mentally disturbed son, and page after page of tortuous prose about the clash between "classic" and "romantic" world-views, was also a surprise best-seller. (Pirsig is fond of reminding people how many New York publishing houses turned it down.) It, too, struck a chord with millions of people by bringing philosophical ideas—some Kant, a little Kuhn and Heidegger, bits of warmed-over Plato—to the popular consciousness.

It is, all the same, an infuriating book, just as *Sophie's World* is: mannered, overwritten, and often excruciatingly portentous or merely boring. I can still remember the combination of dismay and irritation I felt some years ago when, during an overnight train ride from Vienna to Paris, a companion hauled Pirsig's book out of his knapsack so that he and I, after all a philosophy graduate student, could hunker down and discuss it. At Yale the departmental secretary had a rubber stamp she used to apply to misdirected mail which said, in block capitals, NOT PHILOSOPHY. I cannot tell you how many times, before and since that train ride, I have wished I had such a thing in my possession, ready to hand.

But what, precisely, is the problem here? Let's grant that these are bad novels, written not for the sake of art with philosophical ideas included seamlessly (as, say, in Rebecca Goldstein's novel *The Mind-Body Problem*), but didactically, with a crudeness of intention that curdles the milk of fine aesthetic appreciation. Even seen strictly as pedagogical exercises, though, they are not directed at professional philosophers. Why is it that we get so riled by them? We all teach, after all, and that entails a form of popularizing—if done well. Like many philosophers, I occasionally find references to "Star Trek" and even "The Simpsons" useful in getting points across to my students. (Richard Hanley has gone so far as to assess the metaphysical weight of the former TV series in a popular book called *The Metaphysics of Star Trek*.) By the same token, Pirsig's conceptual carving up of his motorcycle into "discrete systems" is not a bad device in epistemology, and Gaarder's *in situ* dialogues are standard fare in many introductory courses.

It is still possible to find yourself on a subway car or in a plane where people are gulping down Pirsig's sloppy prose. But not nearly as many as are reading *The Celestine Prophecy*.

I find that these references are now falling flat with my students, for reasons I cannot fathom. Don't they watch television? What else are they doing when they're not reading my assignments?

Is our disdain just a boundary dispute, a problem of professional possessiveness; or, perhaps worse, pure resentment of commercial success? Well, I think both motives are indeed at work, but there are also two deeper issues raised by academic disdain of popular philosophy, one healthy enough but the other disastrous.

Philosophy is a discipline whose subject is, in many ways, its own possibility. A good deal of specific philosophical argument, in other words, is directed at the very idea of philosophical argument. This is not just a matter of logic or discourse theory being part of philosophy's purview, but also that declarations of what properly "belongs" in philosophy are a central feature of the conversation. We have grown particularly used to this kind of argument in this century, during which logical positivists and other overbearing analytical philosophers have declared huge wads of traditional philosophical speculation, especially anything to do with metaphysics, not so much false as nonsensical—out of bounds. But that is just a late refinement: such in-and-out boundaries have been drawn more or less constantly since the time of Plato, with high points (according to taste) at Montaigne, Hume, and Nietzsche.

That is no cause for worry. Philosophers ought to spend time considering what does and does not count as genuine philosophical reflection. I am open-minded on the topic myself, but I understand why some of my colleagues might wish to relegate some things that call themselves philosophy to the realms of sociology, anthropology, literary criticism, journalism, or in the present case, bad fiction. If they then proceed to denigrate those things too, that's regrettable but not too damaging. A healthy discipline demands the in-group loyalty of its practitioners, and that may sometimes involve the mild denigration of what lies outside.

I'm being too forgiving here.

The second issue, though, is related and more troubling. It is the by-product of the professionalization of philosophy in North American university departments during this century. Under the sour influence of a fetish for analytic precision, philosophy has lately priced itself out of the intellectual market, rendering its hard-won results uninteresting to anyone save a small circle of in-groupers. Partly this comes from science envy—glance at a leading philosophy journal and notice how many of the pages are covered with symbols rather than prose—and partly it is a fondness for what Iris Murdoch once condemned as "dryness": the attitude of arid, thin-lipped disapproval of anything emotional, personal, or ambiguous, which will be familiar to anyone who has ever given a talk to an audience of philosophy professors.

There are exceptions, of course. Some of them, like Bertrand Russell, Martin Hollis, and Thomas Nagel, have pulled off the remarkable double-play of being superb analysts and adept popularizers (though Russell's *The Problems of Philosophy* is surprisingly challenging for a general-interest work). Others, like Richard Rorty, have very publicly turned their backs on the limitations of analytic philosophy and taken up a prominent role as public intellectuals—sometimes to great effect, as in Rorty's recent book, *Achieving Our Country*, in which he challenges "spectatorial" academic leftists to adopt a more activist role.

Still, the problem remains. In contrast to the situation in literary criticism, where readers unmoved by the intricacies of what is usually simply called *theory* may turn back to the pleasure of reading the novels and poems they love, those of us moved by philosophical questions— who am I? why is there something rather than nothing?—must ever grapple with the conflict between amateur and professional thinking. The great works in philosophy are talmudic in spirit, they are an interlocking grid of comment and counter-comment. But a casual lover of wisdom sees academic philosophy as so much hot air, while the professor looks at a Gaarder or a Pirsig and sees only the Cliff's Notes version of great wisdom.

Is there a solution? I think so. Professional philosophers need to remember that the point of philosophical reflection is to think more clearly about issues that matter, human issues. They need to recall (or cultivate, if it is new to them) the conviction that devotion to philosophy does indeed start in wonder. Amateurs of the subject should not be disdained in the name of expertise or professional self-congratulation. Popularizers, on the other side, and the people who are devoted to them,

Hollis, Invitation to Philosophy (1985); Nagel, *What Does It All Mean?* (1987); Russell, *The Problems of Philosophy* (1912).

Rorty, Achieving Our Country (1998): "Leftists in the academy have permitted cultural politics to supplant real politics, and have collaborated with the Right in making cultural issues central to public debate. They are spending energy that should be directed at proposing new laws."

might profitably accept that, as so often, things are perhaps more complicated than they seem.

Let's do *Philosophy for Beginners*, certainly. But let's also remember that in a sense we are all, and always will be, beginners at philosophy.

Extraordinary

See "Dr. Action Man"
(Section III).

Here is a good question: who is America's foremost philosopher? An initial, quite reasonable response might be to wonder whether this is a question without an answer, a title without a claimant. In a society that is, to say the least, not much given to celebrating its intellectuals, it is even perhaps a *stupid* question, a *spurious* title. There *are* imaginable answers, but in the main they range from the banal (Allan Bloom, Mortimer Adler) to the hopelessly professional (David Lewis and Donald Davidson, technical wizards with little reputation outside graduate schools and professional organizations)—the difference turning, presumably, on what one means by "foremost."

What these suggestions fail to capture is what is important about such a title: the ability of a thinker to clarify, and represent, what is special about American life and culture, that which is uniquely and defensibly valuable in the country's patterns and history of thought. A parallel suggests itself. Is there anyone who provides Americans with the same sort of illumination of themselves that was given us by the distinctively Canadian mind of George Grant?

Good answers come from unlikely places. Recently the Harvard philosopher Stanley Cavell has been touted by people of some weight, including George Steiner and Richard Rorty, a thinker with his own claim to the post. To most people Cavell's name will come as a surprise. He is not widely known outside academia, being a self-confessed weirdo, an intellectual "character" who wears his obsessions—Ralph Waldo Emerson, 1940s screwball comedies, Ludwig Wittgenstein—on his sleeve. He is also a writer with no firm place in either philosophy or literary criticism, a critic more often dismissed than read.

In Cavell's hands, however, the obsessions and the obscurity combine

Richard Rorty, "The
Philosophy of the Oddball," in
The New Republic (1989):
"Cavell is among professors of
philosophy what Harold Bloom
is among professors of
English: the least defended,

to form a clear picture of the American soul, its drive for self-reliance and exploration, the pragmatism born of a mind unfettered by tradition. Cavell is thus a true philosopher of the New World, a do-it-yourself prophet of cities on the hill. More important, he is also the Philosopher as Regular Guy, equally happy to talk about TV and Nietzsche, as deeply immersed in the semantics of Hollywood as in those of Heidegger. *America's* foremost philosopher mustn't be some snooty intellectual.

the gutsiest, the most vulnerable. He sticks his neck out farther than the rest of us."

Cavell's path to the American soul follows twin routes, both made obvious in two recent collections of lectures, *This New Yet Unapproachable America* and *In Quest of the Ordinary*. On one hand (call it the left) lies the path of Emerson and Thoreau, those unacknowledged American heroes. Championed by novelists and presidents, adored by generations of real people, these two non-professional thinkers continue to be ignored by the American philosophical establishment. It is hard to imagine a mega-session, multi-paper conference—like recent ones held on John Dewey and C. S. Peirce—being organized around the thought of Emerson. One of the things Cavell wants to know is why that is hard to imagine.

First published in 1989 and 1988, respectively.

Cavell's other hand (call it the right) is more obviously academic and points to the smooth-trodden path of British "ordinary language" philosophy, that concerted attempt by Wittgenstein, J.L. Austin, and others to understand the meaningfulness of the way you and I talk. Here, just as with Emerson and Thoreau, we start with simple things, the features of daily life. Cavell's genius is thus to combine rough-hewn early American thinking with the reality-check of ordinary-language inquiry. Call the result "ordinary guy philosophy."

In making ordinary life his scene of investigation Cavell is only following an old order of philosophical business. The philosopher traditionally puts the world to the question, seeks solutions to large problems by probing the details of daily life. Of course ordinary life seems to have its own agenda, preventing exactly the sort of reflection the philosopher

Austin, "A Plea for
Excuses" (1956): "Certainly,
then, ordinary language is *not*
the last word: in principle
it can everywhere be
supplemented and improved
upon and superseded. Only
remember, it *is* the *first* word."

values by rendering the questioning difficult, outwardly silly, or even dangerous. And considering much of what philosophy's investigating has produced, we may be forgiven for thinking of its "putting the world to the question" in a more inquisitional sense. Tortured, bent, and mutilated, the world the philosopher presents as ours often seems all too alien.

The ordinary therefore turns out to be not as simple as we might have thought. In these collections, Cavell explores the tension between what we desire from the everyday and what philosophy can reasonably recover from it. That he does not resolve this tension is perhaps inevitable, certainly forgivable; that he founders on it, wallows in its uncertainty, is less so. Cavell, proclaimed prophet of the American soul, turns out to be something of a false seer. Consider how by, first, walking briefly down Cavell's right-hand path.

Ordinary-language inquiry is only a late twist on the more general project of recovering the ordinary, and is free of none of its difficulties. Like Cavell, the patron saints of ordinary language, Wittgenstein and Austin, were never able to overcome the tension between the daily world as source of illumination and the daily world as hindrance to inquiry. But their dissections of how we talk give some useful results, often communicated in a language of extraordinary hilarity. Austin, a Peter Wimsey figure in three-piece tweeds, draws his best examples of how language works from the senior common room, the country house, and the garden party. "I am very partial to ice cream," he says, for example, in his essay "A Plea for Excuses,"

Wittgenstein,
Philosophical Investigations
(1953): "Can I say 'bububu'
and mean 'If it doesn't rain
I shall go for a walk'?"

and a bombe is divided into segments corresponding one to one with the persons at High Table: I am tempted to help myself to two pieces and do so, thus succumbing to temptation. . . . But do I lose control of myself? Do I raven, do I snatch the morsels from the dish and wolf them down? Not a bit of it. We often succumb to temptation with calm and even with finesse.

And so we do. However minute and arid, Austin's distinctions are almost always telling. His drawing-room humour is not incidental, or affected; Austin was genuinely amused by the quirks of our language and how we use it. More important, it has things to tell us: about how we misuse language, expect too much of it, investigate it in all the wrong ways.

The humour, and the philosophical weight, of Wittgenstein are more difficult to convey. He is not an ordinary-language philosopher in the usual meaning of that phrase, casting his net wider than a professional amateur like Austin and addressing, if only obliquely, larger philosophical issues. The major work published in his own lifetime, *Philosophical Investigations*, is populated by a series of nameless voices who want to know, among other things, what goes on when someone buys five red apples, whether chairs can think, and how one counts past twenty. Like Austin, Wittgenstein believed our understanding of the world was hindered by false linguistic pictures, many of them owing to philosophy, which hold us in thrall. Only by investigating the grammar of our limitless locutions, the criteria of meaning we all use in the daily round of communication, would we free ourselves of the "bewitchment" of language. How is it that words mean what they do, that they *mean* anything at all? Philosophy was for Wittgenstein a matter of spadework: hard labour in dirty, obvious places. This image also occurs in Austin, but his only personal acquaintance with spades would have been with those of the garden variety. By contrast Wittgenstein, a trained engineer, suffered through a sojourn in the trenches of the First World War.

Despite their attractions—the charm, the philosophical payoff—we may ultimately feel the disappointment of Austin and Wittgenstein. For one thing, ordinary-language philosophy appears harder than we might have supposed. Good examples are hard to come by, and Austin frequently enjoins us to read a dictionary for ideas. More deeply, ordinary-language philosophy appears to generate few genuine *solutions* to philosophical problems. Wittgenstein famously said that "philosophy leaves everything as it is," and there is a deeply conservative bias in his

Austin, "A Plea for Excuses" (1956): "You dropped the tea-tray: Certainly, but an emotional storm was about to break out: or, Yes, but there was a wasp. In each case the defence, very soundly, insists on a fuller description of the event in its context; but the first is a justification, the second an excuse."

thinking. Those seeking reform will look in vain. The celebrated drive to "get clear" on what happens in language appears, on this view anyway, the very model of value-free philosophizing. What happens after the spell of language has been lifted, the enthralling picture shattered, is up to you. Politics happens elsewhere.

The precise position of Cavell, the most prominent American inheritor of Austin's mantel, is relatively easy to track from this point of disappointment. Like many American philosophers, Cavell is in the business of expectation modification. He wants to say, first of all, that ordinary-language analysis shows us that the desire for *solutions* was precisely what had us in chains in the first place. Just say no to those old pictures! More helpfully, he notes that the disappointment we may feel with Austin and Wittgenstein is inscribed in their own works, a driving doubt that wants at every point to know what the point is. They knew what they were doing—or rather, weren't. This may simply be what it is to philosophize: not knowing whether what one does is worth doing. But that is small comfort. We may be inclined to reply to Cavell in the way he says we usually reply to philosophical skeptics: "Thanks for nothing."

Wittgenstein, *Investigations,* Prop. 309: "What is your aim in philosophy?—To show the fly the way out of the fly-bottle."

Ordinary-language philosophy shows us that the everyday world cannot be recovered easily; our quest continues. The obvious monster in our path is skepticism, that philosophical position that makes of our disappointment with philosophy a full-blown theory. Skepticism is the *bête noire* of Cavell's philosophizing. Iris Murdoch said it is always a good question to ask of any philosopher, What is he afraid of? Cavell is afraid that we cannot know whether the everyday world is real, or whether there are (in the language of Anglo-American academic philosophy) other minds. To be precise: he is afraid that we don't know what to do with this condition of not being able to know. That, at least, is my diagnosis of his diagnosis of philosophy, ordinary and otherwise.

Cavell's works deliberately, and sometimes irritatingly, obscure this rather simple proposition, but that is perhaps to be expected of someone who praises oddity as much as he does. In the 1950s Cavell was a clever-clever Harvard graduate student bowled over by the visiting Austin, changing his dissertation topic on the spot to deal with what Austin was saying and what Wittgenstein, his works only then becoming known in America, was labelling unsayable. In the 1980s, and now '90s, he is a clever-clever Harvard professor who rides his stable of hobby horses with the assurance that his merest utterance will find its way between hard covers. Behind the self-indulgent layers of allusion, the tortured parenthesis-ridden sentences, the maddening trendy neologisms—(in)tuition, quest(ion), (re)membrance, and the like—there is genuine humour and warmth in Cavell's writing. But our greatest amusement is reserved for a joke to which Cavell himself is butt and not party. For he is that silliest of intellectual figures, the ordinary-language philosopher who writes incomprehensibly.

Now Cavell is by no means alone in this shortcoming, and there is perhaps no divine ordinance that the investigation of ordinary language should be conducted in plain style. Cavell may think himself akin to the frequently gnomic Wittgenstein, "an extraordinary ordinary language philosopher." But the sin of his unreadability is compounded by a kind of preciousness rarely seen among professional thinkers, a desire to fill the reader in on the various fascinating details of his life and intellectual development. Prefaces are where the worst of these self-aggrandizing remarks occur. His Ph.D. thesis, we are told, circulated in typescript for years among his colleagues (blush). Today he is relaxing by the Pacific at the urging of some committee of graduate students; tomorrow he flies to Vienna—or is it Norway? "One who is as bent as I seem to be on intellectual adventures that require conducting my continuing education in public," he muses in *In Quest of the Ordinary*, "must count on friendly and productive occasions." Were he a more public figure, Cavell would undoubtedly commit the ultimate media-age solecism of referring to himself in the third person. ("Let me just say that Stanley Cavell does not believe in transcendental standpoints . . . ")

Reading Cavell is therefore a trying experience, for more than one reason. Consider a paragraph from *This New Yet Unapproachable*

See "Prolegomena to All Future Prefaces" (Section VI).

217

America, which can be found on the book's back cover and, if that were not enough, once more in one of the lectures printed inside:

> Wittgenstein's appeal or "approach" to the everyday finds the (actual) everyday to be as pervasive a scene of illusion and trance and artificiality (of need) as Plato or Rousseau or Marx or Thoreau had found. His philosophy of the (eventual) everyday is the proposal of a practice that takes on, takes upon itself, precisely (I do not say exclusively) that scene of illusion and loss; approaches it, or let me say reproaches it, intimately enough to turn it, or deliver it; as if the actual is the womb, contains the terms, of the eventual. The direction out from illusion is not up, at any rate not up to one fixed morning star; but down, at any rate along each chain of a day's denial. Philosophy (as descent) can thus be said to leave everything as it is because it is a refusal of, say disobedient to, (a false) ascent, or transcendence. Philosophy (as ascent) shows the violence that is to be refused (disobeyed), that has left everything not as it is, indifferent to me, as if there are things in themselves. Plato's sun has shown us the fact of our chains; but that sun was produced by these chains.

This is about where
most people bail out.

Imagine the effect of reading this sort of thing for several hundred pages, and you will appreciate the fury that Cavell's books can produce among the sane. Yet this passage does, or at least may, mean something. What is it and, more important, why must it be "communicated" in this bizarre fashion?

These are not idle questions. A philosopher of stature must be able to force us to consider the possibility that his or her mangling of our language is to good purpose, bent to some task that cannot be accomplished otherwise. We may—we should—have grave and well-established doubts about this possibility; but it must be held open. In other words, philosophy will not always appear in a form intelligible to everyone, no more than mechanical engineering will. Thus our distaste for the barbarous German style of Martin Heidegger may be mitigated by the realization that his manner of writing is deeply bound up with philosophical convictions we may eventually find compelling. If we do not, then style simply ceases to be an issue for us.

Cavell is no Heidegger, but the critical attention focused on him recently suggests that for some he is America's homegrown answer, the distant next best thing. This is not simply a matter of his self-conscious appropriation of those distinctively American figures, Thoreau and Emerson, though clearly that matters. (Here is the left-hand path.) Despite the central role he finds for them, Cavell's intellectual gaze is not restricted to Americana. The essays in these two volumes, lectures delivered in various academic milieux over the past few years, show Cavell's distinctive mix-and-match style of philosophy as having read everything. Thoreau meets Heidegger, Poe talks to Freud, Wittgenstein and Austin preside over the introduction of Frank Capra to Emerson. Cavell says he "will attempt to fit together into some reasonable, or say convivial, circle a collection of the main beasts in my jungle or wilderness of interests." The common thread in all these disparate positions, names, themes? Why, Stanley Cavell.

I said that the driving force in Cavell's philosophy is skepticism. He is worried about it, it bothers him, he feels compelled to say something about it. This concern goes back at least to *The Claim of Reason*, the big book based on Cavell's Harvard Ph.D. thesis, and recurs in some form in almost everything he writes. So what is the problem? What is he trying to say?

Doubting the world, at least in the Cartesian sense, is the beginning of genuinely scientific inquiry. But a more radical skeptical attitude, say Hume's, indicated for Kant a "scandal for philosophy" that he felt compelled to remedy by splitting the world in two. The line drawn by Kant between appearances and things-in-themselves is thus the great Mephistophelean bargain of philosophy: I will grant you the unknowable if you grant we can at least understand phenomena. The figures Cavell lauds, philosophers and poets and playwrights, are uniformly those who find this bartering of knowledge with doubt distasteful, even dangerous. What is common, he says, is not "their deflections of

Wittgenstein, *Investigations*, Prop. 38: "You really get a queer connexion when the philosopher tries to bring out the relation between name and thing by staring at an object and repeating a name or even the word 'this' innumerable times. For philosophical problems arise when language *goes on holiday.*"

Hume (1711-76) argued that we could not validate the traditional claims of metaphysics, such as causality or the existence of self, because we experienced only sense impressions.

skepticism but . . . their respect for it, as for a worthy other; I think of it as their recognition not of the uncertainty or failure of our knowledge but of our disappointment with its success." They are also, and as a result, those who wish fervently to recover the everyday from the doubt into which skepticism has thrown it in some other fashion. Not science, or metaphysics—so then, what?

The answer, such as there is one, has to do with Cavell's sense of what "the ordinary" is, and his idiosyncratic, even peculiar, reading of the romantic impulse. The recovery of the ordinary is a renunciation of all the "beyond" and/or "before" strategies common in philosophy, the line-drawing that creates transcendental standpoints. Romanticism is thus an acceptance of finitude, a bringing of the ordinary world back to itself. What Cavell finds common in Emerson and Thoreau, Wordsworth and Coleridge, Wittgenstein and Austin is a line of thinking driven towards recovery and acceptance of the mundane. This is living with, rather than living, our skepticism. (Cavell takes seriously Hume's point that living skepticism was not worth the effort, especially if there was a game of backgammon to be had of an evening.) What is rejected here is the drive, call it philosophy as traditionally understood, that takes the ordinary as diseased or limited in a way that could be remedied. Philosophy as remedy gives way to philosophy as, well, redemption—so that Kierkegaard's Knight of Faith, say, exhibiting "the sublime in the pedestrian," is an example of this "(ac)knowledging" of skepticism that Cavell himself cites.

Wittgenstein, *Tractatus,* Prop. 6.54: "My propositions serve as elucidations in the following way: anyone who understands me eventually recognizes them as non-sensical, when he has used them—as steps—to climb up beyond them. (He must, so to speak, throw away the ladder after he has climbed up it.)"

The ordinary, more difficult and problematic than we might have thought, makes genuine acceptance of ourselves a larger intellectual task than non-thinkers think. In the best of these lectures, "The Uncanniness of the Ordinary," Cavell actually approaches intelligibility in saying this, drawing together themes from all his favourite people. There is no clearer statement of Cavell's project than a paragraph from that lecture:

I am not here going to make a move toward deriving the skeptical threat philosophically. My idea is that what in philosophy is known as skepticism (for example, as in Descartes and Hume and Kant) is a relation to the world, and to others, and to myself, and to language, that is known to what you might call literature, or anyway responded to in literature, in uncounted other guises—in Shakespeare's tragic heroes, in Emerson's and Thoreau's "silent melancholy" and "quiet desperation," in Wordsworth's perception of us as without "interest," in Poe's "perverseness." Why philosophy and literature do not know this about one another—and to that extent remain unknown to themselves—has been my theme it seems to me forever.

All of these are responses to the great difficulty in recovering the ordinary, in all its uncanniness. The German word *Unheimlichkeit* gets the meaning better: the world frequently appears unfamiliar, not a home for us. And yet it is, it must be, the only home we have. Ordinary-language thinking, whether done by Emerson or Austin, is best able to show us this problem, but perhaps least able to "solve" it. "An urgent methodological issue of ordinary-language philosophy," Cavell says in the same lecture, "and the issue about which this cast of thought is philosophically at its weakest—is that of accounting for the fact that we are the victims of the very words of which we are at the same time the masters; victims and masters of the fact of words." Language holds us tight—but where else are you going to go when you crave understanding?

Cavell's bestiary-of-thinkers image is imperfect, for it suggests a random collection of animals each exhibiting distinct features. These lectures are more like a three-ring circus, with Cavell as ringmaster and the beasts cavorting to the cracks of his whip. A certain amount of coercion will result, but that has never unduly concerned him. Cavell is more interested in getting us into this mélange of philosophy and poetry, getting us to see that the habitual separation of them is another trace of the hubris (and poverty) of philosophy understood as science. To this end he attempts reforms of the reputation of Emerson and Thoreau, figures commonly passed off as "not serious philosophers." Even Nietzsche, himself a Cavellian hero and surely no slave to professionalism, found Emerson all too casual. "I do not know how much I would give," Nietzsche wrote to Franz Overbeck in 1884, "if only I could bring it about, *ex post facto*, that such a glorious, great nature, rich in soul and spirit, might have gone through some *strict* discipline, a really scientific education. As it is, in Emerson we have *lost a philosopher.*"

Cavell works hard to get us to see that *Walden* and Emerson's *Essays* have important things to say, things at least as important as the work of Heidegger and Wittgenstein, arguably this century's most influential philosophers. He also wants us to see how Shakespearean tragedy, the poems of Coleridge, and the stories of Poe bear on a serious, indeed the most serious, philosophical question: what do we do about not being able to know? But in a way Cavell protests too much. Towards whom are these cries directed? Cavell's fellow professional philosophers? He says, quite correctly, that not all professionals are philosophers, nor all philosophers professional. But are these, as Nietzsche, Wittgenstein, Thoreau, and Emerson all thought, mutually exclusive groups? In other words, is there not a basic disingenuousness in everything Cavell says, coming as it does from Harvard's Walter M. Cabot Professor of Aesthetics and the General Theory of Value?

Part of what Cavell wishes to say—and here we glimpse again why he is supposed to be America's foremost philosopher—is that there is something distinctive about "the new world" that frees us from such old-world quibbles. Or that might. In "Finding as Founding," the second lecture of *This New Yet Unapproachable America*, Cavell notes: "Every European philosopher since Hegel has felt he must inherit this edifice [what commonly goes by the name of Tradition] and/or destroy it; no American philosopher has such a relation to the history of philosophy." This will come as a surprise to many involved in American philosophy. But Cavell's point is that the combined blessing and curse of America is the freedom from the foundations, the foundational

I find this judgment excessively harsh; either I have mellowed with age, or I have come to appreciate better the old but fruitful paradox of the philosopher who denies the possibility of philosophy.

impulse, of European thinking. Philosophy as grasping, controlling, limiting—let's call it metaphysics, just like everyone else—has less hold in America. Therefore it is more easily overcome. And that is what we want.

Well, perhaps. The question at this juncture, and a final question to take away from these offerings, is whether *this* is the sort of overcoming we want. Cavell has been compared, with some reason, to the deconstructionist Jacques Derrida. Their projects are in fact dissimilar, as Cavell hastens to point out, but they share certain tactics. What they also share, and this goes unacknowledged by Cavell, is a tone of self-righteous congratulation about their own perspicacity. Time and again, when everyone else failed to see, failed even to realize they wore blinders, Cavell/Derrida's gaze penetrated to the heart of the matter. Their critics consistently fail to understand them, therefore are dismissed. Professional philosophy is in their view fundamentally flawed as a practice. Yet it continues to provide them with a comfortable livelihood they have no intention of forgoing.

Both are concerned with unpacking the implications and pathologies of language; but there the similarity really ends.

These character faults may not trump what each has to say. Ultimately less forgivable, in Cavell anyway, is a deeper contradiction. Philosophy was put into question because, in so many of its forms, it denigrated the ordinary while elevating itself to kabbalistic status, making its practitioners the high-priests of the transcendental standpoint. In overcoming this deleterious impulse in philosophy—in questing after the ordinary, seeking to redeem the everyday in an acknowledgment of our cognitive finitude—Cavell has succeeded only in separating himself, and his idiosyncratic interests, from the rest of us.

Books

Thanking, Stealing, Making

Praising the culture of books, in the present setting, is probably nothing more than preaching to the choir. But preaching to the choir has its pleasures, and anyway, if publishing numbers are anything to go by, the book culture is in no danger of imminent collapse. The book is still the best-available compact, portable, solar-powered medium of communication; it will continue to thrive. (The questions of quality within that culture, and justice or sense in those numbers, I leave for another time, when I'm feeling more robust.)

As a university professor and a writer, I am obviously a product and a devotee of the Codex Cult, the Gutenberg Gang. So be it. Books are beautiful things, sometimes both inside and outside. They also remain unparalleled in their capacity to do certain kinds of things—notably, make us think. The essays in this section are about book business, from making them to making off with them. "Reading maketh a full man; conference a ready man; and writing an exact man." So said Francis Bacon, and he was a guy who knew what time it was.

Prolegomena to All Future Prefaces

> And now, having broken my resolution never to write a Preface, there are just two or three things which I should like to say a word about . . .
>
> —Thomas Hughes, *Tom Brown's Schooldays* (Sixth Edition)

I am one of those people who prefer reading prefaces to reading the books they preface, and I can only imagine that there are many more where I came from. It's a guilty pleasure, and a guilty secret, but I figure I'll learn more about the author and his or her predilections in a few pages of guardedly self-conscious text than in perhaps thousands of pages of the other stuff.

The title of this essay is a play on Kant's work *Prolegomena to Any Future Metaphysics* (1783).

Where else, for example, is it possible to observe authors in full flights of self-justification, taunting nonexistent enemies or battling off objections yet to find voice? Where else is the economy of thanking and not-thanking so apparent and so calculated? And where else would we gain access, however briefly, to the lives of those devoted to preparing "immaculate typescripts"—the army of secretaries, wives, and other subordinate drudges who sacrificed their wrist tendons and patience to the Great Work? (Sometimes I wish *they* would write the prefaces.) In short, I think it is time for more of us to confess that the preface is often the most interesting part of a book, sometimes even its only redeeming literary feature. In fact, we should think of this confession as emancipatory. Consider how many more books you can read, often while simply standing in the bookstore.

I say this as somebody whose own work has met with a strong reaction of preface-preference. My first book, a work in political philosophy, has its moments of interest and even (I flatter myself) droll humour. But it cannot truthfully be described as scintillating. It nevertheless sports what I consider a pretty jazzy preface—and that's usually all anyone ever reads. I don't blame them. I simply want them to own up and join me. (I also want them, in this case, to buy the book as well. But then, that's between me and my bill-collectors.) Prefaces, like abstracts, should be circulated independently of their books. In rare cases, the book can be ordered later.

What I have discovered, in examining a range of books fictional and non-fictional, is that the great preface archetypes are actually few in number. In fact, I think they can be reduced to four.

They are: (1) the preface that explains, apologizes, justifies, or disclaims; (2) the preface that thanks and/or fails to thank; (3) the preface that rehearses the book (especially useful, these, in rendering the book unnecessary reading); and finally (4) the preface that describes the circumstances of composition in an effort to "humanize" the author. Naturally some masters of the prefatory remark may manage to combine all four features, and clearly 1 and 4 bear similarities in practice. But my research—at home and on the street—indicates that this exhausts the possibilities of prefatory comment. I am in most cases excluding, by the way, introductions and dedications—though these are sometimes interpolated—but including all those things known as author's notes, acknowledgments, or forewords.

The sheer variety of prefaces makes them a worthy subject of study. I can see a doctoral dissertation in it, though no doubt only its preface would really be worth reading. Prefaces can range in length and cogency, for instance, from the extreme of Evelyn Waugh's terse note to *Brideshead Revisited*—"I am not I; thou art not he or she; they are not they"—to, say, the preface to Hegel's *Phenomenology of Spirit*, which is a separate essay entitled "On Scientific Cognition" and a work massive in its own right. This mother of all prefaces begins with a reasonably encouraging disclaimer. "It is customary to preface a work with an explanation of the author's aim, why he wrote the book, and the relationship in which he believes it to stand to other earlier or contemporary

Kingwell, *A Civil Tongue* (1995): "We stood there for what seemed like an age, each of us unwilling to go first, acting out a scene from (as it might be) Noël Coward revised by Ionesco."

treatises on the same subject," Hegel says. "In the case of a philosophical work, however, such an explanation seems not only superfluous but, in view of the nature of the subject-matter, even inappropriate and misleading. For whatever might appropriately be said about philosophy in a preface, none of this can be accepted as the way in which to expound philosophical truth."

Oh, good. And yet: Hegel then immediately moves on to offer a "preface" that comprises seventy-two numbered page-length paragraphs. And it includes (around paragraph twenty-five) the following unfortunately typical passage: "That the True is actual only as system, or that Substance is essentially Subject, is expressed in the representation of the Absolute as *Spirit*—the most sublime Notion and the one which belongs to the modern age and religion. The spiritual alone is the *actual*; it is essence, or that which has *being in itself*; it is that which *relates itself to itself* and is *determinate*; it is *other-being* and *being-for-self*, and in this determinateness, or in its self-externality, abides within itself; in other words, it is *in and for itself*."

All this before the book is fairly begun, and the average reader must quail. By the way, in case quibblers are thinking this is an *introduction*, and therefore disqualified from consideration, let me just say that the book also has one of those. And it's a doozy too.

Waugh's understandable urge to distance himself from the events of his fiction is a common feature among novelists, who often use their prefaces to this purpose. Graham Greene is responsible for what remains my favourite example of this sort of fending off of responsibility, in his preface to *The Comedians*. "I am unlikely to bring an action for libel against myself with any success," he says there, "yet I want to make it clear that the narrator of this tale, though his name is Brown, is not Greene. Many readers assume—I know it from experience—that an 'I' is always the author. So in my time I have been considered the murderer of a friend, the jealous lover of a civil servant's wife, and an obsessive player at roulette. I don't wish to add to my chameleon-nature the characteristics belonging to the cuckolder of a South American diplomat, a possibly

> **Hegel always** takes the fun out of everything.

> **What must** happen to the above- or below-average reader is not something I am right now prepared to contemplate.

illegitimate birth and an education by the Jesuits." You feel, somehow, that Greene thinks the last feature the one he most wants to disclaim. (Speaking as someone who was educated by Jesuits, I have to say you cannot blame him.)

Nathaniel Hawthorne also let himself off the hook with respect to factual accuracy, but in another direction. "When a writer calls his work a Romance," he says in the preface to *The House of Seven Gables*, "it need hardly be observed that he wishes to claim a certain latitude, both as to its fashion and material, which he would not have felt himself entitled to assume had he professed to be writing a Novel." Since today this distinction is little preserved, it is useful that he continues: "The latter form of composition is presumed to aim at a very minute fidelity, not merely to the possible, but to the probable and ordinary course of man's experience. The former—while, as a work of art, it must rigidly subject itself to laws, and while it sins unpardonably so far as it may swerve aside from the truth of the human heart—has fairly a right to present that truth under circumstances, to a great extent, of the writer's own choosing or creation."

Well, okay, but we might be inclined to think Hawthorne protests a bit too much here. Who is he afraid of? Some reporter with newspaper accounts of domestic tragedy in New England? Joseph Conrad had a better idea when, in a late edition of *The Secret Agent*, he openly and insistently attacked the critics who had suggested the book was, because of its violence and degradation, better left unwritten. "I do not regret having written it," he says. "I confess that it makes a grisly skeleton. But still I will submit that in telling Winnie Verloc's story to its anarchistic end of utter desolation, madness, and despair, and telling it as I have told it here, I have not intended to commit a gratuitous outrage on the feelings of mankind." Which does not, of course, preclude an intention to commit an outrage of a non-gratuitous kind, but perhaps that misses the point. It is also hard for us to imagine, today, the kind of response Conrad was fighting off—though perhaps the reaction to Bret Easton Ellis's *American Psycho* is our version of these events.

Alberto Manguel, not a critic given to hyperbole, writes in *Through the Looking-Glass* (1998) that reading *American Psycho* made him physically ill.

Both Hawthorne and Conrad might have been better advised, when inclined to complain about reader reception, possible or actual, to follow the ironic lead of Søren Kierkegaard. In his *Concluding Unscientific Postscript*, Kierkegaard marvels at some length at the great good fortune of public indifference to one's work. "Seldom perhaps has a literary enterprise been more favored by fortune, or had a reception more in accordance with the author's wishes," he begins, "than was the case with my *Philosophical Fragments*. Hesitant and reserved as it is my custom to be in connection with every form of self-appraisal, I dare nevertheless affirm one thing: it has created no sensation, absolutely none." In fact, he says, "the book was permitted to enter the world unnoticed, without fuss or fury, without shedding of ink or blood. It was neither reviewed nor mentioned anywhere. No learned outcry was raised to mislead the expectant multitude; no shouts of warning from our literary sentinels served to put the reading public on its guard; everything happened with due decency and decorum." Kierkegaard goes on to mention that this reception put him at his ease, because no midnight processions of disciples troubled him from his leisure with loud huzzahs and calls for his appearance. "Encouraged in this manner by fortune's favor," he concludes, "I now propose to carry on with my project" and offer a sequel to the earlier work.

Kierkegaard's jauntiness in the face of adversity is enough, for me anyway, to make his book even more attractive than a straightforward preface might have done. And this, after all, is how writers—if not readers—use prefaces: to hook you into reading on. But some of them are remarkably bad at it.

Immanuel Kant, in common with many German philosophers, thought the highest regard one could accord an issue was to consider it *problematisch*—problematic, and therefore worth considering. Even so, the opening salvo in his brick-like *Critique of Pure Reason* is nevertheless a bit off-putting. "Human reason," he tells his presumed audience, "has this peculiar fate that in one species of its knowledge it is burdened by questions which, as prescribed by the very nature of reason itself, it is

Kant himself pronounced this 1781 work "dry, obscure, contrary to all ordinary ideas, and prolix to boot."

not able to ignore, but which, as transcending all its powers, it is not able to answer." Well, thank you for nothing.

And who could feel cheery about reading on when Ludwig Wittgenstein, introducing his *Philosophical Investigations*, notes: "I should have liked to produce a good book. This has not come about, but the time is past in which I could improve it." Wittgenstein is not unbrokenly gloomy, of course, but he's pretty cautious. "It is not impossible that it should fall to the lot of this work," he grumbles in the same preface, "in its poverty and in the darkness of this time, to bring light into one brain or another—but, of course, it is not likely."

You've got to love Wittgenstein.

With François Rabelais we have a writer who is, as a general thing, in a better mood than most, especially more than the philosophers. Rabelais's prefaces are models of the kind of genial leg-pulling best suited (assuming this is your desire) to making the reader forge on. This is J.M. Cohen's translation of the preface to *Gargantua and Pantagruel*: "Most noble boozers, and you my very esteemed and poxy friends—for to you and you alone are my writings dedicated. Now what do you think is the purpose of this preamble, of this preliminary flourish? It is that you, my good disciples and other leisured fools, in reading the pleasant titles of certain books of our invention, such as Gargantua, Pantagruel, Tosspint, On the Dignity of Codpieces, Of Peas and Bacon, cum commento, &c, may not too easily conclude that they treat of nothing but mockery, fooling, and pleasant fictions; seeing that their outward signs—their titles, that is—are commonly greeted, without further investigation, with smiles of derision. It is wrong, however, to set such small store by the works of men." Especially the works of Rabelais? Good on him, if so.

Cheerfulness or gloom about reception frequently gives way to a purpose more self-serving, namely, the doling out of credit for the existence of a book. And here authorial psychology shines through most clearly, creating at a pinnacle the preface—like the gossip column—in which the only thing worse than appearing is not appearing.

Having now appeared in gossip columns once or twice, I must say I no longer endorse this piece of worldly wisdom.

The Harvard philosopher Stanley Cavell is a master of the elaborate list of acknowledgments, some of which run to many pages and detail occasions and conversations stretching back many years. In a preface that thanks several dozen people, what is it like to go unmentioned, or perhaps worse, to be relegated to a catch-all phrase concerning "all those whose names I inevitably forgot"? Cavell grasps the bull by the horns in his usual multiple-clause fashion in the preface to *The Claim of Reason*: "Such a list is something whose personal significance to me is quite out of proportion to its essential insignificance to strangers," he says, "and is thus at deliberate odds with the bright side of the intention to write. But I include it, beyond its sentimental value for me, and beyond its signal that writing has its dark sides, to suggest an answer to those who have been curious whether my tendency toward elaborately detailed acknowledgments hasn't some resonance with my intellectual interest in the concept of acknowledgment generally. What it suggests is that an elaboration of acknowledgment may declare a sense that complete acknowledgment is impossible, perhaps forbidden for one reason or another; and perhaps that one senses oneself for one reason or another to be insufficiently acknowledged." One would have thought that *less was more* when it came to showing the impossibility of full acknowledgment, but not, evidently, with Cavell at the helm.

> **This may** all be true, but it's unbelievably self-indulgent to *go on and on* about it like this.

This issue of full-versus-partial acknowledgment is but one of the paradoxes lurking when one attempts to render credit where it is due in book production. Another is exemplified by John Stuart Mill, who, despite his admirable feminism, never really gave Harriet Taylor her proper place in his writings—on the cover. In a note to *On Liberty* he says: "To the beloved and deplored memory of her who was the inspirer, and in part the author, of all that is best in my writings—the friend and wife whose exalted sense of truth and right was my strongest incitement, and whose approbation was my chief reward—I dedicate this volume. Like all that I have written for many years, it belongs as much to her as to me." And yet, did her name ever appear as co-author? I don't think so.

Fortunately, this sort of give-and-take-away credit has gone out of political fashion. Unfortunately, it has been replaced in some instances

with an aggressive counter-tendency. One contemporary author habitually writes that he will not suggest he could not have written his books
without his wife's help—he could have—but he is nevertheless grateful
for the support. All right, full marks for scrupulous honesty, but it's a
little grudging, no?

A similar note of over-stringent care is struck by some writers who
enjoy flouting the usual convention of thanking colleagues for their contributions but taking responsibility for all errors that remain. As the revi-
sionists never fail to point out, the fallacy in making this conventional
move of acknowledgment is that, if one has indeed relied on the expertise of a colleague, the error could be his or hers and not the author's. True
enough, but those who make a point of saying so strike one as a little
ungracious.

So what avenues remain for the author eager to make a mark preface-
wise? Well, it's still a good idea to give some idea what the book is about.
Of course, this may end up doing more harm than good. Jacques Derrida,
no stranger to impenetrability, opens his famous essay collection *Margins
of Philosophy* with this not-so-helpful comment: "To tympanize—philosophy. Being at the limit: these words do not yet form a proposition, and
even less a discourse. But there is enough in them, provided that one plays
upon it, to engender almost all the sentences in this book. Does philosophy answer a need? How is it to be understood? Philosophy? The need?"

Who knows? Who, perhaps, cares? But you have to admire the notion
that from three words one could engender "almost all" of the following
book. Which parts, one wonders for example, *don't* follow? And how
could we ever tell?

It seems to me that, now considered apart from their very real attraction as a genre unto themselves, prefaces succeed when they efface themselves most. In other words, Thomas Hughes had it right: if one wants
the book itself to command attention, the impulse to air out grievances
and debts in advance should be avoided.

If it cannot be avoided, the surrender should not—as in Hughes's own
pamphlet-length preface to the sixth edition of *Schooldays*—open the

I won't mention his name, but I will tell you that he is now divorced.

floodgates. One should instead follow the example of Charles Dickens, whose preface to *David Copperfield* is a masterpiece of restraint and good sense. "I do not find it easy to get sufficiently far away from this Book," he says, "in the first sensations of having finished it, to refer to it with the composure which this formal heading would seem to require. My interest in it, is so recent and strong; and my mind is so divided between pleasure and regret—pleasure in the achievement of a long design, regret in the separation from many companions—that I am in danger of wearying the reader, whom I love, with personal confidences, and private emotions. Besides which, all that I could say of the Story, to any purpose, I have endeavoured to say in it."

And we love him for saying it.

A statement to which, in an edition published nineteen years later, he sees fit to add only: "So true are these avowals at the present day, that I can now only take the reader into confidence once more. Of all my books, I like this best."

And that, finally, is something worth knowing, both about Dickens and about *David Copperfield.*

When Reality Is
Better than the Dream

For about as long as I can remember I have wanted to be someone who had written a book. Not necessarily someone who wrote books, that is— writing books seemed like an awful lot of work—but someone who had written one, or even a couple. I wanted people to point me out and say, after my name, "you know, author of *The Next Big Thing*." I figure this is a widely shared desire, because it alone can explain all the bad books that people write.

For a long time I didn't do much about realizing this ambition, partly because it seemed pretty fantastic and partly because the actual task held no joys for me. It was the incidental benefits I was interested in, mainly. I spent a lot of time visualizing myself signing the book, standing beside pyramids constructed out of pristine copies of it, catching sight of cardboard cut-outs of me in bookshop windows filled with displays of it.

Eventually I did write a book, I'm happy to say, though not one that will ever grace a window display or form a pyramid beside which I can strike faux-modest poses. My book is a work of political theory, dense with footnotes and published by what is usually called a "reputable university press." I like to think it's not as forbidding as a lot of academic books, having been written in actual English and here and there showing certain signs of wit, but I'll be the first to admit it lacks best-seller potential.

I'm still unsure how I actually managed to get from wanting to have written a book to having written one, but I can tell you that it was no picnic. I think it was turning thirty that did it, because part of the basic

This is what is known as my "pant-weasel" article, on the model of the veteran American magazine journalist whose article on people who put weasels in their pants is the only thing most people remember him writing.

Kingwell, *A Civil Tongue* (1995): "I would like at this point, with your friend deposited neatly into apparent madness, to help myself to the conclusion that a policy of strict truth-telling and truth-seeking is at odds with a life lived among other humans."

version of the book fantasy was that I had written the book by the time I was thirty. Don't ask me why. At one point I had used twenty-six, the age at which the British philosopher A.J. Ayer published his first book, *Language, Truth and Logic.* But eventually—around my twenty-seventh birthday, I think—I decided competing with Ayer was showy and maybe a little foolish.

But anyway, I got around to it, and there it was: my first book, published as it happens just last month. I am thirty-one, so if granted a little latitude I squeaked by the fantasy deadline.

I saw my book for the very first time at an academic conference held in Boston a few months ago, where the publisher had hired out a display table. It wasn't stacked in a pyramid. In fact, a single copy sat in lonely isolation amongst other titles on a wire rack. Nor were there any cardboard cut-outs of me to set next to the stand. (I did a passable imitation of the cardboard cut-out myself, though, and managed to shame a few of my friends into purchases by standing there.) But above all the book was there, a material object of relative durability, and undeniably bearing my name. And I had written it.

It was the American Philosophical Association Eastern Division meeting, where I was looking for, and failing to find, an academic job.

Seeing the book in public that way caused what I imagined are the usual high/low reactions of first-time authors. For several hours I wasn't crazy about the cover design, which I hadn't seen before. Then I flipped through and noticed some editing errors I missed on the proofs, things that made me seem silly. Then I glowed with insane pride for about thirty minutes. Then I noticed that the book was gone.

This is a common problem. I still can't look at p. 36 of that book.

That's right: gone. I had returned to the publisher's display after yet another troll through the other displays looking for friends to shame, and there was no longer a copy on the wire rack. My first, admittedly rather crazy, thought was that the book had proved so popular, or my friends so malleable, that all the publisher's copies had been sold. I didn't know how many he had brought—only about half a dozen, I learned later—but I had a fleeting image of myself as the author of a runaway academic bestseller, the new *Closing of the American Mind* or *Rise and Fall of the Great Powers.*

But no. The book had not been sold, it had been stolen. When I pointed out the book's absence, the publisher looked concerned, but not unduly upset, and he calmly placed a new copy in the empty space on the wire rack. I, however, was reeling.

Stolen! My book—the book I had wanted to have written for so long—had been nicked by some unscrupulous academic colleague! I could hardly believe it. Not, that is, because I hold out very high expectations of the academic community's integrity. I know from experience that scholars will do a fiddle quicker than most people. I've even noticed that people who specialize in ethics seem to be the worst.

No, I was incredulous because I never thought my book would prove that desirable. In my darker moments I had come to terms with the idea that my book might not prove worth paying for. I was prepared for annual royalty statements which claimed that, for some reason, I owed the publisher money. What I hadn't imagined, even in the earliest and most hopeful version of my having-written-a-book fantasy, was that the book I had written would be worth more than its price—that it would, in short, be worth committing a crime for.

I know that I'll see no royalty for that copy of the book, and that there is no guarantee that the thief will actually read my book. He may have mistaken it for some other book, or been moved by a complicated fetish for objects of the peculiar blue-green colour found on my book's cover. But I'm grateful to him anyway, and—I admit it—perversely flattered.

In fact, I now have a new fantasy. The thief of my book (I like to think) is actually a deeply twisted philosophy professor at a small radical college in Montana or Oregon. He has a small but devoted following, who have listened closely to his lectures and as a result have begun stockpiling automatic weapons and freeze-dried food. He returns to them from his trip to Boston, armed with a new book, an object of a strangely compelling blue-green colour whose message he has profoundly, tragically, misunderstood.

When these fanatics break out, quoting my book to the news media as they seize control of the means of production, I will of course have an

Of course this thought is far from crazy—and maybe far from funny—in these pre-millennial, post-Unabomber days.

237

iron-clad defence. "They never paid for that copy of the book, Ted," I'll say. "I'm even more blameless than usual."

Inside, though, I'll be doing cartwheels.

Eric Gill and the Beauty of Character

Some years ago, the British Art Center in New Haven held an exhibition of artwork called "Pocket Cathedrals: Pre-Raphaelite Book Illustration." The exhibition proved how the workaday productions of the Pre-Raphaelites—woodcuts and engravings, line drawings, tireless correction of page-proofs—show their genius most clearly. Though sometimes cloying, especially in their famously overwrought tempera paintings, the Brothers were also genuine and humble labourers of the book-as-artwork, ink-stained and wise in the ways of type and binding. The pinnacle of their book-making was a series of volumes produced by Edward Burne-Jones and William Morris at the Kelmscott Press between 1892 and 1896. Burne-Jones said of the 1896 Kelmscott edition of *The Works of Geoffrey Chaucer* that "[w]hen this book is done . . . it will be a pocket cathedral. My share in it is that of the carver of images at Amiens, and Morris's that of the Architect and Magister Lapicida."

Morris and Burne-Jones produced a number of such cathedrals in the short life of the Kelmscott Press, including versions of several Morris fairy tales. These are not to everyone's taste, for they are cluttered and slightly arch, with Morris's now-familiar floral border designs crowding in on closely fitted blocks of neo-Gothic type. Burne-Jones's woodcuts are likewise brilliant but a bit overwhelming. The typefaces pioneered by Kelmscott—Chaucer and Troy headline—are self-conscious examples of Victorian neo-Gothic revival; though suitable to their task, they are a bit precious. Likewise the Pre-Raphaelites generally, of course. But what struck me about this exhibition was what is missing from it. Looking at a Kelmscott folio page, it is impossible not to think of another great innovator of design and illustration who owed much (frequently more than he would admit) to Morris and his cohorts: Eric Gill.

Looking at these books is a bit like eating a bowlful of honey: way too much of a pretty good thing.

239

Eric Gill had the great good fortune to be born into an era of extraordinary innovation in type design, a field whose most durable contributions date back at least to the eighteenth century and sometimes, in point of origin, to the fifteenth. But the sensibility of early twentieth-century type designers was not bowed by this historical weight, and many of the typefaces now familiar to us originate in a burst of creative activity centred on London and extending roughly from 1920 to 1935. In this era Jan Tschichold, perhaps the greatest unknown type designer, designed the works published in Penguin pocket editions. Stanley Morison, of England's Monotype Corporation, redesigned *The Times* of London in 1931 and made Times Roman the most widely copied serif type in the world. (The redesign also banished the Gothic banner from the *Times* front page, bucking the common newspaper belief that Gothic type is appropriate to announce news.) Also influential was Edward Johnston, who, inspired by the Arts and Crafts movement in England and the crosscurrents of Art Nouveau, designed the "Railway Type" used for the London Underground's famous station signs and posters.

The display face used in the present book for chapter titles, article headings and these marginal notes is similarly inspired: it's called Interstate. The body of the text is in Walbaum.

These designers drew on the tradition that begins sometime between 1440 and the appearance of Gutenberg's first Bible in 1456, when the Mainz job printer perfected a method of casting individual characters and setting them together in blocks to make pages. The idea of moveable type is in retrospect almost too simple to seem momentous: ink was applied to individual forms of letters set up in word formations, then pressed against paper to create in minutes what, by hand, would take hours. The process was still laborious, however. The first perfected keyboard typesetter was demonstrated only centuries later—on July 3, 1886, when the inventor Ottmar Mergenthaler showed the editors of *The New York Tribune* how, by depressing alphabetical keys on a board, they could drop letters into forms that were then covered with molten lead. Before Mergenthaler's invention, all type had to be laboriously set by hand into lock forms, with spacing, to create column lines. Accomplished cold-type setters could sling in hundreds of letters a minute, but it was still a tiresome process. Cold type has, for the most part, gone the way of all things, although it survives in many non-commercial and personal presses. One English professor I knew in college told horrific tales of setting a whole column of cold type by hand, only to slip in fatigue and see the whole fragile thing fall to the floor and shatter into its random, atomic parts: the tenuousness of communication.

Though the technology of type has changed greatly, the essentials of type design itself are not much altered. There are more typefaces now, certainly, but it is a mark of their genius that some of the most common text faces of our era are taken from the master designers of the often quite distant past. The Roman typefaces known as Baskerville and Garamond are named for men of the 1700s, master designers of type and page, men of liberal talent and imagination. Their designs are clear, definite and elegant, copied from the style exhibited in Roman carving and Italian lettering. Bembo, source for the Venetian face first set in 1495, was even older, an Italian monk whose script was renowned throughout Europe for its clarity and definition. Bodoni, still common today, was another Renaissance monk whose script was copied and typed in the 1400s; the Roman type Jenson, first cast in 1470, was also named for another scribe of wide reputation. These designs, so serviceable still, are the great touchstones of typography.

There are few twentieth-century faces that can improve on the integrated perfection of Bembo's style or John Baskerville's type design when it comes to a useful, elegant effect. Only a few have the greatness of Garamond or Caslon. Gill, a modern figure who captures the essence of typography as the art of a Renaissance sensibility, both philosopher and craftsman, stone-cutter and calligrapher, is one of these. Strangely, he is often left out of surveys of modern typography.

This blind spot is difficult to explain. It may be owing to Gill's uncertain commitment to type design, or to his wildly eccentric behaviour. Gill designed at least five typefaces still in extensive use, including the influential sans serif face known as Gill Sans and two beautiful Roman faces, Perpetua and Joanna (the latter named for his daughter). His sculptures, frequently controversial, range from the stations of the cross found

His name was Peter Seary. Anyone who has seen a form of cold type, especially of small point size, will realize the amount of work this represents.

in Westminster Cathedral in London to war memorials in Leeds and St. Antony's College, Oxford, to the famous *Prospero and Ariel* at the BBC Broadcasting House in London. Author of the polemical *Essay on Typography*, Gill is an attractive, heroic figure, a lay monk who carved, lettered, wrote, painted, and sculpted, lived and loved, with irrepressible gusto. He was fond of an argument, given to uttering outrageous sexual information, and an adulterer of extraordinary energy and self-justification. In his frequent excoriations of modern working conditions, and the need to value all workmen equally, Gill was fond of saying that "An artist is not a special kind of man, but every man is a special kind of artist." Gill *was* a special kind of man, but by no means always a likeable one. He was, in the pertinent, non-technical sense, a complete bastard.

Gill was born in 1882 in Brighton to a family of Nonconformist missionaries and preachers and, though he was religious all his life and later professed to follow the Catholic Order of St. Dominic, the morals he learned and practised were anything but strict. His obscurantist *Autobiography* is hazy about his sexual activities, but his obsessively detailed diaries show the startling frequency with which the mature Gill conducted extra-marital affairs, seduced his own daughters, and found sexual release with his sisters, friends male and female, even—on one memorable occasion—a dog. This penchant for sexual experimentation, begun early in manhood, was continued throughout his life and it marks the great separation between the image Gill projected, of the wise and just family man, and the reality he practised, in which *droit de seigneur* and self-serving seduction played a large role.

After his conversion to Catholicism in 1913, Gill lived in a succession of quasi-communal extended families, in Sussex, Wales, and Buckinghamshire. These included relatives and friends, apprentices and associates, and various wisdom-seeking hangers-on. Gill appears to have slept with whomever he fancied in these little communities and otherwise ruled them with a combination of moral terrorism, cajolery, and sheer

Not the Abbey, which is usually a-throng with tourists, but the equally beautiful Roman Catholic Cathedral not far away.

The sexual adventures were all recorded in an elaborate code that Gill developed to keep his sexual proclivities secret.

force of will. His was a charismatic personality, and he found no difficulty in creating and maintaining a cult around it. Young craftsmen flocked to him, attracted by the monkish sparseness of communal life at Ditchling or Capel-y-Ffin and by the apparently profound principles that guided Gill's work.

The pattern of life in these settlements is well documented in the studies of Gill's life. The best of these is Fiona MacCarthy's 1989 biography, *Eric Gill*, a book that effectively dispels the glow of adulation cast on Gill's memory by his uncritical acolytes. (MacCarthy notes several times the degree to which Gill's associates, former pupils, and children seemed ready to forgive him any sin.) The Gill life was one of hard work, eating, and copulating—all carried out with the maximum of energy and minimum of fuss. Household tasks were shared by the women, wives and daughters and visitors, while the men cut stone, moulded clay, or carved in wood. The essence of the Gill settlements is captured in Iris Murdoch's novel *The Good Apprentice.* Like the character Jesse Baltram, a magisterial painter whose home is a kind of Spartan commune revolving around his whims, Gill had the ability to draw people into his orbit and, once there, have them do his will without demur.

Gill did not come to typography until late in his varied career as an architect, stone carver, engraver, draftsman, and sculptor; indeed, in 1924 he had refused the invitation of his close friend Stanley Morison to discourse on the subject in the typographical journal *The Fleuron*, saying typography was "not my country." But Gill's experience with lettering was long-standing, since the bulk of his life had been spent carving Roman letters into stone or wood. He had also done some desultory type design for signs advertising the bookshops of W. H. Smith and Douglas Cleverdon. (The latter became the basis of the Gill Sans alphabet.) By 1925 Gill had begun the drawings that were to become the Perpetua alphabet. The first book set in Perpetua was published in 1929, the same year Gill Sans was shown at a trade show by the Monotype Corporation. The book was Gill's own collection *Art-Nonsense and Other Essays*, a series of attacks on his favourite targets: careerism among artists, industrialism,

Murdoch, *The Good Apprentice* (1985): "'We follow Jesse's example,' said Bettina, 'his rule of order and industry. We have a daily routine.' 'Times of silence,' said Ilona, 'times for rest, times for reading, it's like a monastery.' 'You must let me help you,' said Edward. 'I'm afraid I haven't any skills–' 'You'll learn,' said Bettina."

spiritual deadness in the modern world. D. H. Lawrence, in a review published after his death, called the book "crude and crass" in both thought and execution—a judgment that Gill, in a letter to Lawrence's widow, later admitted to sharing.

At this time, too, Gill's designs for a display type called Golden Cockerel were complete and being used by the publishing house of that name. In 1929, Gill finished the designs of the typeface known as Solus, now little used and probably his least-known contribution to typography. The drawings for the Joanna typeface were begun in April 1930, at a time when Gill's genius was being trumpeted by Morison in his *First Principles of Typography* and the *Fleuron*. Joanna, Gill's most complete success in type design, is commonly defended as "a typographer's typeface," that is, a favourite of experts. Yet it has an immediate attractiveness for any eye. It is a pleasing combination of elegance and playfulness, of clarity and individuality. Robert Harling called it "the most individual and successful" of Gill's typefaces and noted that the letter forms "have character and beauty, discipline and gaiety"—a combination of adjectives that would have pleased Gill. "We would have to go back to the Fell typefaces," Harling continued, "to find a type so wayward in design and yet so easy on the eye."

In the same year, 1930, Gill and his future son-in-law, René Hague (who married Joanna Gill in November 1930), bought the printing equipment that would form the basis of their little company, Hague & Gill. Gill's *Essay on Typography*, printed and designed by Hague & Gill, would be the first book set and printed in Joanna.

In the midst of all this typographical activity, Gill's stone-carving and sculpting work continued, and he suffered a kind of nervous breakdown brought on, one imagines, by excessive work and stress. It is also possible that the imminent wedding of his daughter Joanna was a contributing cause; Gill always reacted badly to the thought of his daughters or lovers finding sexual joy elsewhere than with him. He was discovered one day by his daughter Petra, wandering in the courtyard of the settlement at

Capel-y-Ffin, unable to remember who or where he was. In October 1930 he was hospitalized. It was during this period of comparative rest that, unable to cease work altogether, Gill drafted the *Essay on Typography*. Gill's memory returned fully during his hospital stay, and the *Essay* was completed several months later, early in 1931. A small first edition of five hundred was printed by Hague & Gill in June 1931, and officially published by Sheed and Ward; the second, much larger edition was published in 1936. Both editions are set in Joanna.

It is understandable, if also unfortunate, that Gill's *Essay on Typography* is currently out of print. David R. Godine, the Boston purveyor of fine books, published in 1988 a fine facsimile of the 1936 second edition, printed on laid paper and bound in cloth, of which I was able to find a single copy in New Haven. This edition has not been reprinted by Godine in the years since 1988; no doubt sales were minimal. The *Essay* is not—cannot be—a popular work. It is an intellectual folly, a mixture of the profound and the absurd, frequently badly written and reeking of a slight dementia. It is very much the work of its author. But it is not, despite the breakdown immediately preceding it, the work of an unstable mind. In style and tone, even sometimes in favoured locutions, it is at one with all Gill's writings. The practical advice it contains, which is mostly sound, breaks off from the bizarre speculation and quasi-philosophical insight in which that advice is wrapped.

Consider an example. Gill advocates the use of unjustified right-hand margins, what a typesetter today would call ragged right. The reasons for this should be obvious to anyone who has been enraged by bad breaks in automatic hyphenation or the egregious spacing that sometimes results from narrow column widths. (Any edition of *The Globe and Mail* will provide examples of this, especially now that they have adopted computer typesetters. Some readers collect the most appalling sense-threatening hyphenations for later communication in nasty letters to the editor.) It has long been common knowledge among typesetters that ragged-right margins reduce the number of hyphenated words, control spacing, and therefore make for easier reading.

The marginalia in the present book are ragged right on recto pages, ragged left on verso pages.

245

For most people, and indeed most typographers, the ease-of-reading defence is sufficient here. But not so Gill. Ragged-right is instead here defended against an *encroaching industrial malaise*. Justified margins are a fetish of the perverse mechanical mind that takes pleasure only in hard corners and clean lines, even to the point of ugliness.

The arguments against the "industrial sensibility" are not as straightforward as they might seem at first glance. In our desire to embrace mass production, we are caught, Gill says, between two worlds: the world of old-fashioned hand craftsmanship, and the new world of industrial mass production. Gill says he will not choose between them, as his former associates of the Arts and Crafts persuasion did, but only insist that we do what is proper to each. Therefore mass production methods should not be used to make books that look as though they were hand-stitched or printed on hand-made paper. Offset printing, perfect binding, and acid-free paper, now the norm in quality paperback publishing, would probably have appealed to him. The lovely Godine edition of his own *Essay*

Despite being might, one imagines, have annoyed him.

a beautiful little book.

The *Essay* is thus a polemic against humbug, the hypocrisy of nostalgia for a hand-crafted age. Gill was intimately acquainted with this particular form of bad faith, having spent his early apprentice years in the Chelsea section of London, taking classes in calligraphy and design from Johnston by day and arguing the notions of Ruskin and Morris by night. Chelsea was still Morris country in the first part of the century, steeped in Arts and Crafts sensibility and the vague philosophizing of the Pre-Raphaelites. The Kelmscott Press was in full productive flight. The ideal of these middle-class revolutionaries, some of them of extraordinary

William Blake, "Preface" talent, was a back-to-the-earth alternative to the Industrial Age's "dark

to *Milton* (1804): "And did the satanic mills" indicted by Ruskin. But the passion for beautiful things,

Countenance Divine / Shine created with personal care and dedication, was in some ways a quixotic

forth upon our clouded hills? / one. No revolution resulted from the perfection of Morris's fabric

And was Jerusalem patterns; instead, as so often happens, they were absorbed by the main-

builded here / Among these stream. Mass-produced and fashionable, nostalgia becomes a property

dark Satanic mills?" of the forces it opposed.

Gill was not unique in his ability to recognize this, but he had the courage to follow his own heart to a better place. Soon after he married, he and his wife left the stultifying atmosphere of Chelsea and moved to Ditchling, in Sussex, where the first commune was formed. His ideas changed frequently, and indeed had a tendency to move in whichever direction allowed Gill to realize his immediate object of desire, but the opposition to mass-produced nostalgia stayed with him. The "two worlds" thesis of the *Essay* is only a late expression of an idea that, more than any other, grounded Gill's restive intellectualizing about himself and his craft. "Our argument here is not that industrialism has made things worse," he says in the *Essay*, "but that it has inevitably made them different; and that whereas before industrialism there was one world, now there are two. The nineteenth century attempt to combine industrialism with the Humane was necessarily doomed, and the failure is now evident."

MacCarthy, *Eric Gill* (1989): "Gill's chief battle cry was integration. He objected fervently to what he saw as the damaging divisions in society, the rupture between work and leisure, craftsmanship and industry, art and religion, flesh and spirit."

What practical consequences has this thesis for printing and typography? A clear sense of the separation between the worlds of business and taste, the industrial and the humane, demands that each profess its own standards, and not allow easy compromise to become the norm. "Letters are letters, whether made by hand or by machine," Gill says. "It is, however, desirable that modern machinery should be employed to make letters whose virtue is compatible with their mechanical manufacture, rather than exact and scholarly resuscitations of letters whose virtue is bound up with their derivation from humane craftsmanship." That is, namely, the crafts of stone-cutting and penmanship from which Roman, Italic, and Gothic type styles are all taken.

Gill is not prepared, at this stage, to dispense with these influences altogether. First he tries the path of reform. "There are two typographies, as there are two worlds," he argues. "The typography of industrialism, when it is not deliberately diabolical & designed to deceive, will be plain; and in spite of the wealth of its resources—a thousand varieties of inks, papers, presses, and mechanical processes for the reproduction of the designs of tame designers—it will be entirely free from exuberance and fancy. As we become more and more able to print finer and more elaborate & delicate types of letter it becomes more & more intellectually imperative to standardise all forms and obliterate all elaborations and fancifulness. It becomes easier and easier to print any kind of thing, but more and more imperative to print only one kind."

The model of this "one kind" is perhaps an industrial technical manual, where the strictly functional design matches the matters under discussion. It might also be found in the so-called Swiss School of type designers of the 1960s. Taking Jan Tschichold's principles of cool elegance to an extreme, these designers used only sans serif type, set in close, mathematically regimented blocks that have a peculiar, unmistakably modern coldness. On the other side, the sort of type design left to those few practitioners of humane typography is presumably like Gill's rendition of the *Essay* itself: ragged-right lines, generous leading between lines, use of fleurons, ampersands, and paragraph marks (¶) instead of breaks, and elegant page design of a sort that now looks pleasantly old-fashioned.

Gill suggests that we should find flourishes and fancy lettering nauseating. But if we do, it is typically for aesthetic reasons alone, not because the text under discussion is the product of a large press. Nor would we enjoy the total absence of fleurons and doo-dads in all our texts save those laboriously hand-produced by a small circle of craftsmen. Some developments in typographical sensibility since Gill's time have moved in precisely the opposite direction, mixing faces and point sizes, bold and italic, in an exuberant manner Gill would have considered disgusting. One of the most recent geniuses of typography, Neville Brody, who has designed pages and type for the British magazines *the Face*, *i-D*, and *Arena*, knows no bounds in the mix-and-match approach to setting up type on the page. So popular has this style become that Brody has often expressed his annoyance that his rule of stylishly broken rules is copied without credit almost daily.

On the whole, this trend has lately reversed itself: many magazines, from

Even in the more sedate world of book production, the Gill norm is hard to maintain. Use of the paragraph mark is common in many advertising layouts, effective in, say, the opening paragraphs of a magazine feature, set larger than the rest of the text, though it rapidly becomes tiresome in an extended piece of prose like Gill's *Essay*. So do the ampersands and space-saving abbreviations such as "tho'." Gill adopts them to prevent bad hyphenation breaks, only to go ahead, perversely, and use hyphens anyway. His refusal to use Italic type for emphasis, adopting instead the German convention of s p a c i n g the emphasized word, is equally perverse. Gill is on surer ground when talking about the letters themselves, where he speaks out against exaggeration and in favour of legibility, neatness, and Roman elegance. He decries "the unnecessary and therefore unreasonable mixing of different sorts of letters on the same page or in the same book"—a standard, if rather narrow, rule of design, and one often broken with good results, as Brody shows.

So far Gill's views are sound enough, though perhaps a bit conservative. But in a characteristic *volte face*, he completely undercuts himself. In the final section of the *Essay*, "But Why Lettering?", he argues for the elimination of type altogether. Here we find Gill at his most outrageous, the mind unfettered by the bounds of logic, the man who had railed against powdered custard, trousers, and other dubious symbols of the industrial malaise. "It is simply stupid to make pretence any longer that our letters are a reasonable means for rendering our speech in writing or printing," he says. We should instead employ a more rational system of "phonographs"—a pictorial shorthand. We begin by educating all the current students in phonography, so that a generation hence the revolution will be effected. "Lettering has had its day," Gill concludes grandiloquently. "Spelling, philology, and all such pedantries have no place in our world. The only way to reform modern lettering is to abolish it."

This is a strange statement coming from one the greater part of whose livelihood has come from cutting, drawing, or designing letters. But Gill was nothing if not a bridge-burner. The diatribe against lettering is

Saturday Night to *Sports Illustrated*, have recently adopted conservative, almost classical, type designs.

What, I wonder, would he have made of Tang, the astronaut-approved powdered orange juice that I drank for most of my childhood?

typical of his penchant for the extreme solution. He had an enduring love of invented alphabets, and sketched the so-called Utopian alphabet (a very "rational" series of boxes and lines) after reading and loving Thomas More's *Utopia*. Indeed, Gill was a modern utopian, his various "cells of good living" a succession of failed attempts to realize the perfect spiritual community in the midst of a debased industrial and artistic world. That Gill's own personality and tendency to fad-as-law authoritarianism contributed to the failure of these communities seems not to have occurred to him.

I am more inclined to Gill in his more practical and well-judged moods, the Gill who continued to carve gravestones for money throughout his life, who designed functional and beautiful stamps, pound notes, and coins, and the Gill who loved neatly tied parcels and simple food. This Gill is more attractive than the polemicist who became a figure of fun, a kind of court jester with habitual enthusiasms and rages, his vocal penis obsession a standard joke in artistic circles of the 1930s. It is this more sober Gill who says, in the same section of his *Essay*, "I say a good piece of lettering is as beautiful a thing to see as any sculpted or painted picture." At his very best Gill, like all great typographers, proves this beyond any argument.

The beauty of character is something frequently obscured. It requires an education.

My own love of type began more than a decade ago when I edited the University of Toronto's undergraduate newspaper, *The Varsity*. For those of us on the staff—aspiring journalists and novelists, people avoiding classwork, various hangers-on—this was our first intimate association with the mechanical details of setting type, the bringing of thought to the page. My *Varsity* colleagues fell into two groups in their passionate responses to the process we all called, with suitable awe, "Production." They either hated it or loved it. Since Production happened on Sunday, Tuesday, and Thursday nights, frequently extending into bleary all-night sessions fuelled by a student rocket fuel of Doritos, Gummi Bears, Coke, and gin, enthusiasts were few. From my point of view, fretting about getting our little pile of pasted-up flats to the printer before dawn, Production people were the equivalent of ace relief pitchers. I had strong starters, hot reporters and ace film reviewers, witty editorialists and brilliant cartoonists; but without a good closer I was dead in the water, dead in the middle of the night.

In the midst of these frenetic thrice-weekly all-night production sessions, a few of us conceived a genuine regard for the wonders of typography. The aesthetic pleasure one takes in a well-designed page, a carefully chosen typeface, the dozen crucial decisions that go into making a text *work* as type, is never trivial. After a couple of years spent choosing column lengths, leading, typefaces, and point sizes, I am now unable to look at a block of type without producing a mental typesetter's instruction to match it. Yet text design, like many features of the everyday, effaces itself when it succeeds most. We may pass over thousands of words of type a day, from this morning's *Globe* to tonight's bedside reading, without once feeling the presence of the page designer or typographer. For most people, good typography, in common with many things they love and depend on, is noticeable only by its absence.

At *The Varsity*, a small-budget newspaper not known for its up-to-the-minute machinery, we laboured over ugly box-shaped phototypesetters known as CompWriter IV's. These contraptions worked by spinning a sheet of black plastic on which characters were etched. By the manipulation of various lenses and a small light source, characters of the right point size appeared on a piece of photographic paper. Each key pressed on the board shot a flash of light through a magnified clear-on-black character, slowly creating lines of type and, eventually, columns. The paper was removed from the whirring monster and taken to another, much fouler machine where the paper was quickly developed by a wash of nasty chemicals that frequently ended up in our mouths or eyes. Developed galleys were dried, waxed, and cut into columns, ready to lay down on cardboard sheets the size of tabloid pages.

Some names to honour here: Rebecca Cunningham, Joel Dubin, David Charles Johnson, Paula Kulig, Alison Maclean, Anne Louise Mahoney, Barry McCartan, Karen Shook, Aaron Shuster, Peter Simpson.

We all hated the capricious, overworked Comp IV's, with their penchant for crisis-hour breakdowns and unforgiving natures. They were old, clapped-out, and mean. The alignments were often faulty, making our columns a mess of jumping letters. The developing chemicals stank and made us sick. Bottoms of crucial articles were often a hazy black of totally exposed paper. And only one line of a text appeared on the Comp IV's primitive cursor, so the automatic return routinely sent a dozen mistyped lines per article into the almost irretrievable realm of the typo. Corrections had to be typed again, getting all the particulars (line length, typeface, point size) exactly right, and then cut into the pasted-up column with exacto knives.

> **These tales** of typo-woe are probably hard to believe now; but we are all prisoners of our times, and their dominant modes of production.

I still shiver with the memory of those little bits of sticky-backed photo paper sticking to my hands and arms, limbs already scored with a thousand tiny exacto wounds. I once almost lost a fingertip during a seminar on cut-and-paste layout techniques. Rule One: don't let your fingers hang over the edge of the ruler. Current technology is kinder. Nowadays a little campus journal can produce all their type on a couple of Macintosh computers and a laser printer. No paragraphs of errant news stuck to a forearm, presumed lost. No fingers sliced in 4-a.m. weariness. Yet something has surely been lost in these most recent advances. If nothing else, they take us farther away from the simple truths of setting type and printing. Who among the new breed of computer jockeys, happily selecting "fonts" on their Macs, knows why this is a typographical solecism? How many know the basic relationship among points, picas, and inches?

> **A font** (or receptacle) is a set of type in the same face and size; a face is the entirety of, say, Caslon or Garamond or Bembo type, in all its fonts.

The newspaper pages my colleagues and I produced at *The Varsity* during those long nights were not, perhaps, models of typographical art. We would not have compared them with sculpture or paintings, anyway, though occasionally—with the right amount of white space and enough time to consider—we produced pleasing results. None of us, as far as I am aware, had ever heard of Eric Gill. No doubt we committed one typographical error after another in our ignorance. Yet, struggling over those pages, we closed that great modern gap Gill discerned between the writer of prose and the compositor of type, the gap between artist and worker. For Gill, it was a sign of modern degeneracy that writers and even designers no longer knew how to set type, to see the process of written communication through to its required conclusion. The *Varsity* production room was a workshop where those of us who lasted through the night unwittingly apprenticed to the great gods of type.

There was perhaps not enough sex for Gill's taste—although I cannot be absolutely sure about that; people were often unaccountably absent— but he would, I suspect, have found the spirit of our efforts congenial. Without sentimentality or mawkishness, we perceived the beauty a single character can possess, the undeniable pleasure that comes from a word well formed and clearly presented, the complicated aesthetics of the page.

They may simply have been hiding.

We were not a special kind of people. Like Gill, we were just people with a special kind of love.

Grand Theory Makes a Comeback

To many of us, the figure of the grand systematizing intellectual is forever represented by the character Causabon in George Eliot's *Middlemarch*, that dry and futile stick of a man who has laboured endlessly on a historical *magnum opus* destined never to be completed. We can't help feeling that his very devotion to this outsized task, his lifelong scholarly monomania, is somehow proof that he is unworthy of Dorothea Brooke's love. She belongs with Will Ladislaw, not just because he's young and good-looking but also because he's brief and to the point. *He gets the job done.*

The scholarly Big Book has gone even more out of fashion since Eliot's time. Scholars write big books still, to be sure, and some of them even get read; and sweeping generalizations are easy to come by on the shelves of university bookstores. But few today would dare attempt what Hegel, for example, did when he wrote *The Phenomenology of Spirit*, namely, to encompass all of reality between two confident covers. Nor do intellectual historians blithely help themselves to grand narratives of Progress or Change as they did in Robertson's or Gibbon's day. Indeed, the very idea of the grand narrative is inherently suspect today, and you will find many long books telling you why.

An "incredulity toward meta-narratives" is what characterizes the post-modern condition, according to Lyotard, just the most celebrated of the recent thinkers who have made careers of debunking encyclopedic aspirations. The notion of an encyclopedia in its primary etymological sense, they argue—as of a university itself—is impossible or simply dangerous. Knowledge is never anything but local, contingent, variable, and shot through with power relations. To pretend otherwise—to dress up a particular as a universal—is just the self-serving bleat, or the naked imperialism, of the retrograde class.

254

But post-modernity is less a radical break with modernity than it is an articulation of the specifically self-reflective aspects of it. One of the burdens of modernity is that speculation about its very possibility is often more fascinating than any straightforward pursuit of knowledge, especially for certain adroit thinkers: as parlour games go, the one called High Theory is more fun than most. True, there lurks an imminent logical self-defeat in the post-modern position, familiar from debates about relativism: it is, paradoxically, a grand theory that grand theories are impossible. And if power relations are really the name of the game, writing jargon-riddled books is hardly the way to turn them in your direction.

See "Playing in the Digital Garden" (Section I).

Still, these wrangles have occupied the attention of many a philosopher and critic in the past few decades. And for the rest, there's the popular option of ever more precise and specialized technical debate, most of it a far cry from what mere mortals would recognize as wisdom. Both of these camps, though bitter enemies, seem agreed on one point: grand theory is no longer the thing. If you want Big Books these days you must look not to philosophy or history but to modern (male) American fiction: Thomas Pynchon, Don DeLillo, William Gass, David Foster Wallace.

Which is one reason Randall Collins's new book, *The Sociology of Philosophies: A Global Theory of Intellectual Change* (Harvard, 1998), is such a welcome surprise. At almost eleven hundred pages it qualifies as a big book in anybody's eyes; but it's also a Big Book in the unapologetic global scope of its argument, and in the quarter-century span of its research. Collins, a professor of sociology at the University of Pennsylvania and the author of four previous books, has surveyed the entire history of philosophizing—East and West, ancient and modern—and constructed a sociological theory to explain what we've all been up to these last three thousand years or so.

Mostly arguing and jockeying for position, it turns out.

Collins's findings, amply supported, can be summarized briefly enough. Intellectual innovation is never the product of lone geniuses but instead results from networks of philosophers. Thinkers engage in what sociologists call "interaction ritual chains," which pass influence, and ideas, from one person to another. Writing—manuscript, print, or e-mail—is hugely important to these thinkers, but face-to-face meetings are even more so. That is where they get charges of emotional energy (EE) and new stores of cultural capital (CC), which they will deploy in further creative work.

That justifies academic conferences, I suppose, and perhaps explains why people still walk out if the featured speaker's paper can be read only by someone else because the celebrity is stuck at the airport. But it's only the rosy part of the picture. Collins's sociology is red in mental tooth and claw. Thinkers are constantly out to destroy one another, and philosophers in particular are forever announcing the impossibility of other positions, or even the end of their own discipline. This will-to-kill is the font of all creativity, the well from which new ideas spring, usually as answers to nonexistent questions. "It is typical," Collins says, "for intellectuals to create problems at the very moment they solve them."

There is also a drastically limited amount of space for creative success. The "law of small numbers," culled from the historical evidence, suggests no fewer than three and no more than six major philosophical figures or schools can be on the scene at a given moment. That leaves everyone else in the position of secondary figures (including many you or I would consider major), minor figures (still pretty good), or incidental (the rest). And that's just the people who publish. The vast majority of philosophers, especially in this age of the professional academic, don't even show up on the radar screen.

The law of small numbers means that, when it comes to long odds, making it as a world-historical philosopher puts winning the lottery or entering the NBA in the shade. And unfortunately sheer brain power has less to do with success than we might wish. Early connections to major figures are indispensable, if history is any guide, and pure willpower is probably more important than *nous* in intellectual networks where, as Collins says of one, "the rivalries and jealousies both over preeminence

Which fails to explain why so many scholars have such appalling social skills; or perhaps, perversely, succeeds in doing so—if their meetings are all about accumulations of cultural capital.

Three because there can always be Pro, Con, and Middle Way in any intellectual dispute; six because more than that will break the field entropically into separate groupings.

and over closeness to the favorite resemble the popularity contests of an adolescent social club."

No kidding.

Because clustering is so important for creative disagreement, luck plays a huge role in this. Major creative advances tend to come only when worthy opponents find each other. Success breeds success; but, by the same token, failure breeds failure. Gifted individuals may find the available spaces taken when they try to make a mark, or discover that an early missed opportunity (not getting into Harvard, having to work with a less famous supervisor) curbs all later chances. "Much of the pathos of intellectual life," says Collins, "is in the timing of when one advances one's arguments." The bulk of aspirants to intellectual creativity simply drop from view.

Also, it may be hard to swallow, but contemporary fame correlates strongly with lasting influence. The isolated brilliant scholar, labouring in obscurity only to be vindicated by the ages, is a myth that incidental thinkers use to keep themselves warm at night; it has almost no historical sanction. Chances are, if you aren't famous in your own lifetime—famous in the world at large, that is, not just well thought of in the profession—you just won't make it on the slaughter-bench of history.

It was recently noted that the only twentieth-century philosophers to receive full-page obituaries in *The Times* of London were Bertrand Russell and Iris Murdoch, both widely known for their extra-academic work.

Collins shows a certain unseemly relish in laying down these gloomy conclusions, carefully retailing the long histories of patricide and fratricide, and sketching insane charts of influence and disagreement. (They look like fractal diagrams or the doodles of a paranoid schizophrenic.) "It is," he concludes happily, "the fate of almost all intellectuals to be forgotten, most of us sooner rather than later."

These reflections on the nature of ideas have their own problems, though. There is a constant threat of vertigo in Collins's work, this grand theory of grand theories. He is no relativist, but you can't get over a sense of precariousness, an awareness that even his qualified form of objectivity must, sooner or later, slip back into the mire of intellectual conflict he is at pains to describe. You begin to wonder how Collins can hold himself above the fray, especially if, like me, you indulge the uncharitable suspicion that this thick volume is part of his own attempt to be a shaker. No amount of astringent humour and apparent cheerfulness about the brute, insensate processes of intellectual conflict quite lays these self-cancelling thoughts to rest.

Collins also says that we shouldn't be depressed by his findings. "Our significance as puny human nodes in this long-term network is given not by ourselves," he says, "but by the resonances that make some names into emblems for what has happened at memorable turning points in the flow." By what Hegel called "the cunning of reason," in other words, the good ideas always rise up even if the body count is huge. We're all cogs in the machine.

That's something, maybe a lot. But I for one found this book by turns funny and horrible. Reading it put me in mind of a scene in a Michael Innes thriller in which the protagonist suddenly finds himself in a vast underground library in Oxford, final resting place for thousands upon thousands of forgotten books. He is overcome by the voluminous futility of scholarly ambition: all those words, all those ideas, all that dust. In other words, none of it matters, so you might as well give up.

Near the beginning, Collins mentions Jorge Luis Borges's famous image of the universe as a vast library to which we lack the proper catalogue. He might have done better to heed Borges's tart remarks about the nature of encyclopedic undertakings. They bend into and through one another, and reflect back on the world in an image-multiplying way. For Borges, encyclopedias are unstable, world-eating machines, labyrinthine halls of mirrors, and the history of metaphysics is itself no more than a gantlet of rival esoteric vocabularies. The proper response to this situation is not to sociologize knowledge, as if we could thereby run an end-around on the problem; it is, rather, to cultivate the wondrous, literate skepticism of that gifted genius of language. In other words, none of it matters, so you might as well have a good time.

Of course not many of us are in Borges's league. When he met William Gass for the first time, Borges apparently asked him for the derivation of

---

I could not resist forcing this little piece of self-reference on Collins; nobody, no matter how dispassionate or elevated in tone, can finally escape the gravitational field of scholarly ambition.

Borges likes to quote *The Celestial Emporium of Benevolent Recognitions*: "It is written that the animals are divided into (a) those that belong to the Emperor, (b) embalmed ones, (c) those that are trained, (d) suckling pigs, (e) mermaids, (f) fabulous ones, (g) stray dogs, (h) those that are included in this

his surname. Informed it was from the German word for "alley," Borges said, "Ah. You are just an alley, whereas I am a city." When Gass in turn told me this story I thought: What does that make the rest of us—rats?

Yes, a man's got to know his limitations. I closed page 1098 of Collins's tome, poured myself a gin and tonic, and articulated a secret hope: I'll never be secondary, but please God, give me a crack at being minor.

classification, (i) those that tremble as if they were mad, (j) innumerable ones, (k) those drawn with a very fine camel's hair brush, (l) others, (m) those that have just broken a flower vase, (n) those that resemble flies from a distance."

Two Endings

Looking at Pictures

These last two articles, written half a decade apart, are linked by something of which I was not completely conscious until they were placed side by side: the compelling influence of family pictures. I wonder if other people have the same unsettling experience of looking into the youthful faces of their parents, captured on film, and seeing there something both profoundly moving and somehow disturbing—a feeling at once beautiful and sad. I think they do. I think they must.

The first essay is my attempt, not altogether successful, to wrestle some big questions down to a human level. Much more needs to be said here, but the argument about intimacy strike me as true, and worth repeating as we find ourselves in a world increasingly murderous of intimate connection. I also think the political implications of this argument are not yet fully appreciated, especially by various neo-conservatives, who seem to think everything is working out for the best. I had originally planned to run the second piece (which was written first) without any marginal notes. But I could not resist, in this particular case, giving someone else the last word.

The Future of Intimacy

There is a quality of early-morning light in Vancouver that you don't find in the rest of the country, a Turneresque wash of greys and blues that suffuses English Bay with romantic obscurity and makes the nearby Coastal Range appear like a pod of humpback whales moving out to sea with infinitesimal slowness. It feels like the birthplace of the world—except that between me and that view lie ten blocks of half-completed buildings, shambolic piles of concrete rubble, and the lurking silhouettes of high-load cranes.

I was up this early only because I was still on Eastern Time; thus does westward airline travel create adventitious virtue.

The joggers and rollerbladers, inevitable and ubiquitous here even at 6 a.m., pick their way nimbly through all this ambiguous evidence of Pacific Rim optimism. If there is a downturn in the local economy, one caused (say the right-wing critics) by the "disastrous" tax-and-spend proclivities of the current provincial government—twenty thousand jobs lost in January alone, an eleven percent decline in house prices, a forty percent drop in volume—you wouldn't know it from the many building sites and restaurant patios that will be packed with free-spending patrons in just a few hours. Vancouver really is the every-city of television's "The X-Files," a generic urban location of hustle and intrigue, and it manages to tell a visitor, despite the reservations of conservatives and without saying anything obvious, that it represents the Future. *Pace* the dark-minded Chris Carter, it is a future confident, multi-racial, physically fit, comfortable with technology, and happily, even ecstatically, capitalistic.

"The X-Files" has since decamped to Los Angeles, mostly so star David Duchovny could be closer to his wife, Tea Leoni.

Is it also likely? The economic doomsayers would have you think otherwise, all this pan-Asian and Pacific revivalism so much empty currency-driven puffery. And perhaps they are right: there is quite enough evidence already on the table in other parts of the world—crumbling infrastructures, riots for food, gross disparities in wealth—to suggest that the reality of globalization is not the liberalizing dream of modern economics, with all of us rising to full levels of rational self-fulfilment via fruitful transactions, but instead a nightmare of emergent class conflict, tribal hatred, and technological imperialism.

In Neal Stephenson's 1996 novel *Snow Crash*, a cult phenomenon of cyberpunk action and inventively dystopian speculation, the picture is likewise far from rosy. The book, set in a post-national California of gated communities (or "Burbclaves"), private freeways, and quasi-governmental companies known as franchulates—franchise consulates of global corporations like Mr. Lee's Greater Hong Kong, New South Africa, and the pizza-delivery service doubling as the Mafia, which provide benefits and protection to dues-paying citizens—has become an underground bestseller, one of those defining documents of the culture that never quite show up on the radar screens of network television or mainstream newspapers.

This book should be required reading for everyone, regardless of age or political conviction.

The central action concerns the efforts of L. Bob Rife, a global media magnate, to resurrect an ancient religion (which is also an ancient computer virus) to re-program the brains of the world's population. His point of entry is the Raft, a floating country of refugees, displaced persons, and pirates that moves through the Pacific Ocean on seasonal currents and is moving towards the vulnerable west coast of North America, whose distracted, drug-addled, materialistic, and self-interested inhabitants are powerless to resist. The U.S. federal government has been reduced to a bureaucratic non-entity, Fedland, with the president a glad-handing idiot who can't get anyone to take him seriously.

Now, it might seem capricious to take a science-fiction novel seriously in our efforts to imagine the actual future we face, but as the American philosopher Richard Rorty noted recently with a careful assessment of *Snow Crash* in his book *Achieving Our Country*, visions of the future can have an unusually powerful bearing on the present. An old-fashioned New Deal leftist disturbed by the "spectatorial" tendencies of today's cultural (especially academic) left, Rorty chided the "pessimism" of Stephenson's vision, and lamented its tendency to induce a form of political ennui,

Rorty, *Achieving Our Country* (1998): "*Snow Crash* capitalizes on the widespread belief that giant corporations, and a shadowy behind-the-scenes government acting as an agent for the corporations, now make all the important decisions." Well, don't they?

a sense of impotence because "it's all out of our control," in those who might otherwise convert their detailed awareness of current trends into reformist action rather than spectatorial cynicism. How we imagine the future conditions, in larger part than we know, what kind of future we will actually create.

So what can we say about the future? Any simple dichotomy of optimism and pessimism is too crude to capture the nuances of the issue. Advocates of the bare fork would have us believe that the question of life a hundred years hence is one of either utopia or dystopia, wondrous emancipation or dank enslavement—a form of bipolar thinking that is particularly prevalent at cultural limit-times like our much-discussed, entirely arbitrary, and yet immensely powerful millennium. Both options sport hidden dangers.

The trouble with utopian visions is that they hide the realities of what an economist colleague of mine likes to call "the messy transition." Think, for example, of the blithe elimination of poverty and hunger in Gene Roddenberry's various influential "Star Trek" series. They can also become a platform for intolerant, occasionally violent, social change: witness the dominant political movements of our bloody century. Not least, utopias run the risk of making any actual stepwise reform look paltry, and therefore somehow contemptible, by comparison to an ideal—a contempt that is one source of the cultural pessimism identified by Rorty. It is in this sense that, as the old saying goes, the perfect is the enemy of the good.

Dystopian visions are likewise often an invitation to gloomy inaction, rather than a needed wake-up call. They stunt feelings of hope that might translate into political action. They feed on our fears and anxieties, working them up into fully formed bad dreams of a dark future. They make us feel powerless or overwhelmed, so that instead of acting we quiver in a depressed stasis.

There is good evidence that this cultural pessimism is widespread throughout history, that our current bouts of it are nothing new; but there is also something that must be acknowledged as unique to our

times. In his book *Amusing Ourselves to Death*, the media critic Neil Postman discusses what he calls the problem of "the information-action
ratio." That is, the structure of human responsiveness that determines
how much, and what sort of, information is usefully assimilable by
humans. If someone says to me, "Give me some water," that is a chunk of
data that I can process and, assuming I have some water to give, act upon:
I give the needy person some water. The situation created by our current
mass-information media, by contrast, is that the information side of the
equation is huge, indeed virtually limitless.

This makes not for more action, for no amount of action could process
all that information, but for the kind of overpowering ennui—this
strangely stifling *boredom*—that seems to steal upon us when we think
of how many impossible demands for action the nightly news makes
upon us. It is essential that we bring this situation, and indeed all issues
tangled in the ball of thread we call Imagining the Future—technology,
globalization, environmental changes—down to a level where we can
think about them productively. Consider a small example of how we
might do this.

Anyone who knows me personally is by now aware that my currently
favourite techno-toy, a birthday gift from my wife, is a cordless headset
phone. This little machine has changed my life more than almost any
other piece of technology I use, in large part because it facilitates
the interplay of work and leisure. Using the headset, I approach, or
anyway glimpse, a future in which we all achieve, on demand, what
computer programmers like to call seamless ubiquity: the ability to
access a communications or computation system from any point in a
given environment.

Which means that I am now able to carry on phone conversations not
only from every corner of my apartment, but also can do so with my
hands free, so that I can, say, talk to a friend while signing for a parcel
delivery or do a radio interview while chopping vegetables for a tomato
sauce. Sometimes, in moments of self-indulgent adolescent vanity, I even
imagine I look pretty cool with the headset on. This is surely part of its

I **take** up these
arguments at greater length
in *Better Living* (1998),
chapters 4 and 7.

Boredom again.
Clearly, I'm obsessed.

265

A photographer from *Maclean's* magazine tried to convince me to pose for a photo wearing my headset. No no, I said; I look *geeky*. A photographer from *Time* magazine once tried to get me to jump off a roof.

appeal, at least for men of my generation, raised as we were on Gerry Anderson's Supermarionettes, Captain Scarlet and the Thunderbirds, and with more recent echoes in John Cusack's well-equipped professional killer in *Grosse Point Blank* or Lou Diamond Phillips's in *The Big Hit*— not to mention Val Kilmer as The Saint or Pierce Brosnan as James Bond, Madonna or Bobby Brown on stage during a concert tour. Of course it's entirely possible that I just look geeky, not so much savvy gadget king as stock-control boy at the Gap or greeter at TGIFridays.

The headset is only a small piece of technology, nothing major, but it hints at the real issues in thinking about the future. We have spent a lot of time lately either decrying or celebrating technology, with the hype-masters of *Wired* magazine squaring off against various mild Unabomber-wannabes, but most of us, in thoughtful moments, realize that technology is entirely devoid of interest unless and until it makes some aspect of daily life easier or more interesting—or if it, in rare cases, increases the degree of justice in our world. The base-level facts of existence—that we must rise and face each day, and that at some point this circadian cycle will cease for each one of us—will not be altered by the passage of a century, or a millennium. Whatever changes, these will remain the same. And they cast any technological, economic, and social changes in their only worthwhile light. What happens to the people around the globe, what happens in their daily lives of seeking security, love, and happiness, as we pass into the new era of the twenty-first century?

What particularly fascinates me, in this attempt to bring the Future down to a human scale, is the concept of intimacy, the phenomenon of closeness, one person to another. How is it that we are able to form and maintain relationships, to carry on conversations, that build up a web of interpersonal connections so vast and complicated they can only be captured by the nearly but not quite banal phrase "human civilization"? This daily miracle, which we rarely pause to acknowledge, let alone celebrate, is, I think, the key to thinking about any imaginable future.

It is unlikely that the next hundred years will overcome one of the key features of human life, namely, that consciousness is irreducibly inward,

266

forcing us to find our connections to others by other, outward means. Some people, including some friends of mine, think so—the writer and poet Christopher Dewdney, say, who has lately taken to spreading the gospel according to Transhumanism, in which we upload our consciousness into technology like the Internet. But I rather doubt this. Carbon-based ambulatory organisms like us are, so far, the only ones who evince consciousness, and while that may change in time, I do not think it likely that any form of consciousness will overcome the limits of being trapped inside a physical host, whether carbon- or silicon-based. It is far-fetched to think we will become superhuman clairvoyants like the child chess prodigy Gibson (after the cyberpunk guru and Vancouver resident William Gibson, surely) in the 1998 season finale of "The X-Files."

Dewdney, *Last Flesh: Life in the Transhuman Era* (1998).

Which means that *intimacy* will continue to play its joyful, vexing, complex role in our lives, and that the subtle dialectic of private and public—of the internal monologue of solitude and silence, broken into speech or writing in the troubled land of communication, maybe even communion—will continue to dominate our institutions, occupations, entertainments, and most of all, our sense of ourselves. Our machines will always change, often in ways that technological Whigs will choose to call Progress, but beneath the faster and better wiring our longing for connection will remain the same.

I have been away from home a lot lately, travelling from city to city across this country and south of the border. Last Sunday I had breakfast with my wife in Boston, lunch with a friend in Toronto, and dinner with a colleague in Ottawa. I started writing this essay in Montreal, worked on it in Vancouver, Edmonton, and Calgary, fiddled with the first few paragraphs in Winnipeg, fleshed out some other parts in upstate New York, and then finished it in Toronto. Covering all those miles, trundling in and out of departure lounges, and putting in hours in rental cars, gives you an appreciation for the vastness and variety of Canada: The way cool kids are cool differently in Quebec than on the West Coast. The way provincial politics dominates Edmonton in a way it doesn't in Winnipeg. The way Vancouver has, like Paris, apparently cornered the regional market on beautiful people. The way the smog and the driving habits get worse every year in Toronto.

It also forces an awareness of technology's taken-for-granted gifts, the astonishing privilege most of us in this country enjoy in a world where three-quarters of those now living will die without making a telephone call, let alone fly in a commercial airliner. Many of us now board trans-continental planes with all the excitement of commuters entering a sub-way car, and I boot up my laptop absently in a hotel restaurant, the way I might open a door. Yet these are really the small miracles of modern life, incredible privileges, ones within the grasp of less than a fifth of the planet's inhabitants. And there are many more such mundane miracles on the way, from something as trivial as my headset phone to things that will alter the details of daily life in ways we can hardly guess at.

Because we are ever in danger of forgetting, we must ask: what matters to me, or anyone else, in all this? Well, here is my answer. That I could have dinner with my parents and brothers in Vancouver, the first time in four years we have all been together, my mother passing around old snapshots of her and my father when they were first together—wonderful black-and-white portraits, my father with his lanky good looks and Harry Connick haircut, my mother sprightly at nineteen, the sweet little messages she wrote to him on the back of each photo. That I can check my e-mail in Calgary and read a welcome message from a friend in England that he has a new son. That I can, finally, come home again and find the restful, familiar comfort of my little apartment, the reassuring and human routine of doing the laundry, watering the plants, shopping for food, and cooking a meal for myself.

We all realize, I think, that as humans we find much of our deepest happiness in intimacy, in the sharing of ourselves with each other. This communion is the texture of life, the feeling of cross-hatching beneath our fingers as we run them over the passage of time. There is a mystery here, a deeply human thing that must be acknowledged every now and then before we can move on into this imaginary place we call the Future, a future that is, in the nature of things, coming whether we like it or not. The critic Walter Benjamin once said that we don't move into the future facing forwards so much as we back into it, gazing out over the past. It might be even more accurate to say that we back into it while gazing fixedly down at our feet.

The word "intimate" contains an illuminating contradiction that is worth dwelling on before we take our next backward step. As an adjective, "intimate" means inward or personal: the intimate details of your life that only you can know. It comes from the Latin *intimus*, which means "inmost." There is no farther inward we can go, even in ourselves. In this sense, "intimate" captures the strange opacity of individual consciousness that I mentioned before, that irreducible first-personal character of identity, which is, at some level, impenetrable by anyone outside. (It may often be impenetrable by ourselves too, but that is another story.)

To be intimate in this sense, then, is to be inward: an intimate detail, an intimate thought. But it is also, more commonly, to describe the act of sharing that inwardness with another: an intimate conversation, an intimate friendship. And this hints at the ambiguity in the word, and the concept, intimate. Considered as a verb now, "intimate" also means to declare, to communicate, to send out a message. In English we change the pronunciation to distinguish the two uses of the word, and the verb form derives more proximately from the Latin verb *intimare*, to announce, but the deep connection is clear. To intimate is to share a message, though not always an inward one; to be intimate is to be inward, though not always in a way that can be shared.

This play of closeness and distance, of inside and outside, is at the centre of human life. Trapped, of necessity, inside our own minds, but at the same time recognizing what we take to be other creatures also so trapped, we try, with the crude but wonderful tools of language and touch and expression, to bridge the unbridgeable gap between one person and another. We intimate things and hope, thereby, to become intimate. We

Lewis Carroll, *Through the Looking-Glass* (1871): "'It is a poor sort of memory that only works backwards,' the Queen remarked."

I am often mocked by my students for my etymological tics. But compare J.L. Austin, "A Plea for Excuses" (1956): "Going back into the history of a word, very often into Latin, we come back pretty commonly to pictures or *models* of how things happen or are done."

Austin, "Other Minds" (1946): "It seems that believing in other persons, in authority and testimony, is an essential part of the act of communication, an act which we all constantly perform.... But there is no 'justification' for doing [this] as such."

try to join our private lives together in the public space that lies between us, where meaning resides. It doesn't always work. Sometimes, perhaps often, our words are misconstrued, our intentions twisted, our messages changed in the telling like the comical distortions of the telephone game. But we go on trying because otherwise we are nothing, our stories fall untold and therefore, somehow, unlived.

We also hear intimations from elsewhere. Intimations of immortality, as Wordsworth said, where life and experience hint at the transcendent possibilities buried in our limited selves. The way we can go beyond ourselves, can feel a sense of purpose or belonging that is not illusory because we sense our connection to a scheme of things. It may be a structure of human order, of conversation and narrative itself, rather than anything supernatural; that does not make the feeling of connection any less real. We may also hear intimations of mortality, those whispers of the shade that throw life suddenly into high relief and, if we are listening closely enough, may clarify the possibilities of happiness in this life.

Though there is nothing in the word that demands it, intimations seem almost always to be whispered. They contain hints and suggestions rather than asssertions or policy statements. Which is why they demand a special kind of attention, a disciplined waiting that is both demanding and inherently communal. The philosopher Michael Oakeshott once defined political action as "the pursuit of an intimation." He meant that the substance of politics was a matter not of competing utopian visions or battling grand schemes, but of attending to suggestions for action already contained within the human conversation of which we are a part: claims about respect that need to be lived up to, ideas of equality and justice that must be acted upon, notions of happiness that lie nascent, pre-reflective, in the ore of human life.

Not that I agree with much else in that arch-conservative's political philosophy.

Finding our way into the Future is therefore not a matter of deciding which big picture is most likely. It is not, perhaps, a matter of big pictures at all. Like Socrates' basic question—"What is the life worth living?"—the question of the future is one that starts, that must start, with a thousand smaller ones. What are you going to do today? Tomorrow?

Next month? The future, like life itself, is constructed of the infinite number of present moments passing through our hands. With each one we have an opportunity to pursue an intimation, to make our inwardness responsive to the needs of others like us—and to the field of natural conditions, animate and otherwise, that feed and support us in our pursuit of meaning.

We need ideals to guide us in that responsiveness: justice, primarily, and the respect for other entities on which it is ultimately based. We can no longer, in this world, restrict our pursuit of these connections to other members of our race, our nationality, even our species. We cannot allow the triumph of private life and private goods that has been wrought in **See** "The Mirror Stage" (Section II). these past three centuries of modernity to atrophy the public life and public good that alone makes a society, or a civilization, worthwhile. We therefore have to countenance the possibility that some of the private luxuries we have enjoyed will no longer be tolerable as time goes on, too rapacious of resources, too disproportionate in their distribution, for us to indulge our taste for them any further. Our intimate lives may change in ways we do not always like because we can no longer ignore the voices in our ears—and in our hearts—that intimate we must share even more.

The problem is that if we let the question spin off into trying to imagine the Future as such, a unitary conception of the good life that will for many prove tyrannical, the result can only be an overwhelming set of demands that will, paradoxically, have the effect of deadening our responsiveness, lessening our concern. People defect from responsibility then, hiding in gated communities and surrounding their property with private police forces. This is what Christopher Lasch called "the revolt of the elites," where taxpayers begin to see themselves more as clients than as citizens, able to take their purchasing power for social services elsewhere than to inefficient or redistributive governments.

That revolt is rooted in anxiety, of course, in the perception of threats to security and comfort. But it is also rooted in the loss of substance in the idea of the public good. The anxiety itself, which many of us no doubt feel now and then, is part of the split-brain thinking of our times, with the rival camps of pro and con competing ever more stridently for our attention, telling us everything is wonderful or everything is horrible. It is the subtlest form of millennial anxiety, the kind that seems to come from within and therefore to be perfectly justifiable. After all, it is a dangerous world. True enough. It is, however, the only world we have, and no amount of retreat into isolation will suffice to protect our intimate connections if there are no outward structures of shared meaning or common destiny to support them and give them purpose. We cannot purchase inwardness at the self-defeating cost of social fragmentation.

The challenge is, rather, to get on with the hard business of making this world a *slightly better* place, one step at a time, ignoring along the way the increasingly strident prophets of both certain boom and certain doom. The truth about the Future is, as always, both less spectacular and more demanding than either of those visions. Like everyday life itself.

Who Are These People

in My Parents' Photo?

Like most sons, I have some difficulty thinking of my father as a real person, a genuine fragile cluster of hopes and desires and triumphs. The gigantic authoritarian I recall from my childhood has passed, almost without incident, into being a tolerated old duffer who tells his stories once or twice too often and laughs too hard at his own jokes. Fathers, like priests and presidents, are prisoners of the roles we give them.

Along the way he must surely have had a life. I don't know why I find that so hard to imagine. I have recently been trying harder than usual. My father will be sixty this month, and a few weeks later I will turn thirty. For the only time in our lives, he will be exactly twice my age. And I will be the age he was when I, his second son, was born. This odd conjunction of numbers, more than anything else, is making me apprehensive about entering my thirty-first year.

February 1993.

When my father turned thirty, the world he faced was in some obvious ways very different from mine. Born in 1933, he had watched the Second World War as a young boy. Now, a grown man at thirty, he lived in a society facing major challenges, challenges that would change his world forever. He couldn't have known a U.S. president was a few months from violent death. Or that the Beatles were talking to travel agents. (He preferred Chet Atkins and Jim Reeves anyway.) He did know that Canada was about to get its own flag, would soon celebrate a major birthday, and was more than ever unable to deal with Quebec, his birthplace.

But how much the same, I wonder, was his real life, his life of hopes and dreams? Did he worry, like me, about worldly success and its costs? Did he have misgivings about being a father, about inflicting life on the unsuspecting? Did he ever look at his wife, my mother, and wonder whether he had made the right decision?

I see them in my mind, an image torn from an old newspaper society page. My mother is small and white and beautiful; and my father, crew cut and in an excellent white dinner jacket, a boyish smile all over his startlingly handsome face, looks squarely at the camera. He looks like Montgomery Clift. Can that magic couple really be my parents?

Their story was almost too good—too *Fifties*—to be true. In his early twenties my father was a Christian Brother, and in the summers he worked as a lifeguard at the De La Salle Camp up near Jackson's Point on Lake Simcoe. My mother, fresh from Loretto College on Brunswick Street, spent a summer working in the camp kitchen. Summer romance, and the next thing you know my father, the monk, is going over the wall to chase this blonde beauty. My mother said he had great legs in those days, long and tan.

I find this strangely disturbing. Great legs? Can this really be about sex? This marriage, this family, my own life—the product of some steamy attraction between a Catholic schoolgirl and a good-looking monk? After all, these are my parents we're talking about, the people who (surely?) had sex only the three times necessary to conceive my brothers and me. Bite your tongue.

But the story won't submit to the narrowness of my vision, or anybody else's. The reality of my father's life shines through, even if I can only grasp at the major points. Having taken the plunge into the world, he went further and joined the air-force to be a pilot. But he washed out of flight school when he sent a Lockheed Neptune into a steep dive and left it there. Luckily for him—and for me—there was a flight instructor riding along.

So here he was at thirty, father and husband and air-force navigator and, oddly enough, ex–Christian Brother. The features of a life, to be sure. But I find, thinking about it now, that they don't get me any closer to the man who lived this biographical sketch. Even knowing these things—and who can say how distorted they already are by mythic pressure?—I can't see my father as real.

To the editor: "With respect to this piece, one or two points need to be made. The story about the 'steep dive' is entirely apocryphal. I, and several of my fellow students, washed out because our instructors didn't understand us, and in any case it was a de Havilland Chipmunk, not a Lockheed Neptune."

He is instead an image, created from a series of remembered photographs like the wedding shot. I recall an image of a tall man with a crew cut, wearing a Ban-Lon shirt and pegged trousers, holding my older brother and me on each knee. There is a handsome young flight lieutenant in air-force blue. A laughing sportsman in chinos and high-tops, beer in one hand and fishing rod in the other.

Beneath the images lies something I can't see, and it is, after all, everything. What he thought about, what scared him, his plans and hopes that are today nothing but barest memory. Was he funny? Did he yell at people? Did he care about clothes, or music, or food? Did he dream of writing a novel? Or winning a lottery? Did he think about life's darker things, about madness and death and violence? Did love ever desert him?

It is all opaque, and perhaps better that way. It comes easily to us to say that knowing someone else is impossible. But the very ease of the commonplace obscures the tragic dimensions of our ignorance, the terrible isolation of human life. Assigning people to roles—father prominent among them—is one of the ways we cope with the limits of our own knowledge.

But now, my father's life frozen for the moment at sixty—which is twice thirty—I am moved to attempt life's gravest task, the recovery of what is gone. At thirty, I am a man like my father was before me. And his thirty-year-old ghost has questions for me, too: What do you care about? What shape does *your* life have? What do *you* hope for?

I'll try to answer, if I can.

"**At least** with regard to my sons, the correct attitude preceding 'old duffer' should be 'tolerant' rather than 'tolerated'. I rarely repeat stories unless the audience contains at least one individual who has not heard the story. I laugh at my own jokes when, as is invariably the case, they are exceedingly funny."

"**I raise these** points only in the interest of accuracy. I was pleased to see, however, that the writer got 'good-looking' and 'startlingly handsome' correct."

Sources

Beginnings

"Running Low on Posing Pouches? Come to the Cabaret," from *The Globe and Mail* (2 March 1995). "The Party That Ended Too Soon," from *The Globe and Mail* (12 February 1991). "On Hitting the Chic and Missing the Buss," from *The Globe and Mail* (26 June 1992). "Brideshead Revisited, Revisited," from *The Globe and Mail* (22 August 1992). "When East of Bay Is a Foreign Land," from *The Globe and Mail* (4 April 1998). "Finding Your Way," from *Shift* (November 1998). "On Style," from *Azure* (November/December 1998). "Playing in the Digital Garden: Getting Inside by Going Outside," from *Descant* 30: 2 (Summer 1999).

Politics

"Insanity Lurks on the Campaign Trail," from *The Globe and Mail* (15 September 1992). "The Voice of the Pundit Is Heard in the Land," from *The Globe and Mail* (12 October 1994). "Graven Images," from *Gravitas* (Winter 1995). "Six Scenes of Separation: Confessions of a Post-Facto Trudeaumaniac," from *Trudeau's Shadow: The Life and Legacy of Pierre Trudeau* (Toronto: Random House, 1998). "The Mirror Stage: Infinite Reflections on the Public Good," from *Nijenrode Management Review* 13 (November/December 1998) and *Queen's Quarterly* 106: 1 (Spring 1999).

Screen

"The Intellectual Possibilities of Television," from *The Chronicle of Higher Education* (12 December 1997). "The Uneasy Chair," from *Saturday Night* (November 1996). "Sad About You," from *Saturday Night*

(March 1997). "Homicidal Tendencies," from *Saturday Night* (April 1997). "Dopes on a Soap," from *Saturday Night* (February 1998). "Buffy Slays Ally," from *Saturday Night* (May 1998). "Dr. Action Man," from *University of Toronto Magazine* 24: 1 (Fall 1996). "The Nihilistic Noir of a Reservoir Pup," from *Gravitas* (Spring 1996).

Speed
"The Storyteller's Game," from *The Idler* (January 1992). "X-Rated Sports," from *Shift* (August 1996). "Sportspace," from *Descant* 24: 2 (Summer 1993). "Fast Forward: Our High-Speed Chase to Nowhere," from *Harper's* (May 1998).

Thinking
"Ten Steps to Creating a Modern Media Icon," from *Adbusters* 20 (Winter 1998). "Warning: The Topic Today Is Boredom," from *Adbusters* 23 (Autumn 1998). "Wonder Around," from *Adbusters* 22 (Summer 1998). "The Future of Jurassic Technology: Housing Culture at the End of Time," from *Muse* 15: 4 (Winter 1998). "The Fiction of Philosophy," from *The Chronicle of Higher Education* (5 June 1998). "Extraordinary," from *The Idler* (January 1991).

Books
"Prolegomena to All Future Prefaces," from *Descant* 26: 4 (Winter 1995). "When Reality Is Better than the Dream," from *The Globe and Mail* (18 February 1995). "Eric Gill and the Beauty of Character," from *Descant* 26: 3 (Fall 1995). "Grand Theory Makes a Comeback," from *The Globe and Mail* (10 October 1998).

Two Endings
"The Future of Intimacy," from *Maclean's* (1 June 1998). "Who Are These People in My Parents' Photo?" from *The Globe and Mail* (16 February 1993).